Growing Bulbs

The Complete Practical Guide

Brian Mathew

B.T. Batsford Ltd, London

ACKNOWLEDGEMENTS

I would like to thank all those friends and colleagues who have enthused with me through the years about bulbous plants, stimulating my interest and often generously sharing their plants with me. I must also acknowledge the great service provided by those in the nursery trade who propagate and distribute an enormous number of bulbs each year, making them available to a wider public and increasing the general awareness of these fascinating plants. Nursery traders are frequently blamed for the decimation of bulbs in the wild but without their propagation skills a great many more would be collected. The conservationists must also be praised for their concerns about the plants we love, so let us hope that these various interests can become increasingly complementary rather than in opposition. Finally, I would like to thank my editor, Gerard McLaughlin.

First published in Great Britain 1997

© Brian Mathew 1997

All photographs are by the author unless otherwise indicated.

A CIP record for this book is available from the British Library.

ISBN 0 7134 4920 9

Designed by David Seabourne
Printed in Hong Kong

For the Publishers

B.T. Batsford Ltd
583 Fulham Road
London SW6 5BY

Contents

1 *Tulipa* 'Red Riding Hood'

Introduction

Most of my writings on the subject of bulbous plants have been largely devoted to the bulbs themselves rather than their cultivation, although I have tried to give some indication as to their requirements in the space available. This book is intended to reverse the emphasis, with much more information on cultural needs and less of the descriptive matter. Thus, to some extent it will form a companion volume to *The Larger Bulbs*, *Dwarf Bulbs*, and the successor to the latter, *The Smaller Bulbs*, but it is much wider in scope including the frost-tender and tropical bulbs, propagation methods for the amateur grower, and the various problems which one inevitably encounters during the course of bulb growing. The book is intended not so much for specialist bulb growers, who will already know much of what is included in the following pages, but for the enthusiasts who are 'on the up', and ready to try out a wider range of bulbs and eager to add to their knowledge.

Before we start on the more detailed side of cultivation it is important to look at 'bulbs' within the context of the whole plant kingdom: what they are, where they fit in the overall scheme of the plant world, why they are what they are, where they occur in the wild and the type of habitats in which they grow naturally. Apart from being interesting, all this knowledge helps us to understand the requirements of the bulbs we are striving to make happy in the artificial surroundings of our gardens. So first let us take a look at the world of bulbs, beginning with the term 'bulb' itself in order to define what the coverage of the book will be.

Understanding bulbs

CHAPTER 1

Definition of the term 'bulb'

The group of plants which gardeners and nurserymen regard as 'bulbs' consists of a range of subjects which are brought together because they all possess an underground swollen storage organ, thus allowing the plant to go into a period of dormancy during a period of adverse weather, usually drought. They are not necessarily true bulbs in the botanical sense and it is a fact that there is no all-embracing term which includes all those plants which we loosely refer to as bulbs. I like to think of them as anything which a nurseryman can dig up, dry off and post to you in a packet; a very unscientific definition but more or less true!

It should be mentioned that there is another word for 'bulbous' plants which might be encountered in the more botanically inclined literature since it is currently quite a popular term with botanists; this is 'geophyte', meaning any plant which has its growing point situated below soil level, thus including all true bulbs, corms and some tubers. However, this excludes many of their relatives which have their growing points at soil level, such as the rhizomatous irises, so here again it is not a useful all-embracing term for 'bulbous' plants in the sense of the nurseryman and gardener. Many of our 'bulbous' plants belong to the group of plants known as petaloid monocotyledons (see page 3), but not all of them, and many petaloid monocots are non-bulbous, so here again this is not an all-inclusive term. So, we just have to accept that there is no accurate term which we can use for this group of plants and we are left with 'bulbs' as the snappiest and most convenient. No one, I am sure would be attracted to a book entitled 'Smaller Petaloid Monocots' any more than they would to 'Smaller Geophytes' or 'Smaller Swollen Underground Storage Organs', so my books on the subject have all had 'bulbs' in their titles even though corms, tubers and rhizomes are included in their con-

3 *Crocus tournefortii.* Bulbs can burst into growth quickly after a long dry period.

tents. Similarly, a person buying a book with 'bulbs' in the title would not expect *Crocus*, *Gladiolus*, *Colchicum*, *Iris* and *Cyclamen* to be excluded because their underground parts consisted of corms, rhizomes or tubers.

4 Various types of swollen storage organ, referred to collectively as bulbs.

Why have a swollen storage system at all?

The great majority of bulbous plants experience a long dry summer followed by a cooler, damper winter, and the swollen storage system is the way in which they have adapted during the course of evolution to cope with this particular regime of weather conditions. Another group of bulbs have adopted the reverse sequence, a cold, dry winter during which they are dormant, followed by a warm, wet summer. We will look at the world distribution of bulbs later on (see page 6), but briefly it is true to say that the great majority of bulbs occur wild in these two types of climate. There are relatively few in those areas of the world which are damp throughout the year, such as the humid tropics and the cooler temperate regions, since there would be little point in possessing a storage organ. The few exceptions do not necessarily break the general rule

and if we look more closely at their habitats we can usually find an acceptable explanation for the fact that some plants possess bulbs in spite of the fact that they occur in areas which have some rainfall right through the year. Of course, in the perverse world of plants where, it seems, almost anything is possible, there are exceptions and I can think of a few bulbs which grow with their swollen part actually under water: *Crinum natans*, for example, in West Africa, has its bulb in stream beds with the leaves trailing along in the current and the flowers sticking up out of the water on a stout stem! I can only suggest that plants such as these are left-overs from previously dry times and as the climate changed to a damper one the plants adapted to their new environment but retained their bulbous character; if the plant was not actually disadvantaged by having a bulb there would be no selection pressure to lose it. However, these odd rare examples do not alter the overall fact that 'bulbs' must have evolved in response to a long dry period during which time it was necessary to go into a period of dormancy.

Another major advantage of having a swollen storage system is that it enables a plant to make immediate use of a change in the weather to start into growth and flower within a very short period. With many bulbs the period of so-called dormancy is actually the time when the flower buds are being formed ready for the coming season, and it is a particularly important time which gardeners should understand. Bulbs from areas with hot, dry summers actually need that warmth for their resting bulbs in order to initiate the formation of buds, and if for some reason, perhaps an exceptionally wet, cold summer, the temperature does not reach the minimum requirement, buds will almost certainly not form and the plants will be 'blind' the following season. For this reason the storage arrangements at the nurseries where the bulbs are grown are fairly important. Similarly, in the garden, some bulbs do not thrive if other plants grow up and cover them while they are at rest in summer, shading the soil and keeping it too cool for bud formation.

Relationship of bulbous plants to others

To gain a greater understanding of the world of bulbs it is interesting and, I think, necessary, to know how they fit into the overall scheme of the plant kingdom. For the purposes of this essentially practical book I will take a very simple classification which, although basic, is quite adequate to illustrate this point. Firstly, the whole kingdom of plants may be divided into the non-flowering plant groups such as ferns, mosses, liverworts etc., and the flowering plants, the seed-bearing group to which the bulbous plants belong. The flowering plants can be divided into two, the Gymnosperms or conifers, and the Angiosperms; obviously our bulbous plants belong to the latter group since there are no, to my knowledge, bulbous conifers! The Angiosperms may be further subdivided into two: the Dicotyledons, which possess two seed leaves, or cotyledons, which can often be seen clearly when their seeds germinate (think of germinating bean or cabbage seeds); and Monocotyledons, which have only one seed leaf (e.g. onions, sweet corn, bluebells etc.). Most 'bulbous' plants, in the wide sense of the term, belong to the Monocotyledons. It is useful to follow our family tree one stage furthur and split the monocots into those which have flowers with no petals (e.g. grasses, sedges) and those with obvious petals (in monocots these are more often referred to as perianth segments). This group can be referred to as the 'petaloid monocots'.

5 Some monocotyledons are non-bulbous. Here, at the RHS Garden, Wisley, a border has been successfully devoted to them.

It has to be said that the division into petaloid and non-petaloid monocots is not clear-cut (the rushes, for example, have reduced 'petals'), but it is convenient for our purposes to recognize this division. Nearly all of the 'bulbous' plants which we commonly grow in our gardens belong to the petaloid monocots, but there are a few others which are lumped in with bulbs even though they may be non-petaloid, or in some cases not even monocotyledons. Examples are the tuberous-rooted aroids, which have a showy spathe surrounding a lot of tiny flowers rather than showy petals on each flower, tuberous-rooted Anemones, *Cyclamen*, some *Oxalis*, *Eranthis*, and some *Ranunculus* (all of these belong to dicot. families). These are normally offered for sale by the bulb nurserymen and to some extent require a similar sort of treatment to bulbs in cultivation. It should be pointed out here that, conversely, by no means all petaloid monocots are 'bulbous', for example, *Kniphofia*, *Agapanthus*, *Hemerocallis*, *Alstroemeria*, and many of the *Allium* species and *Iris* species which have rhizomes with many perennial (often rather fleshy) roots. A few petaloid

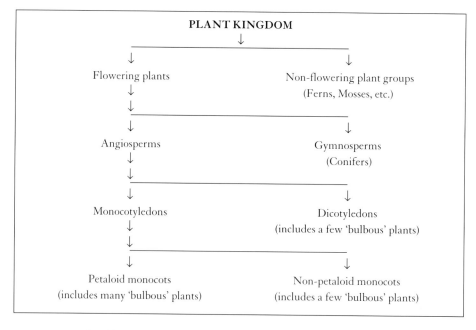

PLANT KINGDOM
↓

↓	↓
Flowering plants ↓ ↓	Non-flowering plant groups (Ferns, Mosses, etc.)

↓	↓
Angiosperms ↓ ↓	Gymnosperms (Conifers)

↓	↓
Monocotyledons ↓ ↓	Dicotyledons (includes a few 'bulbous' plants)

↓	↓
Petaloid monocots (includes many 'bulbous' plants)	Non-petaloid monocots (includes a few 'bulbous' plants)

monocots are shrubby (e.g. *Philesia*), some are climbers (e.g. *Lapageria*, *Smilax*, *Dioscorea*) and some reach almost tree-like proportions (some *Yucca*, *Dracaena* and *Cordyline* species). The position of our 'bulbs' in this elementary scheme is shown the above diagram.

We have established that most of our bulbous plants are petaloid monocotyledons, but it is also interesting to look at some of the reasons why they are grouped together. Apart from having only one

seed leaf the true leaves of most monocots have parallel veins resulting in narrow or strap-like leaves whereas dicotyledons commonly have a netted system of veins.

The flower parts in monocots are nearly always in multiples of three, with 6 'petals' or perianth segments, 3 or 6 stamens, 3 chambers, or locules, to the ovary, etc.; dicotyledons, on the other hand, frequently have their flower parts in 4s or 5s, although some have a rather indefinite and variable number, such as the *Ranunculus* family. A quick look at the tulips, irises, lilies and daffodils will confirm these simple facts.

Within the group we have defined, the petaloid monocots, the next division for all practical purposes is the family, and there are three families in particular which we will encounter frequently with regard to garden plants: the Iris family (Iridaceae), the Lily family (Liliacae) and the Narcissus or Amaryllis family (Amaryllidaceae). The families are then divided into genera, such as *Narcissus*, *Iris*, *Crocus*, *Lilium* etc., and

6 The leaves of most monocotyledons are parallel-veined.

each of these contains one or more species such as *Narcissus tazetta*, *Crocus speciosus* and *Lilium martagon*. The species may be furthur fragmented into subspecies, varieties, forms, and in the case of garden plants, cultivars.

What are bulbs, corms, tubers and rhizomes?

Bulbs

In the true botanical sense, a bulb is a storage organ consisting of concentric fleshy scales attached to a solid piece of tissue known as the basal plate; this is actually a compressed piece of stem which produces roots from its base and to which the modified leaves, or scales, are joined. In a dormant bulb these scales enclose the growing point of the plant which, towards the end of the dormant period (e.g. in late summer) will contain all the primordial parts of the aerial shoot for the coming growing season, that is, the stem, the true leaves, bracts and flower buds. The buds in turn house all the floral parts, and if a daffodil bulb is cut in half lengthways in late summer it will be found to contain quite well-developed buds in which the stamens can be clearly seen, although flowering time is still several months away. The bulb represents a complete 'packaged plant' just awaiting the right sequence of stimuli, in the form of moisture and temperature requirements, in order to begin to grow.

Corms

Corms also consist of a piece of condensed stem, but in this case the stem forms the major part of the organ and there are no scales attached to its apex. Since they are stems, corms usually have secondary buds situated on the outside in addition to the main ones at the top; these axillary buds often remain dormant unless the main shoot is broken off or damaged when they may be stimulated into growth. Corms are usually covered by dry papery or fibrous 'tunics' to protect them, and their axillary buds, and to prevent them from drying out too much. In fact an inspection of, for example, a *Gladiolus* corm will reveal that these secondary buds are situated in the axils of the tunics, these tunics being modified leaves. Most corms are replaced annually, the old one shrivelling away as it is used up at the expense of the developing shoot, and a new one forming on top of the old towards the end of the growing season. In *Crocus* and *Gladiolus* corms this can be easily seen if a plant is dug up half way through its growing season, when both old and new corms are clearly visible. These two genera have corms which produce roots from the base, or rather in a ring around the base, whereas some others, for example, *Gynandriris*, produce their roots from the base of the new shoot, so that they appear to be emerging from the top of the corm. A *Colchicum* also has a corm which is replaced annually but here the shape is quite different, being rather elongated and lop-sided with a 'foot' at the base, and there are no lateral buds on the surface of the corm. In fact, it may be incorrect to refer to this as a corm since it is not very similar to the true corms which are produced by members of the iris family (*Crocus*, *Gladiolus*, *Moraea* etc.) and it may be more accurate to refer to it as a tuber. However, it is a non-scaly organ, unlike a bulb, and is replaced annually.

Tubers

Many familiar garden plants possess tubers, for example, dahlias, potatoes and cyclamen. These are fleshy, non-scaly, structures which may or may not have resting buds on their surfaces and are clearly not all the same in structure and origin. The tubers of the potato and some *Tropaeolum* species do have buds ('eyes') which are capable of producing aerial growths, and these are obviously stem-derived tubers. Others, such as the tubers found in some species of *Liriope* and *Asphodelus* appear to be root-derived and have no resting buds. In others it is not at all clear (to me) whether they are modified stems or roots; here is an excellent subject for study – a survey of storage systems! Coupled with this group are fleshy roots, which are clearly also intended for storage purposes, in *Roscoea* and some eastern Asiatic *Iris* and *Allium* species.

Rhizomes

Although in general rhizomes do not come within the scope of a book on 'bulbs', many of the plants which possess rhizomes are petaloid monocotyledons, the non-bulbous irises being a very good example. A rhizome is a stem which runs along just on the surface of, or just under, the ground and usually has reduced leaves (scale-like) along its length, in the axils of which are carried resting buds. *Convallaria*, the lily-of-the-valley, produces very long thin underground rhizomes whereas the familiar tall bearded irises have short swollen ones resting on the surface of the soil. In fact, rhizomes and corms are very similar in structure. I like to think of a corm as being a very compressed rhizome in which the internodes (the spaces between the resting buds) are extremely short: stretch the whole thing out and the result is, more or less, a rhizome! Corms, as mentioned above, are of annual duration, but in the case of rhizomes the older parts die away and are replaced at the growing end, so there is really not much difference, except that the rhizome has the power of locomotion, to steadily move on into new soil. Some *Crocus* species (*C. nudiflorus*, *C. kotschyanus*, *C. gargaricus* subsp. *herbertii*)

produce rhizome-like structures (usually referred to as stolons) as well as corms, as do some *Gladiolus* species and *Schizostylis coccinea*.

Bulbs in the wild, their distribution and habitats

Bulbous plants are to be found in most countries in the world, so in a sense they are widely distributed, but this gives a rather false impression of the situation. The majority of them are in fact clustered in certain areas, not scattered more or less evenly all over the globe. If we look at the areas where they are most plentiful we find, understandably, that they are in areas which have an alternating wet-and-dry climate – hence the reason for having a storage organ, to tide the plant over to the next rainy season. In temperate regions the wet periods may be in summer or in winter, but in tropical regions, where there are no large temperature differences through the year, they are just wet or dry seasons. Of course, there are bulbs in other places, and almost every country has a few native ones, but the overall pattern is that they are very much more plentiful in some regions than in others.

Winter-growers

Looking at the distribution of the majority of bulbs we find that, broadly speaking, there are five main areas for winter-rainfall bulbs:

a)   the Mediterranean region and eastwards through south-western Asia to Central Asia as far as the extreme western Himalaya.

b)   the western United States, west of the Rocky Mountains.

c)   the South West Cape of South Africa.

d) the south-western part of Western Australia; for some reason which I cannot explain, most of the petaloid monocots in this area have not developed swollen bulbs or corms but instead have tough rhizomes and, often, a mass of roots.
e) the western slopes of the Andes, especially Chile; parts of Argentina also have a climate which seems to have promoted the development of winter-growing bulbs (e.g. *Ipheion uniflorum*).

The position is a little more obscure when dealing with the higher altitude bulbs where, although bulbs may be essentially 'winter-growers', they do not really start to grow much, and certainly not above ground, until the warmth of spring.

Summer-growers

There are fewer summer-rainfall/winter drought areas, perhaps three main ones:
a) the monsoon temperate regions of the Himalaya and China, where, for example, there are many *Lilium*, *Nomocharis* and *Allium*.
b) Central America, notably Mexico, extending northwards into Texas and including Guatemala.
c) the East Cape region of southern Africa, extending northwards through the eastern side of southern tropical Africa.

Bulbs from tropical latitudes

The tropical regions which have well-defined wet/dry seasons include tropical South America, especially parts of Brazil and adjacent parts of northern Argentina, Bolivia and Ecuador; the whole of eastern tropical Africa (sometimes, for example in Kenya, there are two wet seasons each year). These regions have also developed a large number of bulbs which, for the purposes of cultivation in temperate gardens,

may be treated the same as the summer-growers, keeping them dry and frost-free in winter.

Natural habitats of bulbs and their relevance to cultivation

Since bulbous plants have largely evolved in response to dry periods it is to be expected that the majority of them occur in rather open situations, any competing vegetation being either shorter than the bulbous plants or fairly sparse and therefore providing little shade. Many bulbs grow on hillsides, rocky areas and flat sandy plains where the drainage is good, because of sloping ground or the nature of the soil. Even if, as is often the case, they are embedded in sticky clay during the growing season, the conditions are never stagnant and the soil subsequently dries out, sometimes to the point of being almost baked in the sun. Although they do occur often amid other plants, the bulbs flower and complete their growing cycle before the accompanying vegetation has fully developed.

Some bulbs, however, do grow in habitats which are more densely clothed with vegetation, sometimes in lush grass meadows or shaded by trees and shrubs in woodlands. It may seem at first unnecessary for a plant to have a storage system

7 Many bulbs grow naturally in turf. *Crocus vallicola* and *Colchicum speciosum* in Turkey.

8 A few bulbs prefer shade. The bluebell is a good example.

in such situations, but in fact these areas can be quite dry in summer, although not sunbaked.

Woodland bulbs grow mainly beneath deciduous trees and shrubs and there are several good examples such as *Galanthus*, *Erythronium*, and *Eranthis*. These make their root and aerial growth during the autumn, winter and spring while the trees are 'dormant', using little moisture themselves and allowing rain and dappled sunlight through the canopy of branches to the ground below. In spring the trees burst into growth, using more and more moisture as the season progresses and shading the ground; by this time the bulbs will have completed their growth cycle and are seeding and dying down for a period of dormancy. In gardens, we can supply similar growing conditions, Erythroniums, for example, being ideal bulbs for planting in semi-shade beneath deciduous shrubs for an early display.

The same comments apply to bulbs which grow in meadowland. The grass is fairly inactive in winter, and usually reasonably short, so the bulbs do not have to compete for light and moisture; as spring passes the bulbs die down and the grass begins to grow vigorously, using up excess water so that the soil is relatively dry at the height of summer. Many bulbs grow in grassland, from low meadows to high alpine turf, and

a knowledge and understanding of the conditions under which they grow in the wild may well help us to place them in the most suitable positions in the garden. A piece of rough grass (as opposed to mown lawn) can provide an attractive and appropriate home for a wide range of bulbs, for example, *Narcissus pseudonarcissus*, *N. poeticus*, *Camassia* species, several *Crocus* species and some Ornithogalums.

On the whole, bulbs which occur in the shade or in damp grassland will not thrive, and may not survive at all, if their bulbs are planted in areas which get hot and dry in summer. If they are lifted they should never be stored in dry heat.

To recap, the cultivation of bulbs therefore falls into several categories, although these do overlap to some extent depending upon the local climatic conditions where the garden is situated:

Shade-lovers, of which there are rather few in relation to bulbs as a whole, can be treated as such in gardens, but in the colder areas with low light intensity they should be given more open situations than in areas which get very hot and dry in summer; conversely, in regions where the latter conditions prevail, it may be necessary to give them shadier positions in order for them to survive the dormant period.

Those bulbs which occur naturally in grassy places, constituting rather more than in the above category, can also be used very effectively in grass in gardens. Bear in mind, though, that the type of soil in the garden in which the grass is growing, and the climate, have a great bearing on which species can be successfully cultivated.

Bulbs from open habitats, probably constituting by far the largest number, need to be grown in well-drained, sunny positions; in the case of those which die down for the summer months, care must be taken that not too much summer vegetation grows up and shades the resting bulbs, since this can result in a lack of flowers due to the soil temperature being insufficiently high to induce bud formation. Many *Tulipa*, *Crocus* and some *Fritillaria* and *Narcissus* species fall into this category and are ideal for the open, sunny border requiring no special treatment other than reasonable drainage. The extreme of this type of habitat is where the bulbs occur in hot summer countries in open situations, with no or few other companion plants, thoroughly dry and sun-baked during their dormant period. The cultivation of these may be rather special-ized, except for those gardeners living in areas with climatic conditions similar to those of the plants' native lands. Gardeners in Britain, for example, cannot grow many of the bulbs from Iran and Afghanistan in the open ground without protecting them from the combination of wet and cold in winter (in the wild they are mostly under snow and are thus in a state of relatively dry cold storage) and summer damp, when they should be dry and sunbaked. However, a certain amount of success can be achieved by choice of position: a raised bed or rock garden, for example, can give that extra sharp drainage which results in drier, and thus warmer, soil allowing a wider range to be cultivated; a bed against a warm, sunny wall may supply the necessary

protection and summer baking for some subjects which are otherwise quite unsuc-cessful in other spots in the garden.

Covering a raised bed (thus resulting in a bulb frame) provides the means by which gardeners in the cooler, temperate regions can grow a much greater range of bulbs since this allows considerable control over the conditions. A stage further is to grow bulbs in individual pots or other containers in a glasshouse so that each group, or even each species, can be given separate and detailed attention. The unheated glass-house (often referred to as an 'alpine house' in Britain, although this term should really be reserved for a house which has almost continuous side and roof ventilation) is a very convenient method of growing the smaller hardy bulbs, while the provision of heat opens the door to a whole range of fas-cinating tender bulbs from the subtropics and tropics which, for many 'temperate' gardeners, are impossible outside.

In the next chapter we will look at the cultivation of bulbs in these various garden situations in more detail, starting with the 'shady end' of the scale, working through to those which are suitable for naturalizing in grass, on to those for open, sunny borders, raised beds and rock gardens, and finally dealing with those which are likely to require the protection of a glasshouse in all but the most favoured areas. One must remember, however, that in these 'favoured' areas, a suitable climate for one set of bulbs may mean that another group cannot be grown successfully. There are gardeners in various parts of the world who can cultivate wonderful subtropical Amaryllids outside, but snowdrops, which clearly revel in a miserable British winter, are a great rarity!

9 Most bulbs grow in full sun in soils which become hot and dry in summer. *Tulipa montana* in Iran.

CHAPTER 2

Cultivation of bulbs

General considerations

Bulbs, as we have established earlier, have evolved in order to act as storage organs through dry periods when it would be disadvantageous for a plant to have aerial growth because of drought or scorching sun which would lead to desiccation. The possession of a bulb is a very effective way for a plant to overcome an adverse period and means that it has plenty of food reserves locked up for a quick start when that period is over. Hence, many bulbous plants start into growth very rapidly after rain has fallen, some of them flowering immediately, thus making the maximum use of what is often a rather short growing period before the next dry season. This quick start is facilitated by the fact that there is already a flower bud present within the bulb. For many bulbous (cormous, tuberous etc.) plants the so-called 'dormant' period, when bulbs have no top growth and sometimes no roots either, is an important time when flower buds for the following

season are laid down within the growing point, which may be buried deep inside the bulb. In order to do this, many species of bulb need warm temperatures before they will actually initiate flower buds. For the major crops, such as Hyacinths, bulb growers have established what the optimum temperatures are, so the stores where the bulbs are kept before they are sold are temperature-controlled, resulting in a product which already has the capability of flowering, long before the customer receives it; all that the gardener has to do is supply moisture and nutrients and success is guaranteed, at least for the first year!

It follows that if a plant is designed for a specific set of conditions, in order to cultivate it well we must try to reproduce those conditions, at least the more critical of them. The most important is to provide moist growing seasons and dryish dormant seasons, much as the bulbs would experience them in nature, but there are fairly distinct bulb groups and an understanding of these is essential for successful cultivation.

10 *Hymenocallis harrisiana*. A tender bulb requiring specialized cultivation.

BT Batsford Ltd.
Freepost WD240
Braintree
Essex
CM7 2BR
ENGLAND

b

We'd like your thoughts...

Growing Bulbs: The Complete Practical Guide

Thank you for purchasing this book. We hope you enjoy it. While you're reading the book you can use this card as a bookmark. Then, we'd like your comments so we can continue to publish books which will interest our readers. Please fill out this card and return it to us.

Your reaction to this book:

_____

_____

_____

Where did you buy this book?

_____

Your profession:

_____

Name: _____ Mr/Mrs/Ms/Miss/Dr Other:

Address: _____

Postcode: _____ Country:

http://www.batsford.com

Winter-growers or summer-growers?

Although mentioned above (see page 6–7), this is such a basic part of bulb-growing that a little repetition is, I hope, forgiveable. The bulbs which we grow in our gardens have come to us from all over the world, and from a wide range of climates, soils and habitats. There is, however, one fundamental aspect of bulb growing which we need to address before going on to the subtleties such as soil mixes, how warm to keep them etc., and that is when to start them into growth. The majority of bulbs can be placed into two broad groups for cultivation purposes, the 'winter-growers' and the 'summer-growers', and it does not matter where they come from or are transported to; a winter-grower from the predominantly winter rainfall South West Cape region will continue to be a winter-grower in the northern hemisphere and likewise the summer-growers from the primarily summer-rainfall East Cape will continue to grow in summer, wherever they are. This is because the winter-growers have evolved to commence growth in response to the effects of increasing moisture and falling temperature after a warm summer drought, whereas the summer-growers respond to increasing spring and summer temperatures and summer rainfall after a cold, and sometimes also dry, winter. It is essential to think in seasons rather than months, since the use of named months is meaningless when a change of hemispheres is involved. For example, the advice 'start watering crocuses in September' would be correct for gardeners in Britain but totally wrong for someone in South Africa where September is in early spring. On the other hand, 'start watering crocuses in early autumn' would be correct (or roughly so) for either hemisphere, even though there may be a 6-month difference between the autumns in the two hemispheres. It is often

a rather tricky operation to transfer bulbs from one hemisphere to another; their growth cycle is 'out' by 6 months and it takes a while for them to readjust. Nevertheless they will do so in time since they are, at least those from temperate regions are, quite fixed in their behaviour. Bulbs from the more tropical areas are not programmed in the same way, so we will look at the two groups separately.

Bulbs from temperate regions

In temperate regions the wet and dry periods usually coincide with cool and warm periods as well, and these four factors combine to give two types of climatic conditions in which the majority of the world's bulbs occur:

Category (1) bulbs (the winter-growers): cool, damp winters and warm, dry summers.

Category (2) bulbs (the summer-growers): cool, dry winters and warm, damp summers.

This is an over-simplification, but applies to a very large number of the bulbs we cultivate. When brought into cultivation the bulbs from these temperate regions will continue to behave in the way in which they have always behaved, even if a change of hemisphere is involved. If they are moved from one hemisphere to another they merely change their cycle of growth by 6 months to fall into line with the timing of the seasons (in at least the first year after importation they may, however, be somewhat confused). They are fixed in their behaviour and will often start growing at the appropriate time of year, even if water is not available. Colchicums from the Mediterranean region will start to flower in autumn whilst still in packets in the garden centres, and similarly Ixias and Tritonias from the South West Cape will begin to push up shoots long before they are planted and supplied with moisture. Nurseries sometimes offer corms of Freesias and Sparaxis, both of which are naturally winter-growers, in spring for planting out for a summer flowering. In these cases the corms have been stored artificially warm and dry to simulate an extended summer dormancy. Once planted in spring they will grow during the summer if given plenty of moisture, but after that one season they will try to revert to their former winter-growing habits unless the corms are lifted and stored again, warm and dry for the winter; in my experience this seldom works, for they are always striving to make growth in their accustomed autumn-winter period and just become weaker and weaker if they are forcibly prevented from doing so.

The climatic category (1) includes the much-loved (by plants as well as humans) Mediterranean climate which promotes such a wealth of plants, not just bulbs. Areas of the world with this 'cool-winter rain (or snow) and warm-summer drought' climate include the Mediterranean region itself, eastwards through Iran and Afghanistan to the central Asiatic mountain ranges and the extreme western Himalaya. The western United States to the west of the Rockies, especially California and Oregon, also have a primarily winter-rainfall/summer-drought climate. Switching to the southern hemisphere, the western slopes of the Andes, particularly in Chile, also receive winter rainfall from the Pacific, as does the South West Cape region of South Africa, and the southwestern part of Western Australia. All of these areas contain very many petaloid monocots, and a great number of them 'bulbous' in the wide sense of the word, although for some reason few of those from Western Australia have developed swollen storage organs, many of them opting for a tough rhizome with a mass of wiry roots. There are other smaller areas with this type of climate, for example parts of eastern Argentina and adjacent Uruguay, where there are some familiar subjects such as *Ipheion uniflorum* and several *Nothoscordum* and *Zephyranthes* species.

Bulbs from the climatic category (2) behave in the reverse way; these are dry and cool in their dormant period in winter and warm and damp in the summer. The regions where the summer-growers have evolved are perhaps not quite so well-defined as for the winter-growers but we can pick out the monsoon, summer-rainfall areas of eastern Asia, where there are many lilies, Central America, notably Mexico, from whence come many species of *Tigridia*, *Milla*, *Nemastylis*, *Bessera*, *Rigidella* etc., and the East Cape region including Natal and Lesotho where there are many interesting and garden-worthy summer-growing 'bulbs' such as *Rhodohypoxis*, *Eucomis*, *Galtonia*, and *Gladiolus*. Cultivation of these summer-growers in cold-winter areas is a simple matter since their bulbs can be lifted and stored dry away from frost during the dormant period, so the question of hardiness is not so much of a problem as it is with the winter-growers.

Tropical and subtropical bulbs

Although they are dealt with later in Chapter 3 (see page 39), this is also an appropriate time to mention the subtropical and tropical bulbs since they are rather different in their behaviour and are not nearly as set in their ways. They do not experience such marked cool and warm periods as the temperate regions; their seasons are wet or dry, without the accompanying dramatic temperature differences. Their flowering period coincides with rainy seasons and if the rains fail they just stay dormant until it does rain. Thus, in cultivation, providing they are given alternating wet and dry periods, most tropical bulbs can be started into growth at any time, although for those of us gardening in the cooler temperate climates it is most convenient to treat them as summer-growers so that less artificial heat and light will be required; they can then be kept dormant and dry away from frost in the winter. This behaviour accounts for the widely differing flowering times which are quoted for some of the tender bulbs. The more tropical species of *Hippeastrum* ('Amaryllis'), for example, can be grown for a winter display or kept dry and dormant and then started into growth in spring for a summer display. So, as a very general rule, the bulbs from subtropical and tropical areas can be treated in the same way as the summer rainfall bulbs of category (2), but there may be a particular reason (e.g. Hippeastrums for the Christmas market in Europe and North America) for inducing them to flower in winter. Areas of the tropics where there are a significant number of bulbous, cormous and rhizomatous monocots include tropical South America and east tropical Africa, and there are a few in the Northern Territories of Australia; it is mainly the drier parts of the tropics where they occur in their greatest numbers, of course; there are very few 'bulbs' in the forested areas, most of them occurring in seasonally dry grassland or semi-desert.

Buying and planting time

On the whole, the decision as to when to buy and plant bulbs is out of the hands of the gardener, since the nurseryman will dictate this. The winter-growing bulbs (that is, the great majority of those in general cultivation, the tulips, crocuses, colchicums, daffodils etc.) are on sale in early to mid-autumn, while the summer-growers (for instance the large-flowered gladiolus cultivars, lilies, *Galtonia*, *Tigridia* and *Eucomis*) are available in the shops in spring. The more tropical bulbs are usually also sold in spring. In most instances they are best planted as soon as they arrive, but there are a few points to note.

Autumn-flowering bulbs, such as *Crocus*, *Colchicum* and *Sternbergia* need to be obtained and planted in late summer if they are to perform properly in their first season after planting; so often they are seen trying to flower in their packets on the garden centre shelves. Good nurserymen make a point of sending these out earlier than the spring-flowering bulbs.

Tulips are more resilient with regard to planting time than many of the other bulbs; they are best planted in early to mid-autumn but if it is not convenient this can be delayed until late autumn or even early winter without harm to the bulbs; of course in cold-winter areas it may be necessary to get them in early before the ground freezes.

Summer bulbs should be started into growth in late spring or early summer. However, many of these are not frost-hardy so planting should be delayed until the soil has warmed up. I find that it is best to get them off to a good start by planting them in small pots and keeping them in a frost-free glasshouse to get the roots growing; as soon as the warmer weather arrives they are planted out into their summer-flowering positions.

Lilies are often offered for sale in autumn but some growers store them over winter and supply the retail nurserymen with bulbs for spring planting. Providing that the bulbs are in good health, have some good roots attached and have not been dried out too much, there does not seem to be much difference in the subsequent performance between autumn- and spring-planted bulbs. Notable exceptions are *L. candidum* and *L.* x *testaceum* (and other

'Mediterranean' species) which have an active growing period in autumn; these need to be planted in autumn.

Some South African 'bulbs' such as *Sparaxis* and *Ixia*, although normally winter-growers which should be planted in autumn for flowering in winter and spring, are sometimes offered for sale in spring for a summer-flowering. These are corms which have been stored artificially dry and warm over winter to hold them back; in my experience they will behave as summer-growers only for the first season, then try to revert to their winter-growing habit, so these should really be regarded as short-term plantings for one season, although one could try lifting them in autumn and storing them dry and warm for the winter.

Planting

There are no particular rules about planting techniques for bulbs; as the great and unforgettable rose grower Harry Wheatcroft once said at a lecture, when asked how to plant a rose bush: 'well, you dig a hole, put it in and put your foot on it'! With bulbs, I would perhaps omit the foot. There are special bulb planters on the market but I have a very shiny unused one in my shed which has been there for many years; a trowel is quite adequate, or a spade or fork for larger quantities. I was once lecturing on the subject of bulbs and explaining how to plant bulbs for a naturalized effect in grass (see page 21) when a rather elegant and obviously wealthy lady in the audience remarked that on their estate they planted them with a JCB mechanical digger; so the means of planting really does depend upon the scale!

I find it very useful to line the bottom of the planting hole with a layer of yellow sand on which to sit the bulbs; this may help with drainage at the bottom of the bulb, but the main purpose is that at lifting time all one has to do is dig down and find the sand; the extent of the sand shows the extent of the planting, thus avoiding lengthy searching through a heap of soil for all the small bulbs.

Planting depths and distances

Bulbs in the wild tend to be very specific in the depths at which they occur. In the case of many species, from the seedling stage the young bulb or corm produces a fleshy root (distinct from the 'proper' roots) which bores a hole downwards beneath the developing bulb; then, at the end of the growing season, the root shrivels and pulls the young bulb down into the gap. This happens each season until the bulb is at its 'working depth' when it will commence flowering. In cultivation this will also happen with bulbs which are grown from seed; bulbs will often end up at the bottom of a seed pot and, if left untended for several seasons, I have known them to go out through the drainage hole and into the soil beneath! Mature bulbs bought in for planting, or grown in pots, are not quite so critical in their depth requirement, although sometimes even these will make contractile roots if they are planted too shallowly, and they will often do this at the expense of flowers.

Depths

A general rule of thumb is that bulbs should be planted about 2 to 3 times the depth of the bulb itself, the depth of soil being measured from the surface down to the tip of the bulb; only the fat 'body' of the bulb should be measured, ignoring the long tapering neck which some bulbs possess. For example, a large bulb 5 cm (2 in) long needs about 10–15 cm (4–6 in) of soil above it, a small one like a crocus, only 1.5 cm (0.6 in) long, about 3–4.5 cm (1.2–1.8 in). In light sandy soils which dry out quickly they should be planted at the deeper end (3 x) of this scale, in heavier soils at the shallower end (2 x).

In very cold-winter areas where the ground freezes hard to a considerable depth it will be necessary to plant them deeper and mulch them with loose litter (bracken etc.) for the winter months. There are notable exceptions, for example, nerines, which need planting shallowly if they are to flower reliably. These exceptions have been noted in the A–Z section in Chapter 7. Some shy-flowering bulbs, which tend to split into many small bulblets or cormlets, can be encouraged to flower and not to split up by deeper planting; this sometimes works with, for example, *Crocus sativus* and *Iris danfordiae* which are notorious for this behaviour; try them at about 8–10 cm (3.2–4 in) deep as an experiment.

Distances

This partly depends upon what effect is required; if a dense solid mass of flowers is needed, the bulbs will obviously be planted close together. As a starting point the distance can be about 10–15 cm (4–6 in) apart for the larger bulbs and 5–10 cm (2–4 in) for the smaller ones, but this should be varied for very large and very small species; large trumpet lilies, for example, may need as much as 30 cm (12 in) between bulbs if the flowers are not to be crowded together, while tiny romuleas or even the smaller crocuses might well look rather silly if spaced 5 cm (2 in) apart. For mass effects, such as scillas planted beneath shrubs, the bulbs can be almost touching.

Soils, drainage and potting mixes

It never fails to amaze me that one can acquire bulbs from all over the world and bring them together in one garden where,

on the whole, they will grow reasonably well in one basic type of potting mix, bearing in mind other important factors such as hardiness and light/shade tolerance of course. This is remarkable, especially in view of the fact that many bulbs are endemic to quite small areas, often with rather precise conditions. However, defining what the basic soil mix should be is another matter altogether! Do a tour of the enthusiasts' potting sheds of the world and one would find, I feel fairly certain, just about as many recipes as there are enthusiasts, so it is really a case of trying to work out what factors they have in common.

Soils

Firstly, the soil provides a physical home, protecting the bulb from frost, extreme heat and drought, predators and diseases. It also gives support to the roots and the aerial shoots as they grow and develop, the former seeking moisture and nutrients and the latter raising the leaves above ground to make use of the light and air and the flowers to give rise to seeds for future generations. Obviously the soil acts as the medium for carrying the moisture and nutrients which the roots seek, and also air, since roots, like other living tissues, require oxygen if they are to remain healthy and active.

Drainage

Ask any bulb enthusiasts what is the most important factor in making up a good bulb soil, and most will say 'drainage'. This is of prime importance and there are very few bulbs which will survive in permanently stagnant moist conditions – in fact few plants at all – and even in areas where bulbs appear to be thriving in saturated soil one will usually find that it is only seasonally moist, such as in mountain meadows receiving water from melting snow. *Crocus gargaricus*, for example, is often virtually

11 A layer of sand assists drainage and acts as a marker when lifting the dormant bulbs.

under water at flowering time but by mid-summer the alpine turf will have used up any excess moisture, the ground will have dried out and the corms will be awaiting the onset of cooler, damper autumn weather to start rooting again. To achieve good drainage in an artificially prepared soil mix one needs to have gaps in between the various particles making up the compost; it is fairly obvious that if there are no, or only very fine, gaps the drainage will be reduced to a slow seepage downwards and some water will probably be retained for a long time by capillary action; if it remains too long the soil will become sour and the roots will probably die. Compacted clay soils, consisting of very fine particles packed together, soon become waterlogged and take a long time to dry out; coarse sandy soils have plenty of gaps through which water can seep and soon dry out. A useful thought to have in the back of the mind when making up bulb beds or potting mixes is that a good soil sample should consist of about 50% solid matter, and 50% gaps (the gaps accounting for approximately 25% water and 25% air which will vary somewhat according to how recently water was applied).

Potting mixes

When making up a potting compost it is important to bear in mind the sizes of all the particles involved. If one has a very fine particle soil mix (some commercial bags of 'John Innes Compost' which I have purchased are extremely fine with quite poor drainage) and adds coarse grit to it in an attempt to make it drain better, the effect may not be as favourable as expected since the fine particles merely fill the gaps between the pieces of grit and the drainage is much as before. In cases such as this a very high percentage of grit has to be added to achieve the desired results, perhaps as much as 75%. So, the aim is to achieve a structure which is granular – 'light and fluffy' is a phrase which one hears fairly frequently, and it is very descriptive.

A good all round mix for the majority of bulbs is:

2 parts (by volume) loam
1 part leafmould (or moss peat if this is not
    available)
2 parts coarse sand/grit
Fertilizer
Lime: sometimes

The following comments about each of these ingredients may be helpful:

LOAM

This is a variable substance but try to choose something which does not have the consistency of clay, or is very sandy. Many amateur gardeners use the soil which is in their garden for this purpose since it so expensive to keep buying in ready-made compost or good new loam. Left-over pieces of turf from lawn re-shaping can be stacked up for a season then used as the base for potting composts and this can be very successful. It is usually advocated that the materials should all be sterilized by some method, steam or chemical. This is an added problem for the amateur and a good incentive to buy ready-made potting soils which should already be sterilized. I have to say that although I would agree that all the materials should obviously be as weed, disease and pest-free as possible, one of the best bulb growers I know does not use sterilized soil, and does not wash his pots before re-use either!

LEAFMOULD OR MOSS PEAT

(I have not yet experimented sufficiently with coir to comment usefully). Leafmould helps to keep the mixture more open and provides additional nutrients. However, it is not something which everyone has access to although it is not all that difficult to obtain or make, providing that there are a few trees around. Moss peat serves as an alternative but I would avoid using black sedge peat which seems to remain much wetter than the rather granular and very light moss peat. I am not convinced that the humus content is very important, certainly for those bulbs which inhabit open situations in the wild; humus is often a very minor constituent of the soils in which they grow naturally. As an experiment one year I dispensed with humus altogether, except for the small amount occurring in the loam itself, and the bulbs really did do extremely well; extra grit was added to make up for the fact that there was no humus to help lighten the mixture. Perlite, or any of the similar preparations, can also be used to lighten soil mixes, although I have found that bulbs can easily become over-desiccated during hot, dry spells in their dormant period if the soil is very loose. Obviously in the case of woodland bulbs, such as erythroniums, there is a greater proportion of humus in the soil in their natural conditions and this is taken into account when mixing composts. To some extent this also applies to the mountain meadow bulbs like *Crocus vallicola* and some of the *Narcissus* species where the alpine turf may be quite peaty.

GRIT OR SHARP SAND

This is another very variable substance and one must really shop around and work out which is the best available in the area. The nomenclature is very unpredictable; one firm in our area sells 'sharp sand' which does have sharp pieces in it but also has a high proportion of fine as well so it really needs sieving, while another firms sells a very desirable and sizeable grit as 'extra coarse sand'. When I travel to other parts of the country giving lectures I usually try to call in at local garden centres to pick up a bag or two of grit to see what local variations there are; the answer is that there are many.

FERTILIZER

To the above 2:1:2 mix is added a balanced fertilizer at the rate of about 5 oz (1 gm) to 10 gallons (45 litres) of compost; these rates are not very critical and one will find greatly varying recommendations in literature. For those who cannot be bothered with scales, I measured out various powders and found that as a rough guide, making use of familiar objects, this would be 1 teacup (not a mug or a Turkish coffee cup!) of fertilizer to 5 buckets (the average sized bucket of 2 gal or 20 litres) of soil.

There are ready-mixed 'potting base' fertilizers available, or a general garden fertilizer can be used, providing that it has roughly equal proportions of N (Nitrogen), P (Phosphates) and K (Potassium); the percentages are usually shown on the side of the packet. I avoid the use of straight organic fertilizers such as bone meal and blood, fish and bone since, in our garden anyway, they most definitely attract foxes which start digging in search of some perceived goody at the bottom of the hole.

LIME/CHALK

If the bulbs which I am potting are known to come from particularly alkaline conditions I add ground chalk, lime, or 'dolomite chalk' if I can get it, at the same rate as the fertilizer. On the whole a potting compost which is neither markedly acid nor strongly alkaline (a pH of 6–7.5) seems to suit the great majority of bulbs. Michael Hoog, who successfully cultivated so many unusual bulbs in Holland, strongly advocated the use of dolomite chalk, finely ground dolomitic limestone, which he scattered on to the bulbs as they were planted (especially recommended for irises); however, this is not very freely available and I normally resort to the use of 'garden lime' from the local garden centre.

VARIATIONS

I vary this basic mix to 1:1:1 for bulbs which occur in damper conditions, or in woodland. Of course one can play about for hours trying to produce soil mixes which approximate to those in which certain bulbs are found in nature (if this information is known) but I have little evidence to suggest that this has any great effect!

READY-MADE AND SOIL-LESS POTTING MIXES

The quicker route to all this is to buy ready-mixed potting mediums. In my experience most loam-based ones need adapting for successful bulb growing, in the form of extra grit/sharp sand to improve the drainage. Loamless composts can give good results, and I have grown very good fritillaries in a peat-based compost in the past, but on the whole I would say that they are best for growing plants which are robust with vigorous roots, taking up a lot of moisture; winter-growing bulbs, especially the small species, do not use up a great deal of water, even at the height of their growing period, and peaty, moisture-retentive composts can stay damp for long periods, especially if used in plastic pots. Another problem arises in summer when they are dried out: peat-based composts shrink much more than loam-based ones and the dormant bulbs can easily become desiccated.

Bulbs in the garden

CHAPTER 3

In order to have some system to this chapter I have arranged the various categories of bulbs in order of amount of exposure they might require or tolerate (shade →full sun) combined with the degree of hardiness (outdoor cultivation →glasshouse treatment), starting with the bulbs which can be grown outside in the shadier parts of the garden, moving on to those which can be grown out in the open, but are still shaded to some extent by grass, on to those which require more exposure and little in the way of competition in the open, sunny border

Bulbs in the shady garden

There are few bulbs which will survive in deep shade and, even if they do survive, will almost certainly not flower. However, if there is a certain amount of sunlight filtering through trees or shrubs, even for a part of the day, then there are quite a number of possibilities. It may at first seem odd that there are some bulbs which are adapted to growing in shade, since, as we considered in an earlier chapter, most bulbs have evolved largely in response to the need to overcome an adverse climatic period, usually in the form of a long, dry summer following a damp winter. A review of the conditions in a deciduous woodland will explain this apparent inconsistency.

The great majority of bulbs in temperate regions are 'winter-growers', making their new roots in autumn and winter, followed by leaves and flowers in spring, then dying down again for the summer. In a woodland, the trees and shrubs shed their leaves in autumn, are leafless and more or less dormant during winter, then produce a new crop of leaves for the summer. At the time when the bulbs make their growth, moisture can filter through the canopy to the ground beneath; the trees do not require it so it is available for the bulbs and other small shade-tolerant plants, and light can filter through to allow the leaves of the

12 *Trillum chloropetalum*. Successful cultivation of bulbs is largely a matter of choosing the right spot.

smaller plants to photosynthesize. In the late spring the bulbs begin to die down and the trees and shrubs come into active growth, shading the ground beneath and using up large quantities of moisture; hence the soil, although shaded and probably quite cool, is actually relatively dry for the rest of the summer and the possession of a swollen rootstock provides a means of overcoming these adverse conditions. Obviously there are not nearly as many shade-loving bulbs as there are from the open, sunny hillsides, but there are some important and very attractive ones which we can exploit to the full for our gardens. These winter-growing bulbs which are suitable for shaded situations differ from those which need full sun in that during their rest period in summer they do not require a great deal of warmth in order to form flower buds. Whereas the sun-lovers will not form flower buds, and may even die, if kept cool and moist in their dormant period, the shade-lovers may be adversely affected by hot, dry conditions while they are at rest.

The temperate summer-growing bulbs which are adapted to shade (there are relatively few) tend to come from winter-cold or mountain areas where they overwinter in the dormant state because of the cold, often under snow, then grow and flower in summer in response to increasing warmth

and moisture availability from melting snow and summer rainfall. Many of the lilies of Asia and North America are 'programmed' to this climatic pattern and provide us with some of the horticulturally most important summer bulbs which can be grown in dappled shade.

There is, of course, not just one type of shade. In Mediterranean climates there is warm, dry shade beneath trees and shrubs where some bulbs shelter out of the burning summer sun; *Cyclamen hederifolium*, for example, is usually to be found tucked away in scrub or on shady banks where it does get dry in summer but not baked. In gardens it is thus a superb plant for dry shade (even under pine trees), just as long as it gets enough winter dampness to stimulate its growth and support the leaves until late spring; normally this will not thrive in permanently damp shade or heavy moist soils in the garden. On the other hand, some bulbs are natives of fairly damp woodland – some *Galanthus* and *Erythronium* species for instance – and these will grow well on the damper, heavier soils in the garden. Before planting any particular species of bulb it is worth trying to find out the natural conditions in which it occurs in the wild but, nevertheless, it always pays to experiment in varying conditions; in the world of plants one can always disprove any theory!

Although the following list of suggestions contains those which one would normally think of as shade lovers, it is important to remember that in some particularly warm regions, or where the light intensity is high, it may be necessary to provide shade for bulbs which in other cooler or duller areas would be planted in full sun.

13 Partially shaded areas provide homes for those bulbs requiring cooler, moister conditions.

Bulbs suitable for dappled shade:

Anemone apennina, blanda, nemorosa, ranunculoides

Camassia, most species and cultivars

Cardiocrinum giganteum

Chionodoxa, all species

Cyclamen coum, hederifolium, purpurascens, repandum

Eranthis hyemalis, cilicica, x tubergenii

Erythronium, most species and cultivars

Galanthus, most species and cultivars

Hyacinthoides hispanica, non-scripta

Leucojum aestivum, vernum

Lilium, most species and cultivars; not L. candidum

Nomocharis, most species

Scilla bifolia, siberica, 'Tubergeniana'

Trillium, most species

Bulbs in grass, and naturalizing bulbs

I have always enjoyed seeing and growing bulbs in a grassy situation for they often look far more natural than in a bare, cultivated border, although the number of species which will actually flourish in grass is limited. However, there are quite a lot which are natives of meadows or alpine turf, and can be naturalized in any patch of grass which is not going to be treated as a formal lawn and closely mown throughout the year. On the other hand, few people have enough space in the garden to allow their area of bulbs-in-grass to develop into a hayfield during the summer, and most will want to keep it trimmed down from late spring onwards. A combination of tidy lawn and rough grass is a useful compromise, and if one is prepared to leave a section of grass there is quite a range of bulbs which can be used to provide a delightful feature in the garden. If it is a sizeable area, an informal winding path can

be kept mown through the grass between the bulbs or, alternatively, a path of stepping stones of irregular paving or slices of tree trunk can be provided.

The majority of hardy bulbs which we grow in gardens are spring- or autumn-flowering ones which are dormant in summer, so these fit in well with such a plan. In the same way that trees and shrubs use up excess moisture, grassland can also provide a suitable environment for certain bulbs by drying out the soil at the time when the bulbs are dying down. Conversely, when the bulbs are in growth in the autumn to spring period, the grass is growing very slowly and is not competing for the available water.

One great advantage with bulbs in rough grass is that the area can be used during the summer, at least for sitting on, but when bulbs in borders die down they leave a bare patch, and little else can be done with the area since it is not good practice to cover them with other plants. In borders, flower bud formation may be affected if there is a lush growth of summer vegetation keeping the soil cool and damp, and summer perennials may need watering in dry weather just when the bulbs should not be wet; grass, on the other hand, can be cut short at this period, allowing the sun through to warm the soil to some extent. From early autumn onwards through to late spring or early summer the grass can be left to grow, providing a pleasant neutral foil for the bulbs when they are in flower and also some support for those with slender tubes such as the crocuses and colchicums which can get battered down by rain and splashed with mud when growing in the open border. It has been said that mice and squirrels do not dig up crocuses which are growing in grass as readily as they do those in the more cultivated parts of the garden but I have no convincing proof of this.

The question which most people need an answer to when contemplating growing bulbs in this way is when to make the first cut of grass in the spring. Ideally this should not be until the bulbs have completed their growth cycle, that is when the leaves have developed fully and begun to turn yellow, and perhaps also when seeds have been shed, although this is usually about the same time or shortly after. After this, it is actually beneficial to cut the grass to allow the sun to get through to warm the soil. Normally, using daffodils as an example, this would be towards late spring or early summer; they tend to retain their foliage longer than most other bulbs, so provide a useful standard to work with. It was found in some comparative experiments in a trial at the Royal Horticultural Society's garden at Wisley that the minimum safe time between flowering and cutting the leaves was 6 weeks; any period less than this resulted in loss of vigour of the bulbs and a reduction of flowering in the following season caused by weakening of the bulbs. Some bulbs, for example Winter Aconites, Chionodoxas, *Scilla bifolia*, Crocus and Snowdrops complete their growth cycle much more rapidly than Narcissus, so for these it might be possible to cut the grass much earlier, within about 1 month. After the initial cut of the grass which, in view of the height it will have reached, may need to be by hand, 'strimmer' or a strong rotary mower, the grass can be mown conventionally right through until the autumn.

Of course, if the intention is to naturalize bulbs in grass and allow them to self-seed to form a colony, then it is necessary to leave the grass uncut until the seed pods have ripened and shed their seeds. This might be well into summer with the later bulbs. The capsules can be left to scatter their seeds with nature's resulting informality and uncertainty, or the seeds can be collected and sown so that a crop of young bulbs is available for planting out when large enough. The first method is by far the laziest route but the second is likely to lead to a larger number of flowering bulbs in a shorter time, perhaps blooming a year or two earlier than those which have to compete with the grass before reaching maturity. If a planting of bulbs in grass is left to its own devices to produce a naturalized effect one should not expect any of their seedling offspring to flower in under three years, but from then on a new batch of flowering-sized bulbs should be added to the population each year if all is going well.

Most hardy bulbs are planted in autumn soon after they are received from the nursery. Planting in grass is perhaps not quite as straightforward as in the open border but it presents no great difficulty. A bulb planter can be used, which takes out a core of turf and soil, but with such a tool only one or two bulbs can be planted at a time. I prefer to mark out a sizeable piece of turf with a spade and slice underneath it, then roll it up like a rug, dig the soil beneath and plant the bulbs, then roll back the 'carpet'. If the soil is not suitable, for example, poorly drained, this is the time to improve it by working in coarse sand and/or moss peat before planting the bulbs. Fertilizer can also be added; a light dressing of a balanced one with roughly equal proportions of nitrogen, phosphate and potash (NPK) is fine, avoiding those with a high nitrogen content since these will encourage the grass, which will become too lush. About 1 oz per square yard is sufficient.

If a new area is being grassed over for the first time the bulbs should, of course, be planted before the final rolling, raking and seeding takes place. Autumn is a good time for lawn preparation as well as for bulb planting so both operations can be carried out together.

For random plantings or an informal, naturalized effect in grass it is often recommended that the bulbs are scattered by hand and then planted where they fall. However, with the smaller bulbs and corms, having scattered them it is not always easy to find all of them, and there is always the danger of treading on some of them whilst planting others. Large bulbs like Narcissus can be dealt with in this way without the problem. However, in general I regard this method as too disorganized and it does not necessarily give rise to pleasing results. Although it sounds a contradiction in terms, in my opinion it is better to plan the informality, taking nature as an example. In the wild, large populations of bulbs are seldom of uniform density, some areas thick and others very sparse, and a smallish colony may consist of a dense central 'core' of many plants, becoming more thinly scattered towards the edges of the patch. This effect is to my mind more attractive than a solid drift, and it is easily achieved by starting to plant at the centre of the proposed colony and placing the first bulbs close together, then increasingly farther apart as you work outwards. Random mixtures of bulbs seldom look very satisfactory so it is best to separate the different species or varieties, although the patches can be merged and overlapped in an informal way. The planning stages can be done on paper or actually on the site, but in the latter case I think it is best to put the bulbs in boxes or trays and move them around, bearing in mind the colours and heights until the envisaged effect is achieved; then planting can take place. If planning on paper it is sometimes helpful to have on hand a set of colour photos of the bulbs to be planted; these can usually be easily obtained by searching through a few nursery catalogues and cutting them out. By arranging these in different ways, pleasing associations can be worked out before purchasing the bulbs. I am sure that the nurseryman would approve of the mutilation if an order was forthcoming!

The type of grass is usually dictated by what is already on the site and on the whole it is not worth trying to change the make-up of an existing patch of grass since what is growing there is probably natural for the area. However, the grasses may be very coarse ones which swamp the bulbs, so it may be worth killing off the existing patch using a contact weedkiller (hormone type, if they are very persistent creeping grasses) and re-sowing. When starting a new grassy area there is a choice of seed mixes and it is better to select one of the finer mixtures, avoiding those with any of the tougher coarser species. However, the choice partly depends on what is likely to survive best in the area, different countries and climates usually requiring different grass mixes; with the finer grasses it is possible to try out some of the smaller bulbs instead of being confined to the larger more robust varieties. In general it may be said that if the grass grows well, then the soil will also be suitable for bulbs. Grass does not thrive in dense shade, waterlogged or dusty dry conditions, and neither will bulbs grow in such situations. There are many bulbs which will grow satisfactorily in grass, the range depending partly on the underlying soil type and the fineness of the grass. In turf consisting of coarse strong growing grasses on heavy soils it is not really sensible to try the very small bulbs since they will rapidly become swamped in the spring by the developing grass. In these conditions it is better to plant the more robust types such as the taller *Narcissus*, *Colchicum*, *Ornithogalum*, *Leucojum aestivum* etc. On lighter, well-drained soils it is quite likely that the grasses will be finer and less vigorous so that it will be possible to try some of the dwarf bulbs like Reticulata Irises, *Crocus*, *Romulea*, *Scilla*, small *Narcissus* species, *Tulipa* and Alliums. Anyone lucky enough to have an area of sloping grassy ground with water seeping through it, especially in the spring, might well find that they have the ideal spot for some of the dwarf *Narcissus* species, particularly *N. bulbocodium* and *N. cyclamineus*. Nevertheless, whatever the conditions, it is worth experimenting with a few bulbs of anything which can be spared, and it sometimes comes as a pleasant surprise to find that a bulb which has been cosseted in a pot under glass for many years 'takes off' and thrives when planted out. Several successes in our own garden have been achieved by mistake, usually when old potting compost containing overlooked bulblets has been used to fill in uneven areas in the rough grass at the bottom of the garden. It is unexpected events such as this which make gardening such great fun.

The following bulbs which I have tried, or have seen doing well, in grass all flower in autumn or spring. The summer-growing bulbs are on the whole not very suitable and make it almost impossible to cut the grass. There may, however, be a case for planting a patch or two of something dramatic, such as a group of Lilies, which will liven up the area later on when all the other bulbs are dormant and most of the grass has been cut; being tall, they are very easily avoided when mowing. I have seen clumps of *L. monadelphum* (or *L. szovitsianum*), *L. pyrenaicum* and *L. martagon* growing happily in such conditions but there is scope for experimentation here, perhaps with some of the very robust and relatively cheap Asiatic hybrids.

Bulbs suitable for growing in grass include:

Anemone blanda
Allium: *A. hollandicum*, *A. aflatunense*, *A. stipitatum*, *A. moly*
Camassia: any species
Chionodoxa: any species and cultivars
Colchicum: *C. autumnale* and its varieties, *C. byzantinum*, *C. speciosum* and its varieties, especially the large white

'Album', and any of the robust hybrids such as 'The Giant', 'Lilac Wonder' and 'Rosy Dawn'
Crocus: spring-flowering: *C. angustifolius* (*C. susianus*), *C. biflorus*, *C. etruscus*, *C. chrysanthus* and cultivars, *C. sieberi*, *C. tommasinianus* and cultivars, large Dutch selections of *C. vernus*, 'Dutch Yellow' ('Golden Yellow', 'Yellow Mammoth', 'Yellow Giant' etc.). Autumn-flowering: *C. banaticus*, *C. kotschyanus*, *C. laevigatus*, *C. nudiflorus*, *C. pulchellus*, *C. serotinus* ssp. *salzmannii* (*C. asturicus*), *C. speciosus* and its various forms
Erythronium: *E. dens-canis*
Fritillaria: *F. meleagris*, *F. pyrenaica*
Galanthus: *G. nivalis*
Hyacinthoides: *H. non-scripta*, *H. hispanica* (*campanulata*)
Leucojum: *L. aestivum*, *L. vernum*
Muscari: *M. armeniacum*, *M. neglectum*
Narcissus: *N. bulbocodium*, *N. cyclamineus* and its hybrids, e.g. 'Tete-a-Tete', 'February Gold', *N. poeticus*, *N. pseudonarcissus* variants and any of the larger trumpet and large-cupped daffodil cultivars
Nectaroscordum: *N. siculum*, *N. siculum* subsp. *bulgaricum*
Ornithogalum: *O. nutans*, *O. umbellatum*
Scilla: *S. bifolia*, *S. mischtschenkoana*, *S. siberica*
Tulipa: *T. sylvestris*, *T. sprengeri*

Bulbs in the border and sunny wall beds

Borders

In our progression from the shadier areas of the garden to the open, sunny places, the next position to consider is the more highly cultivated border where there is likely to be a mixture of hardy perennial plants, mostly summer flowering, perhaps a few shrubs and some annuals sown into any gaps. Bulbs can be extremely useful in these areas for extending the season into early spring and perhaps also autumn. Some of the summer bulbs are also valuable and, as far as cultivation is concerned, fit in rather better than the autumn-winter-spring bulbs in that they require water in summer at the same time as the accompanying plants, whereas the latter are summer-dormant and prefer to be dryish.

Spring bulbs are, of course, often used for seasonal bedding displays, sometimes on their own, sometimes in association with other plants; the whole bed is then cleared and replaced with another set of plants for another season. For success, the beds need to be in an open situation and the soil well-cultivated and reasonably freely draining, but there is no difficulty in getting good results since the bulbs are normally purchased fresh each year and will already have flower buds inside. If bulbs are to be kept for another year they should be treated more carefully, the soil fed with a balanced NPK fertilizer, and the bulbs lifted after they have died down naturally and stored dry and warm (but not in full sun) for their dormant period.

In the case of perennial borders, spring bulbs can be used as seasonal bedding in the same way, but planted more informally, in small groups in gaps between the perennials; this can work quite well, extending the flowering season considerably. Many gardeners, however, prefer to plant up bulbs on a more permanent basis. The only borders where bulbs are likely to be successful on a long-term basis are those where there is little disturbance; bulbs planted in beds which are dug over from time to time are a nuisance and rarely thrive; anyone who has had to dig between perennials in winter will sympathize, for it is highly annoying to spike bulbs at every stroke of the fork! The ideal sites are among small shrubs and long-term perennials such as

hellebores, peonies, the smaller euphorbias and michaelmas daisies, where the bulbs can settle in and increase into clumps or seed around. The choice of bulb will depend upon the site; for the dappled shade near shrubs, any of those bulbs mentioned above for growing in shade (page 21) are suitable. In the sunny spaces between low-growing plants at the front of the border, crocuses, the smaller bulbous irises and the shorter hybrid daffodils (especially the 'cyclamineus hybrids') can all be very successful, while farther back the more robust daffodils and tulips can be used; tulips will only thrive if the soil dries out and warms up when they are dormant, so for perennial plantings these need to be placed in open positions where the adjacent plants are those which do not need too much extra water in summer, for example on the sunny side of drought-resistant plants such as *Cistus*, *Ceanothus* and *Cytisus*.

Summer bulbs can be used in the same way; most of these are taller and are therefore very useful for planting farther back in the border where their flowers will push up through other plants. Lilies are the

14 Bulbs grown in formal displays can be lifted and stored dry for the summer. Tulip 'Grevel' and Viola 'Joker'.

15 Sunny borders are good places for bulbous plants as long as their dormant bulbs are not shaded too much in summer.

obvious example, for they do best where their bases are shaded by other plants, but there are other striking subjects, such as *Crinum moore*i, *C. × powellii* and the many *Crocosmia* cultivars. In cold-winter areas where some of the summer bulbs are not hardy it is easy enough to lift them and store them frost-free for the winter months; bulbs such as *Eucomis*, *Galtonia*, *Gladiolus*, *Tigridia* and some of the South African *Ornithogalum* species fall into this category.

For the longer term bulb plantings in borders, feeding will be necessary; this can be done at the end of the dormant season, just before growth recommences and again after flowering, as a light sprinkling of a balanced fertilizer, or as a top dressing of a soil mix containing the same fertilizer; the latter method is useful if the bulbs have a tendency to work to the surface.

Sunny wall beds

For those in the colder climates, sheltered beds at the foot of sunny walls and fences are often treasured sites where the slightly more tender plants can be grown, and particularly those bulbs which require a baking in the sun in order to get them to flower well. In colder gardens (such as our own here in southern England), *Amaryllis belladonna* will only flower if given a site such as this, whereas in warmer regions it is sometimes so 'at home' that it will become almost naturalized. Other 'bulbs' which may need similar positions are *Dracunculus vulgaris*, *Fritillaria imperialis*, *Iris unguicularis*, *Narcissus tazetta*, *Nerine bowdenii*, *Scilla hyacinthoides*, *Sternbergia lutea* and *Tulipa saxatilis*; some of the frost-tender summer bulbs will also do well in such a site, as long as there is enough moisture available in their growing period, and with the extra protection may well survive the winter; *Tigridia pavonia*, for example, is hardy through most winters here if planted against a sunny house wall.

Bulbs in raised beds, the rock garden and bulb frames

For those smaller bulbs which would get lost in the open border, or need extra sharp drainage in order to dry out during their dormant season, the provision of a bed which is raised above the surrounding soil might well prove a good method of cultivation. This can be achieved as a rock garden or as a more formally-shaped raised bed; in areas where there is rainfall at the 'wrong' time of year, when bulbs need to be dry, the raised bed can be covered to provide a purpose-built bulb frame. These three garden features will be dealt with together, since they are in fact very similar in application and construction.

A rock garden is, in effect, a series of raised beds put together in an informal way so as to provide a feature in its own right, not just as a place to grow plants. However, in addition, if considerable thought is given to its construction, it can provide a very varied range of habitats for any small plants, as well as bulbs. A rock garden which I once constructed, with this aim in mind, included (of course) pockets of soil at varying levels facing in different directions, so that some were hot and sunbaked and some were tucked behind large rocks for those plants which preferred cooler conditions; a few small deciduous shrubs were planted for shade, there was a sharply drained area of 'scree', and a small piece of meadow for naturalizing bulbs. It could have been extended to include a pond and stream, which would have increased the range of habitats, but from the point of view of growing bulbs this would not have added much value since few bulbs require very damp sites. All this was in an area of not more than about 30 m x 20 m (100 x 65 ft).

Raised beds are much simpler to construct, and although they do not have quite the same visual impact, provide very good conditions in which to grow the great majority of smaller hardy bulbs. The main point of building such a bed is to raise the area above the natural soil level for the purpose of providing better drainage, at the same time facilitating viewing and maintenance of the small plants growing in it. Tiny crocuses, romuleas, irises and so on, which can be almost lost out in the main borders of a garden, can be appreciated at close quarters and, depending upon how high the bed is raised, such jobs as weeding can be made much less of a chore. Even in areas where the natural soil is already well-drained, or the summers are dry, it may still be an advantage to have a raised bed for the smaller bulbs for this very reason.

Soils for raised beds and rock gardens

From what has been said about drainage it follows that the soil mix for bulb beds and rock gardens must have a good proportion of grit or sharp sand incorporated into it.

A rough guide to the type of mix which would be suitable is: 2 parts loam (or the local garden soil): 1 part moss peat (coir or leafmould will suffice if the current worries about peat reserves prove to be well-founded): 2 parts grit or sharp sand. Obviously the garden soil will differ widely from place to place, so it is a case of using common sense and adjusting the proportions accordingly; if the soil is already sandy, then the proportion of grit/sand can be reduced and more peat added; if it is a heavy clay, the percentages of grit and peat are increased. The aim should be to get a crumbly type of mix which will not stick together and form a hard sticky ball if it is rolled together in the hands. Having achieved this, some fertilizer is required, and a balanced (NPK in about equal proportions) commercial flower fertilizer would be suitable, avoiding those which have a high proportion of nitrogen. There are many improvements which could be made to this mix but, for a rock garden, it is likely that a considerable amount will be required, and this is probably the cheapest answer. A ready-made, loam-based potting medium could be purchased, and mixed with extra grit on a 1:1 basis but,

16 Even a small rock garden can provide a wide range of habitats.

although very satisfactory and involving much less work, it would probably work out much more expensive than a home mix. One great advantage of buying in such a mix would be that it had been sterilized; to home-sterilize enough soil for a rock garden would be too great a problem for most amateur gardeners.

For the great majority of bulbs a soil which is slightly acid to slightly alkaline will be suitable (pH 6–7.5); they appear to be not particularly fussy in that respect. Although a lot of the Mediterranean and western Asiatic bulbs are natives of lime-stone regions, often growing in alkaline red clay soils, they seem to do equally well in cultivation, using this area of south-east England as an example, in conditions as diverse as the acid sandy soils of the Surrey heaths and the chalk-rich gardens of the downlands. It is noticeable, however, that in some gardens a particular species will increase while in others it will survive. The reasons for this are seldom obvious. A good example is the old favourite, *Crocus tom-masinianus*, which is virtually a weed, albeit a very nice one, in some areas, while in others it is very well-behaved or is even rather reluctant to grow. Our own garden belongs to the latter category, this lovely little species staying in neat clumps as planted, whereas a friend regards it as a pest and is constantly removing it from his rock garden. It would be interesting to study individual species such as this to try to ascertain what it is about the soil or micro-climate which leads to success or failure; a complete cultivation dossier on each of all the species of bulb in cultivation would be a wonderful project, but life is too short!

Raised beds

It is logical to deal with these first since they are more simple to construct than rock gardens, although the basic principles are similar. Firstly the site and the materials must be chosen. The site, for most of the dwarf bulbous plants, needs to be out in the open where there is good air movement and plenty of light, although to some extent this will be dictated by local conditions as it is difficult to make sweeping statements which will cover anywhere in the world. In Britain, for example, the gardener needs to choose a site in full sun to try to compensate for the low light intensity in winter and spring when most of the smaller bulbs are in growth; in parts of Australia or South Africa it might well be necessary to choose a semi-shaded site so that bulbs from Europe and western Asia can survive the intense sun. Even in Britain I have known dormant bulbs to get 'cooked' during a very hot period in summer whilst they were dormant; the very sandy soil mix just got too hot and they literally boiled in their own juices; however, this is a very rare occur-rence in our climate!

The material used to construct the bed will depend partly on what is available, per-sonal taste and whether aesthetics come into the decision at all. The purpose of the surround is to raise the bed and keep the soil in place, so it may be made of wood, stone, concrete, brick, plastic or anything else to hand. Railway sleepers, for example, may be readily available in some areas while in others a beautiful walling stone may be the most convenient material. The height of the bed is also largely a matter of preference; in areas where the natural soil is reasonably well-drained it is unnecessary to raise it more than about 15–30 cm (6–12 in) above ground level whereas over heavy clay, 30–60 cm (12–24 in) would be much better. A higher bed can be built, making a garden feature of it, and this has the advan-tage that the walls can be planted up with crevice plants as an added attraction, but such a bed can cause problems for the non-bulbous plants in that it may be too deep for their roots to reach the subsoil and, being raised so much above soil level, it may dry out too much for them to survive during long dry spells.

The shape of the bed can be varied to fit in with the overall plan for the garden, from a formal square, oblong or round, to any irregular shape with sinuate walls to match or complement the shapes of any other beds or garden structures. So the message is that any material, height or shape will suffice as long as it results in a well-drained area for growing bulbs.

All gardens have pest problems to some degree but some suffer much more than others. Digging and burrowing creatures can be a real nuisance – squirrels are the worst here – and it may be necessary to take some action. The raised bed can be adapted to provide some degree of protection by using a fine mesh galvanized wire netting. Before filling the constructed bed with soil it is lined with netting on the bottom and sides; then it is filled with the soil mix to within about 5 cm (2 in) of the top of the bed, the bulbs are planted and another thin layer of soil is placed over them. More netting is then placed over the top so that it links with the sides leaving no gaps. This can then be hidden from view with a final layer of soil or grit. The bulbs will grow up through the mesh without hindrance, but creatures attempting to burrow down will be discouraged if not prevented altogether. Undoubtedly this adds quite a lot of work and is a nuisance whenever one wishes to dig up some bulbs, but in really badly affected areas it may be the only answer, short of poisoning the local livestock, which gardeners are increasingly reluctant to do. There is one other distinct advantage to those who open their gardens: it does deters those members of the public who seem to think that plants, unlike other possessions, are community property!

For the more functional 'botanical collection' bulb bed I prefer to plant in straight lines, using perforated pots (see page 35), making lifting so much easier when the time comes to refurbish the bed. It is also a good plan to alternate the various types so that there are very different-looking bulbs adjacent to each other; that way, if something does spread into its neighbour, it will be easier to separate them out at replanting time. If a more informal effect is required it is also a good plan to separate like bulbs, and with a bit of planning the seasonal interest can be spread all over the bed rather than confined to certain areas at certain times of year.

A raised bed such as this may be the perfect answer to growing bulbs in areas where a dry rest period cannot be guaranteed in the normal garden soil but, if such a feature is planted solely with bulbs, is likely to be a bit of an eyesore when they are dormant. It is therefore preferable to incorporate a range of other plants which will enjoy the same sort of conditions and provide interest at other times of the year, not necessarily flowers, but at least some interesting foliage effects. There are plenty of suitable 'rock plants' which, once established with their roots well down into the subsoil of the bed, will survive long dry periods; this is essential, since watering when the bulbs are dormant will completely defeat the purpose of providing a bed which dries out! It is also important to choose plants which will not become large and leafy, spreading over the dormant bulbs and keeping them cool when they should be warm and dry. So, the best types are those which occur naturally in hot, dry areas and have small leaves with compact growth, thus providing interest while covering only restricted areas or casting a minimal amount of shade. Plants from Mediterranean-type and steppe climates, those areas with high light intensity and seasonal drought, are high on the list of suitable subjects. There is plenty of choice: examples include species and cultivars of *Thymus*, *Acantholimon*,

Dianthus, *Astragalus*, *Helianthemum*, *Helichrysum*; the choice will depend somewhat on the local climate and in turn what is hardy in the area.

Aftercare of raised beds

A raised bed can be left to its own devices, except for the usual weeding, for as long as the bulbs and plants in it are doing well and not outgrowing their space. Inevitably some will grow better than others and require lifting and dividing; eventually the whole bed will require replanting, perhaps after 3–4 years. On the whole, with such a bed it is better to collect the seeds rather than allow them to fall and spread naturally. Certainly if the bed houses a valuable collection of bulbs this is essential, since they will rapidly get thoroughly mixed as the more vigorous species seed into clumps of others. Aftercare really is a case of common sense gardening; feeding with a well-balanced fertilizer will help to maintain vigour, and a commercial fertilizer with roughly similar proportions of NPK is suitable for this purpose, applied in late winter in the case of the 'winter-growers' when they begin to grow strongly at the onset of warmer weather. The summer-growers can be fed in late spring or early summer. If, for some reason, flowering is rather poor, it is worth trying a high potash feed instead, or even 'sulphate of potash' itself. Rather than trying to make a generalized statement about application rates, I would say that it is always best to follow the rates recommended on the packets. On the whole if the bulbs are healthy and flowering well it is better to leave them alone, but if they start to dwindle, become congested or flower less freely, then it is time to empty the bed and start again with new soil. This is carried out at the same time of year as the initial planting, towards the end of the dormant period so that they will begin to grow again soon after planting.

A raised bulb bed can be much more than just a utilitarian construction for the cultivation of bulbs. Planted with a range of dwarf bulbs and associated plants chosen for a long display it can make an interesting and rather unusual garden feature.

Rock gardens

Apart from being an attraction in its own right, the rock garden is a useful home for those bulbs which require sharp drainage but at the same time do not mind a little competition from other plants. Especially suitable, of course, are the dwarf bulbs, many of which are mountain or rock plants in the wild, although not necessarily from very high altitudes; the species and varieties of *Crocus*, *Tulipa*, *Iris*, *Muscari* etc., are ideal for the colder-winter areas, while in milder climates many of the Cape bulbs, which are not hardy in Britain, are suitable. This combination of rock plants with bulbs works best in the case of the 'winter-growing' bulbs which grow and flower in the autumn-winter-spring period when there are few rock plants in flower, the latter providing their display during the late spring and summer. Creeping or carpeting plants such as alpine *Phlox*, *Antennaria* and *Thymus* can be planted over some of the more tolerant bulbs so that there is a longer season of interest; the flower stems of the bulbs receive some support and the blooms are to some extent protected from soil splashes during heavy rain; this is particularly useful with some of the autumn-flowering bulbs such as *Crocus* and the smaller *Colchicum* species. Many of the more specialist bulbs, however, will not stand much competition and need to be planted between other plants; when they die down for their period of rest it is wise to keep that patch of soil free from other plants which might keep the soil shaded and too cool for the bulbs to ripen and set flower buds for the next season. Any bulbs which are native to areas which are hot and dry during the summer are likely to need a warm rest period if they are to perform well.

Not all of the rock garden needs to be sunbaked, however, and in fact it is essential to have a few larger plants as well to provide shade for those plants which normally grow in cooler spots. Dwarf shrubs are very much in keeping with a rock garden, providing a little dappled shade and, from the point of view of the bulbs, they actually perform a useful purpose in helping to use up excess moisture in the soil when the bulbs are dormant in summer.

This is not the place to go into detailed construction methods for rock gardens; there are specialist books available on the subject, but it is appropriate to mention the rock and soils. The choice of rock is largely a matter of personal preference and what is available in the area. If a very informal effect is preferred, then 'misshapen' rocks such as waterworn limestone and tufa are fine, whereas the sedimentary rocks like sandstone often have a more rigid appearance and must be laid so that there is a convincingly natural stratified effect. As far as the bulbs are concerned it matters very little, providing that there is good drainage but, at the same time, plenty of moisture available during the growing season. It is therefore important to arrange the rocks so that they form pockets of soil, preferably tipping slightly back into the 'hill' of the rock garden so that water falling on it will be trapped and fed back into the pockets. The 'plum pudding' rock garden, which one sees all too often, consisting of a heap of soil with rocks pushed almost haphazardly into it, not only looks awful but, even worse perhaps, any water which falls on it immediately rushes off down between the rocks to the lower parts, washing away some of the soil and leaving the bulk of the rock garden dry. The well-constructed rock garden catches water so that the plants grow well, but at the same time the soil is well-drained so that it never becomes waterlogged and sour.

Having constructed the rock garden and mixed the soil, the pockets are filled to the top and watered well to settle the soil in before planting. A top-dressing of grit, gravel, or crushed pieces of rock to match the stone of the rock garden, is a nice finishing touch but is best left until after planting. On soils which are very heavy and poorly drained it may be necessary to put a layer of gravel, clinker, crushed brick etc., into the bottom of each rock pocket before topping up with the mixed soil, just to make sure that the drainage is sharp.

Planting bulbs in the rock garden

Planting time for bulbs is dictated largely by their availability: autumn-winter-spring bulbs are on sale from late summer onwards for planting in autumn, whereas summer bulbs are available in the nurseries in spring for immediate planting. Few summer bulbs are grown in rock gardens since most of them are tall compared with the autumn-winter-spring bulbs, and there is, in any case, plenty of colour from other non-bulbous plants during the summer season. There is a place, however, for a few tall species, for example some of the smaller-flowered and more graceful *Lilium* species such as *L. pomponium*, *L. tenuifolium* (*L. pumilum*), *L. mackliniae* and *L. martagon*; these may be on sale in autumn or spring. Apart from the marketing of dormant bulbs, there is an increasing range, certainly of the smaller bulbs, on sale in pots when in bud or in flower and these can be planted as soon as purchased. There is no great advantage in buying them in growth other than that the effect is instant and you can see what you are buying; it is also, perhaps, easier to associate them with other plants rather than trying to imagine how a particular association is going to turn out in six months time.

The actual planting does not differ in any way from planting bulbs in any other sort of bed, but the placing of the bulbs might benefit from a slightly different approach. A rock garden, to be effective, should consist of fairly informal plantings; to my mind it is better to avoid solid blocks of one species, colourful as they may be, and place a few bulbs away from the main colony, both to the sides and on the next shelf below as if the colony is seeding itself around. In addition to the unnatural appearance, the large solid planting will, of course, leave a bigger bare space when the bulbs die down.

Bulb frames

A bulb frame is normally used for the autumn-winter-spring growing bulbs (see page 11), although one might, in cold-winter areas, also construct such a frame in which to grow summer bulbs with a view to keeping them dry in winter and slightly protected from frost. The bulb frame is, in effect, just a raised bed with provision for some form of transparent covering. In the case of the winter-growers, which is the group of bulbs we will discuss here, the lights are fitted when necessary, either for protection from inclement weather in winter or to keep off excess rain in summer when the bulbs are supposed to be dormant and warm, or perhaps both. Although it is perhaps not the most attractive of garden features, the bulb frame does represent an excellent method of growing summer-dry bulbs in areas where this cannot be guaranteed. In most of the cooler, temperate countries the summers are just not warm enough or dry enough to 'ripen' some types of bulb, and they will either not flower or will die out altogether if planted in the open garden. However, with slight protection such as a bulb frame can

provide, a whole range of delightful bulbs can be grown successfully, including such treasures as the Oncocyclus and 'Juno' irises, a wide range of *Tulipa* species, many of the more unusual fritillarias, rare crocuses, the Middle Eastern and Central Asiatic tuberous anemones and *Corydalis*, and the lovely western North American *Calochortus*.

The comments made above about the construction of a raised bed apply more or less to a bulb frame, but the materials and shape are dictated by the type of frame coverings to be used. These can range from, at the simplest end of the scale, sheets of corrugated plastic to more expensive but more permanent metal-framed structures, a number of which are on the market. These last types have the advantage of providing more headroom for the bulbs to develop properly, whereas using lights which are laid flat on the frame it is only possible to grow the shorter species. Plastic sheeting is perfectly adequate providing that some provision is made for weighting it down or fixing it firmly, and this can be quite difficult. Being light and flexible it flexes up and down in windy weather and can 'wriggle' out from underneath any weights which are placed around the edges. Therefore it is best to attach stout string or plastic-covered wire at both ends and stretch it along the frame to hold the sheets down in the centre as well as at their ends. Even the heavier metal-and-glass frames need attaching to the basic structure in some way. If a long-term bulb frame is planned, it is cheaper in the longer run to go for a glass construction since plastic needs to be replaced from time to time and, even if it does not crack, it inevitably becomes scratched and transmits less light. A heavy duty clear plastic should be chosen, and one which is claimed to be stable in sunlight or it will discolour rapidly. I have found that even the good quality corrugated plastic sheets will go 'cloudy' if stacked one on top of the other in sunlight in summer so, when not in use, always cover the lights or place them in shade.

The frame itself can be made from a variety of materials – whatever is the most convenient in the area – such as brick, concrete or manufactured concrete blocks, stone, treated wood or railway sleepers. In the last century the renowned George Maw, of Crocus fame, constructed his bulb frames by making the surround of earth and resting the lights across the walls so that the frame was rather like a moat without the water; this must be one of the cheapest bulb frames possible, but one would have to make sure that it was raised well above the surrounding soil or it would become even more like a moat!

Since bulb frames are usually practical rather than ornamental it is wise to plant in rows and keep a plan for reference; also it is best to prevent things from seeding into each other, otherwise chaos will surely result. If seeds are not wanted the flowers can be 'dead-headed' as soon as they begin to fade but otherwise, keep a careful watch and collect them before they are shed from the capsules. There is always a good demand from friends for seeds, and the various specialist societies are very keen to acquire any surplus seeds, so I would recommend saving them. As far as the actual planting is concerned, I prefer to use the perforated mesh pots which ensure that the bulbs do not grow into each other and can be lifted easily when necessary. Alternatively, slates or tiles can be sunk into the soil vertically to act as dividers between the various species.

In the case of most of the winter rainfall bulbs the annual sequence of treatment of a bulb frame consists of keeping the lights on through the summer months, in order to keep the dormant bulbs warm and dry, then removing them in autumn and giving several good waterings to encourage root action. In late autumn, or when the wetter, colder weather arrives, the lights are

17 A bulb frame for bulbs which are summer-dormant and require protection from excess rain.

replaced for the winter to give some degree of protection from the elements. The soil should retain enough moisture through winter to make it unnecessary to water very much, so management through winter is really only a case of checking to see that no pests are causing damage, that the frame lights are clean, allowing as much light as possible to pass through and that there is plenty of air through the frame on all but the coldest nights; this will very much depend upon the local climate conditions and the hardiness of the bulbs which have been chosen. The aim of all this is to grow the bulbs as 'hard' as possible without actually freezing them to death; this way they will be more in character and less likely to succumb to diseases such as botrytis. A problem which we experience in England is that in winter we have alternating warm and cold periods in which the light intensity is often poor so that bulbs in frames tend to appear above ground very early and become etiolated. These simple practices are therefore important. When the warmer spring weather arrives, the frame lights can be removed altogether and the bulbs watered freely and given liquid feeds of a potash-rich fertilizer; the type sold for tomato-growing is ideally suited. If the weather is reasonably good the frame lights can be left through flowering and seeding until the foliage begins to die back in early summer, unless of course there is some very bad weather which might damage the blooms. The leaves dying back is a sign that the time has come to start to dry off the bulbs for the summer, so the coverings can be replaced to keep off any summer rain. Here again, local conditions will dictate what is actually done; in areas with very hot summer weather it is best to apply some shading as the bulbs may actually cook, although if this is the case then there is probably no need for a bulb frame anyway!

Bulbs growing in such a frame can be left for three or four years, or as long as they are continuing to grow well, but it is a good idea in the interim years to feed them in late winter with a granular balanced NPK fertilizer; this will filter down during watering through the spring months. The slow-release pelleted fertilizers are also useful and could be applied in autumn.

Replanting a bulb frame is best carried out in late summer or early autumn, just before root growth is about to commence again. Although a slow and laborious business, this is, like repotting, a time to find out what has increased in size or number and whether you are doing the right thing; although the bulbs are dormant, a great deal can be learned about them and their cultivation at this time.

Bulbs in pots and other containers under glass

The attraction of growing bulbs in pots is that they can be given individual treatment and extra special care; they can be moved around for display or for showing when in flower, then stacked away during their

18 Although hardy, small bulbs are often better in a cool glasshouse. (Photo: courtesy Alan Edwards).

dormant season and the space used for something else. In the case of the smaller or more esoteric subjects, they can be viewed close to, and they are more readily accessible for photographing. Frost-tender bulbs, such as the many lovely Cape bulbs and the more tropical subjects, can be grown in pots under glass in areas where they would otherwise be impossible to cultivate. For those who grow specialist collections of bulbs, perhaps a lot of species of one genus, it is also much easier to keep them separate when in pots than if they are all planted out in the open ground. On the other hand, there is much more work involved in maintaining bulbs in pots since they require more frequent watering, feeding and mostly need repotting every year; there is also the provision of frames or glasshouses to consider, with all the accompanying maintenance work.

Clay or plastic?

Pots are basically made of clay or a plastic, and individual growers have their own preferences in this respect; the choice may be a case of availability or expense. Both can be used successfully but there are various points to consider which may almost dictate which type is used. Clay pots are porous and will dry out quicker than plastic ones; this is an advantage in the case of bulbs which rot off at the slightest sign of excess moisture, for example the Juno group of irises when grown in damp winter climates like that of Britain. Plastic pots do not dry out through the sides and can stay damp for an undesirably long time after watering when the weather is dull and humid; on the other hand, in areas where rather dry mild conditions prevail when the bulbs are in flower, it might be

19 Lattice pots provide an easy method of planting and lifting bulbs, without the root restriction of a normal pot.

preferable to use plastic pots to maintain a more uniform degree of soil moisture.

Potting soils, top dressing, repotting and feeding

Potting soils and their constituents have already been dealt with in Chapter 2; the only additional comment is that if plastic pots are used in damp climates it might be necessary to increase the sharpness of the drainage to counter the fact that there is no water loss through the pot as there is with a clay one. It is very popular, especially with hardy bulb enthusiasts growing specialist collections and those who show their plants, to cover the surface of the pot with grit. This gives a very attractive finish, helps to stop the soil panning down during watering and keeps a sharply drained surface layer around the neck of the bulb. On the other hand, it is not easy to see when the plant needs watering and it also reduces evaporation from the surface, so these are matters to consider when deciding whether or not to 'top-dress' with grit. Repotting is best undertaken every year for most bulbs but, if this is impossible, a good compromise is to scrape away the surface layers down to the level of the bulb and top dress with new potting soil; this is very much quicker than repotting and does give you a

quick sight of the bulbs to check on how they are doing. In the case of the larger bulbs in sizeable containers, such as lilies, this may be the only practical way of dealing with them, and also with those bulbs which are best left crowded and undisturbed in their pots, for example, some of the *Cyrtanthus* and nerines (these cases will be commented upon under the genus entry in Chapter 7). The best time for repotting (and top-dressing with new soil) most bulbs is just before they are watered at the end of their dormant period, when they are ready to start rooting again; they can, however, be successfully 'potted on' without disturbance into a larger pot when in growth; the worst time is probably just as they die down at the start of dormancy since they will then lie in dry loose soil for the remaining dormant period. The volume of soil in a small pot is quite limited so it is wise to give a liquid feed periodically during the growing season (at least once a month); the high potash liquid fertilizers sold for use on tomatoes are excellent for bulbs. If flowering is poor it is also worth trying light feeds of potassium sulphate ('sulphate of potash') which is very soluble in water. Alternatively, if this is a chore, a few granules of a slow release fertilizer can be scattered on the surface after repotting and this will become available steadily through the season as the pots are watered.

Plunging pots

On the whole it is best to plunge pots, both clay and plastic, and certainly the smaller-sized ones, up to the rims in sharp sand, gravel, or some other similar material depending upon availability. This keeps the temperature at root level more uniform, an important point in cold-winter areas in unheated frames and glasshouses since bulbs in pots are far more vulnerable to frost than they are planted in the open ground. In the case of clay pots, plunging

also keeps the moisture levels more uniform, although as mentioned above, this may not necessarily be desirable in very damp climates for certain bulbs.

Heating, ventilation and lighting

In cold-winter areas it will be necessary to provide some form of heating in winter if tender bulbs are to be grown; for example with almost all of the the fascinating South African 'winter-growing' bulbs from the South West Cape it is necessary to keep the glasshouse frost-free, while at the same maintaining a well-aired and not too damp atmosphere. On days when the vents cannot be opened because of the heat loss it is useful to have a small fan to circulate the air. There are various heating systems available – electric, gas, oil – but it should be borne in mind that those involving any form of combustion will lead to moisture formation which may be undesirable in countries which already have a high air humidity. Here in southern England, I find that in most winters the condensation is quite a problem so I prefer to use a fan-blown electric heater which has the fan running all the time and the heating element thermostatically controlled to cut in at the lowest desirable temperature; this deals effectively with both heating and ventilation. The more tropical subjects do not appear to need the air circulation to the same degree as the temperate winter-growing bulbs and I find that these grow well enough in a section of the glasshouse which has a tubular convection heater without a fan. Bubble plastic can be used to reduce heat loss to a minimum, but this does cut down a little on the amount of light reaching the bulbs and those which are in growth in the winter do tend to get rather 'drawn up'. In areas of poor winter light intensity, extra lighting can be provided using purpose-made natural daylight lamps.

Bulbs in pots for an early display indoors

Successfully forcing spring bulbs such as hyacinths for an early indoor display relies on a rather elementary principle. Bulbs bought in autumn for this purpose will have buds already formed inside – that is the nurseryman's job – so all the grower has to do is provide the necessary stimulus. No bulb will perform without water, and without roots it cannot take up water, so the message is to first encourage good root growth and the rest will follow almost automatically. Once the bulbs have a good root system forcing can begin, but if this is attempted too early, before there are sufficient roots, the aerial shoot may not expand properly and the flowers may well abort.

Bulbs such as hyacinths which are essentially 'winter-growers' start to root in late summer/early autumn when moisture levels increase and the temperature falls, so the first thing to do on purchasing bulbs for forcing, usually in early autumn, is to pot them, water them and place them in a cool position. The ideal position is a shaded frame or open bed in a shady part of the garden where they can be plunged up to the rims in sand, peat, gravel, or whatever is available; the plunging helps to maintain a steady temperature and, in the case of clay pots it stops them drying out. The pots are then kept just damp while the roots develop. By mid-autumn an inspection should show that the roots are beginning to emerge from the drainage holes (if this is not happening, turn one pot upside down and tap out the soil to see if there are roots); there may also be signs of the aerial shoot starting to grow as well.

Hyacinths

These are the most popular subjects for forcing for an early display, and are among the most successful. For flowering in mid-winter (Christmas in the northern hemisphere) it is necessary to buy prepared bulbs and plant them fairly early in autumn, in fact soon after they first arrive in the garden centre is a good rule. After potting, as above, they need a cool period of about 9 °C (48 °F) for 8–11 weeks; if the temperature is much above this, planting is best delayed until it has fallen to nearer the optimum of 9 °C (48 °F). Commercial growers who are producing early flowers for market follow a fairly rigid regime of time and temperature, but for the average gardener growing a few for the house, the final forcing into flower is best left until the bud is seen to be pushing up out of the leaf rosette; that way it will be most likely to develop properly. For flowers in late winter or spring, ordinary untreated bulbs are quite adequate. It is best not to mix varieties in a pot or bowl since it is quite likely that they will develop at different rates and not flower together; some people prefer to grow hyacinths singly in pots, then select those which are all at the same stage for planting together in a container just as they come into bloom.

Paperwhite Narcissus

These are very rewarding to force for indoors since they do not require the prolonged cool period beforehand; bulbs purchased and potted immediately can be in flower in as little as six weeks. It is best to buy a number of bulbs and split them, potting them up, say five to a 15 cm (6 in) diameter pot over a period of time to provide a succession of flowers. The first of these can be prepared as soon as the bulbs come in to the garden centres in early autumn, and the rest follow at fortnightly intervals for as long as the bulbs last out, up until late autumn or even early winter; kept in a warm, dry place they will not come to any harm and should not start growing until potted and watered. Paperwhites are liable to become rather tall and fall over so I prefer to give them plenty of light all the time to keep them as stocky as possible, however, it is usually necessary to provide a stake and tie them loosely to it as they develop.

Other bulbs for home forcing

Some bulbs sold for forcing are fine for the purpose providing they are not warmed up too early. Crocuses, the various cultivars of *Iris reticulata* and some of the shorter earlier-flowering tulips are good examples; they look delightful on the windowsill in the early spring but can be a failure if the simple rules are not followed. With these, the cool-growing period is essential for the roots to form and the pots are best placed in a light cool position for the buds to develop;

20 Tropical bulbs such as this *Hippeastrum* make excellent container plants for the conservatory.

they must not be brought into the warmth indoors until the flower buds can be seen, preferably with a little colour showing, otherwise they are likely to abort. Freesias for forcing are bought as pre-treated corms and these need to be planted in early autumn in a frost-free glasshouse. Hippeastrums (still sold as 'Amaryllis') are also given a heat pre-treatment by the commercial grower so that when they are planted (they are often sold already in containers) and watered they will begin to grow quite quickly without any cool period since they are tropical bulbs; a growing temperature of about 20–25 °C (68–77 °F) is suitable.

Treatment of forced bulbs after flowering

After flowering, the treatment of forced bulbs depends upon what is intended for them in the future. If they are to be discarded then they may as well go into the bin immediately, but most people keep them with a view to planting them out in the garden. In areas with fairly mild winters they can be planted out (not hippeastrums, of course, which are tropical/subtropical) into the open ground as soon as they have finished flowering, either straight into the final position in which they are required or into a 'nursery bed' where they can complete their growth cycle. In areas where there is hard frost this will not be possible so it is best to keep them in a cool, light place – cool greenhouse or conservatory is ideal – and feed them regularly with a liquid high potash fertilizer (as for tomatoes) until they die down naturally. This way, reasonably strong bulbs can be achieved which can be planted out for flowering in either the next season or the one after. Hyacinths are quite successful if treated in this way and can give years of pleasure out in the garden; their racemes of flowers become looser and more graceful, standing up well to the weather.

Tropical bulbs

As explained elsewhere (see page 12), tropical bulbs are somewhat different in their cultivation requirements than those from more temperate climates in that they do not experience marked seasonal temperature changes and respond mainly, if not completely, to the availability of water. In the tropics, bulbs are subjected to much the same temperature range throughout the year, perhaps in some instances a little lower during the rainy seasons, and the main fluctuation in temperature is between day and night; those at the higher altitudes are likely to experience quite a substantial range during a 24 hour period. Thus, unlike the 'temperate bulbs' which are fairly fixed in their growth patterns as 'winter-growers' or 'summer-growers', the bulbs from tropical latitudes can be induced, more or less, to grow at any time of year by witholding water and giving a warm rest period, then starting them into growth again by watering. The temperate, winter-growing bulbs will mostly stay in growth for about eight to nine months, then die down for three to four months; the summer-growers have a rather more equally balanced regime of about six months in growth, six months dormant. A lot of the tropical bulbs, however, appear to be able to complete their growth cycle in a shorter period of time and then stay dormant for as long as is required to see them through to the next rains. In some instances (e.g., some South American Amaryllids) it is possible to make use of this in cultivation and get two crops of flowers in one year from the same bulb; a minimum rest period of about two months is necessary, so assuming a growth period of about four months, two complete cycles can be completed in one year. Most growers, including myself, tend to stick to one cycle per year, keeping the bulbs in growth longer by watering and feeding. It makes sense to treat them as summer-growers with the dormant period in winter, the reason being that in temperate zones, which is currently where the great majority of bulb enthusiasts are situated, the light intensity is poorer in winter and much more artificial heat is required to keep the temperature up to the required level during the winter months; bulbs which are dormant in winter can be stacked and kept warm in a much smaller space (such as the airing cupboard) than if they are growing.

The cultivation of tropical bulbs is not really very different from the hardier species. They require a freely-draining potting soil and respond to potash-rich fertilizers. Many of them are potentially much more robust in their growth than their generally smaller, hardier (especially the winter-growers) counterparts, so they tend to require larger containers of good depth to accommodate the strong roots.

Miscellaneous matters

CHAPTER 4

Staking

This of course only applies to the taller bulbs which might be damaged during inclement weather, and since all of the autumn-winter-spring bulbs are fairly dwarf, staking is only necessary for the large summer flowering ones such as the lilies and gladiolus. Especially vulnerable are the highly bred cultivars, often bearing much larger flowers than their wild ancestors, or with many more flowers on the spike.

At the time when bulbs are planted there is no above-ground growth and a lot of tall canes would look very insightly, so I prefer to put in a small cane or stick which acts as a marker to show where the bulbs are planted. Later, this can be removed and the full-sized cane pushed into the same hole, thus avoiding the danger of spearing through the bulb or damaging the roots. This also has the advantage of marking the site so that nothing else is planted over the top of the bulbs by mistake before they have emerged. The main cane needs to be slightly shorter than the expected total height of the plant, thus giving maximum support but without the bare top of the cane standing up above the plant spoiling its appearance. Bulbs in a border are usually viewed from only one side, so it is best in this case to place the cane at the back of the clump, or in the centre, where it will not be too prominent. Normally one cane per bulb will be necessary but with, for example, closely planted lilies in a container or a group in a border, I find that one stout cane in the centre is sufficient; garden twine is then used to tie each stem loosely to this central support in a maypole fashion. When tying stems to a cane never pull them tightly against it or a stiff unnatural effect will result and the twine may well cut into the stem.

At the end of the season when the bulbs have died down, and are lifted for storing, the canes may be removed and these can also be stored in a dry place; treated in this way, they could last for several years. With more permanent plantings (e.g. lilies) the canes

21 *Lilium parryi.* Some of the taller bulbs may require staking.

are best removed as well but, as with the original planting, it is a good plan to mark the position where the cane was with a small stick so that it can be replaced next season without the risk of damaging the bulb.

Labelling and recording data

Most people who are enthusiastic about growing plants like to know what their botanical names are, how they were acquired, perhaps the country of origin and the habitat, when the seeds were sown, etc. On a small scale it is easy enough to remember the details but with a large collection, perhaps containing several different varieties of one species, or various samples from different sources, it is necessary to keep some sort of record. Visitors to the garden might well wish to know the identity or source of a particular plant, and even the best memories fail at times, so there are good reasons for labelling or recording the details in some form. Labelling has another advantage in the case of bulbous plants which disappear below ground periodically in that labels mark their position. Labels can be metal, plastic or wood, or even pottery, but I think that the last two can be discounted for the purposes of a sizeable collection, pottery on the grounds of expense (lovely for small herb gardens!) and wood because of the need for frequent replacement or re-painting; hardwoods can be used, and are very long lasting, but are neither cheap nor easily obtained. Plastic labels have the great advantage of being inexpensive and easy to write on. I prefer to use an ordinary HB pencil which lasts well and does not fade in the sun like some of the 'permanent' marker pens; waxy pencils work reasonably well but seem to have no advantage over the standard 'lead' type. The big disadvantage of many of the plastic labels is that they do not stand up to weather and last only a few years before becoming very brittle and snapping easily. However, they are perfectly adequate for labelling on a temporary basis. I use large numbers of them, especially for seed pots since the seeds may not germinate and thus a more expensive label will not have been wasted. I find that most breakages in plastic labels are a straight snap across at ground level, thus the important part with the writing on is lost; the answer to this is to write on the labels twice, once at the top in the conventional place and once right at the bottom, so that even if the top end goes missing there is still another chance of finding out, for example, important information about the accession number or collector's name and number. There are on the market some plastic labels which are said to be weather resistant, staying pliable rather than becoming brittle; I have not used these for more than a few years so I cannot confirm nor refute these claims. There are also laminated ones in which the name is scratched with a sharp point through a black layer to the white underneath; these are clear and durable but I find it is a slower job to do the writing.

This brings me to metal labels which, although expensive, are very long lasting; as an example, I still have easily discernable labels written after an expedition to Turkey in 1965. I wish that I still had all the bulbs to go with them! So, the initial outlay is greater but in the long run these metal labels may work out much cheaper. There are several types on the market, mostly finished in grey which take pencil or permanent markers very well, but there are copper ones as well which are written on with a ballpoint pen leaving the name indented; these are not as easy to read, although a pencil can be used to go over the name to make it stand out more so. The ink markers give excellent clarity but it is important to ascertain whether the manufacturers consider them to be fade-proof and waterproof; I have not yet found one which does not fade after a couple of years, so pencil is still my first choice.

One big problem with the smaller labels, which is what one uses for most bulbs, is that there is not a great deal of label in the ground so they are relatively easily removed, by the heaving action of frost, sometimes birds, and I have even known them to be scattered by strong winds. This is annoying in a collection where there are a lot of similar species, or different accessions of the same species, growing close together, so one may have to resort to other tactics. Some people use pieces of stout wire pushed deeply into the ground with a loop at its top end to hold the label; not very attractive but very resistant. One could have two labels for each plant, one metal as the above-ground marker, and a small plastic equivalent, either in the bottom of the pot or buried in the soil alongside the bulbs; the latter will last for many years when underground, protected from sunlight and frost.

Recording planting positions and data

If labels are frowned upon in the garden – and they do look fairly awful when the bulbs are dormant – the alternative is to do away with them and have a planting plan of each bed so that individual items can be identified. If graph paper is used, it is useful to mark in the positions of any permanent features such as trees or shrubs, then it is quite easy to identify the smaller plantings. I have occasionally in the past, when time allowed, made quick sketches of beds, as well as having each plant labelled, a real belt-and-braces approach, but this ideal is seldom attainable. On the whole I prefer to have a good label with as much information as possible – name, origin, collector or source, date acquired or date sown, etc., so

that I do not have to come into the house every time I need to know something about a particular plant which has attracted my attention. In addition to this I keep as good records as time will allow, either in a file (sometimes just the seed packet or accompanying letter) or, more recently, on the computer, although the updating of this every time something arrives through the post or dies is quite time consuming. I find the chore of this comparable with making up my annual income tax returns – well, not quite as awful!

Hardiness zones

It is currently popular to try to allocate hardiness ratings to plants, and I can appreciate the reasons for doing so. The only problem is that very few bulbs have been really adequately assessed with regard to hardiness, so the recommendations given in books must be regarded as very rough guides only, mostly guesses. Whether a plant is hardy in a particular area or not very much depends upon the site chosen for the garden, and on the site for the plant within the garden. Even within a small area here in south-east England, the climate varies markedly, and what grows well outside on the warm, sandy soils a few miles down the road will not necessarily survive in our garden which is on a heavy, wet clay and sloping to the north. Countries with relatively uniform cold, dryish winters with snow cover can sometimes grow bulbs which are considered impossible in the open here, where the combination of widely oscillating temperatures and frequent rain, alternating with frosty periods, can be disastrous. In choosing bulbs for growing outside in the garden it is not just a case of selecting those which are said to be suitable for, for example Zone 8 (our quoted zone); the actual site chosen within the garden is probably an even more important factor in its survival. The success or otherwise of a particular planting lies very much in choosing just the right spot, and only experience of one's own garden will tell us that. To find those 'special' spots which are slightly milder (or slightly colder, since some bulbs prefer that) I try to remember to have a look around on a white frosty morning to note where the frost has not reached (or conversely where it lies longest) – it is surprising how many places there are, often quite small patches adjacent to conifers or other shrubs and alongside walls and fences, not always exactly where one would predict; these are the places to save for those bulbs which need just that extra little bit of protection. The colder places are for those high altitude bulbs which are better if they are kept dormant for as long as possible in the spring, for example *Scilla rosenii*, *Corydalis bracteata*, the alpine *Erythronium* species and the small Himalayan lilies. Experimentation such as this is all very much a part of the great fun of gardening, but success is often based on very personal experiences and what is correct for one garden will quite likely be totally incorrect for another!

Smoke treatment

Much has been written on the subject of treating bulbs with smoke to make them flower more reliably (and often earlier) and I do not propose to go into any great detail here. It has long been known that certain bulbs can lie dormant in the soil for many years, then burst into flower almost immediately following a fire. The reasons for this have been discussed for decades – extra potash fertilizer, loss of competition, blackening of the soil so that it heats up, and so on – and it is now generally accepted that it is at least in part to do with the gases released during combustion, seeping down through cracks in the soil to the bulbs beneath. This has been adapted for commercial purposes; the burning over of fields containing narcissi has been carried out for perhaps over 50 years but more recently smoke has been applied to bulbs whilst in store; it is thought that it is the ethylene (perhaps also the carbon monoxide) content of smoke which is the most active consituent, although research is still being undertaken in this field. Several different bulb crops have been shown to respond to smoke treatment, including *Narcissus tazetta*, *N. papyraceus*, *Freesia*, *Ornithogalum thyrsoides* (chincherinchee) and *Iris* (the Dutch iris cultivars). In the wild, there are reports of various bulbs flowering in response to fires, including: *Amaryllis*, *Cyrtanthus*, *Haemanthus*, *Watsonia*, *Crinum*, *Boophane* and *Gladiolus*; I have seen *Gladiolus ukambanensis* (*Acidanthera laxiflora*) in Kenya and *Calochortus macrocarpus* in Washington State flowering well in blackened soil following shortly after fires.

For those who wish to experiment, burning straw, leaves etc. generates ethylene, as do ripening fruits. I have tried burning straw in my glasshouse when the bulbs were at rest but I cannot say that there was a marked difference in flowering afterwards; however, this is a quite unfair test since the whole matter was conducted on a very unscientific basis through lack of time. Although it is hardly to be recommended, as a rough guide, the smoke should be so thick that you cannot see your thumb at the end of an outstretched arm – a passing comment from a colleague in the agricultural advisory service many years ago! The period of time should be several hours, but as far as I know this is not critical. A more recent commercial treatment involves spraying with ethephon which has the same effect. Anyone interested in this subject is recommended to read the article by Andrew Tompsett in *The Plantsman* 7 (1985).

Pests and diseases of bulbs

To cover all pests and diseases which can damage bulbs would be a book in itself, so on the whole I would recommend one of the specialist books on the subject, applicable to the country concerned. However, there are some problems which are quite widespread and a few comments on some of the common ailments might be helpful. The main point to make is that a strong healthy plant is less likely to succumb to an infection, and a weakly plant has little in reserve to withstand attack by pests, so cultivation methods are of prime importance. In some instances, virus infections may be masked if the plants are growing strongly enough, for example, with many irises and lilies, of which the stocks are commonly infected in cultivation. So, the basic message is to get the cultivation correct.

Amateur growers have, in general, far less serious problems than commercial growers who often bring together large numbers of the same or similar plants in one area, thus creating a banquet for specific pests or diseases; on the other hand, specialist enthusiasts may well have only one bulb of a very rare species, so it is just as important for the amateur to keep a close watch for signs of trouble. The methods of control are, however, often very different; working on a small scale, the amateur can often employ physical methods, such as hand-picking of pests, whereas the large commercial growers will be obliged to use sprays and dips, or effective chemicals which are not available to the amateur; they may also employ specialist techniques, such as hot water treatment of bulbs, which are scarcely worth while for a small collection of rare species.

Pests
Larger pests

Bulb growers around the world experience a great many different larger pests which nibble, trample, uproot, dig and eat their bulbs, from moles, voles, rats, squirrels,

22 *Fritillaria verticillata*. Strong, well-grown plants are resistant to pests and diseases.

23 When buying bulbs it is usually fairly obvious which are the best!

birds, cats and dogs up to deer, and there is really no magic answer to these problems; it is really a case of working out what is the best protection in each case. On a small scale I find that, with the range of smaller pests which we have, a physical barrier is the only real answer, in the form of a fine wire mesh. This can be used as a surround for frames and glasshouse doors and vents, or buried under the soil after planting the bulbs to prevent animals digging down to find them (one well-known British garden used to employ this method to stop the public from digging down as well!). Where underground pests such as moles are a problem it may be necessary to completely enclose the bulbs in mesh, or line the entire bed with it, below, above and round the sides; root and shoot growth is quite unimpeded and a galvanized mesh lasts for many years. The only alternative is to kill the creatures by some means but, even for those who are not squeamish, this is likely to be an on-going job and, often, the damage has already been done by the time one is alerted to the fact that there is a problem.

SLUGS AND SNAILS

Slugs and snails can be devastating; there are species which attack the young shoots, leaves and flowers and others, potentially much more serious, which work underground eating and sometimes hollowing out the bulbs. There are plenty of very effective mollusc-killing pellets and liquids on the market but their effects on other wildlife are of concern; I have not seen any definitive study of this question. Some say that birds and hedgehogs are killed if they eat dying snails and slugs, while others say that they would need to eat hundreds before there were any ill effects. I have only once seen a thrush eating a poisoned snail in our garden, and I have no personal evidence that slugs form a significant part of a hedgehog's diet; I have tried collecting slugs (not poisoned ones!) and placing them next to a semi-tame hedgehog but it showed no interest whatsoever; maybe they were of the wrong type. The various preparations reputed to act as mollusc birth controls appeared not to have any effect when I tried them for a season, but perhaps a longer term is needed; with the current immense populations of these pests which we have in our region, something a little more immediate and drastic is required. On the whole, I prefer not to use poisons around the garden, and I must admit that I am not entirely comfortable about biological controls since there is at least one classic example where the control has resulted in a worse problem. Garden cleanliness can go a long way to helping with mollusc problems since they like to hide in damp places under stones, heaps of leaves etc. I go around in winter and find these places, disposing of a great number in short space of time and thus reducing the breeding populations for the coming year; occasionally the large clusters of rounded eggs are found as well. These can be despatched by whatever means the conscience or degree of squeamishness will allow; I have taken to putting mine in the rubbish bin for transport to the tip. Attacks on the bulbs can to some extent be discouraged by encasing the bulbs at planting time in sharp sand.

24 A search around the garden will reveal the hiding places for snails.

APHIDS

Aphids are a universal problem and can cause loss of vigour, and distortion of the leaves and flowers. They are also capable of transmitting virus diseases. Although squashing or picking by hand might work on a small scale it is usually necessary to control them by spraying whenever they are seen, or even on a regular basis as a preventative. There are many proprietary sprays for this purpose. It is best to vary them occasionally to discourage the build-up of resistant strains, switching from chemical to chemical and from systemic to non-systemic. On any particularly choice or rare plants it is worth testing a few leaves first to see if there is any susceptibility to the spray; I have, for example, found problems with some *Oxalis* and *Tropaeolum* species.

CATERPILLARS

There are many different caterpillars which can cause damage, mainly to leaves and flowers. These are mostly easy to control by spraying, or hand-picking on a small scale. Some of the moth caterpillars are a nuisance and cause severe damage which is often wrongly attributed to slugs; those known in Britain as cutworms are nocturnal, hiding below soil level or under leaves during the day and then crawling up after dark, chewing the stems, leaves or flowers, one caterpillar capable of causing considerable damage. They love hiding at the base of clump-forming plants such as *Iris unguicularis* where there is a lot of protection. A soil pest-killer dusted around the base of the plants is effective but they are also very easy to find after dark with a torch since they seem to stay in one place and attack the same plant night after night. They squash very juicily!

NARCISSUS FLY

This is a serious and widespread problem, not confined to *Narcissus* but capable of attacking the bulbs of a wide array of amaryllids – *Lycoris*, *Galanthus*, *Nerine* and *Pancratium* have also been attacked in our garden. The larva of the large narcissus fly eats out the bulb from the inside, one large grub per bulb; with the small narcissus fly there are often several per bulb. The flies, looking like small bees, lay their eggs in spring on the necks of the bulbs, the resulting larvae then eating their way into the bulb and hollowing it out during its dormant season; the first indication of the presence of the grubs is either when the bulbs fail to grow, or at lifting or repotting time when the bulbs are found to be soft or completely rotten. Some small measure of control can be obtained by raking over the soil as the bulbs die down, thus closing the gap left by the shrivelling leaves through which the flies could gain access to the bulbs; on a small scale a collection of pots could be covered by a finely woven material to prevent the flies from settling – the very light 'fleece' material produced for protecting early vegetables would be very suitable for this purpose.

The flies are only active on warm, sunny days and are reputed to avoid shaded areas, so the provision of shading material is another recommended preventative. Dusting the necks of the bulbs with a soil pest-killer (e.g. pirimiphos-methyl) may also help, applied in spring/early summer. Some specialists, and commercial growers, soak the bulbs in chemicals (the most effective are not available in Britain) before planting, or they use hot water treatment which involves placing the bulbs in a container of hot water for a given length of time at a specified and uniformly maintained temperature; the margins for error are small – too high a temperature, or for too long, and the bulbs are killed, insufficiently high, or too short, and the pests are not killed; the temperature most frequently used for *Narcissus* is 44.4 °C (111 °F) for three hours for the control of bulb fly grubs and nematodes (for control of narcissus fly grubs alone, a one hour treatment is sufficient); this is carried out in early to mid-summer. However effective, this is not a simple treatment to be taken lightly; the bulbs need to be 'pre-treated' at 18 °C (64 °F), as well as the treatment itself. On the whole it

is much better for small-scale growers to keep to the simpler methods of prevention and control, even if they are not 100 per cent effective.

MEALY BUGS

These can be quite serious, especially with bulbs grown under glass, and particularly those which have a tight cluster of leaves; tropical and subtropical amaryllids seem to be particularly prone to attack. The greyish, waxy-coated bugs get into the fairly inaccessible places at the bases of leaves and cause damage which results in disfiguring or distortion of the leaves and loss of vigour in severe attacks. On a small scale the bugs can be removed using a fine paint brush dipped in surgical spirit, otherwise try spraying with a systemic or contact insecticide sprayed with some force into the affected areas.

VINE WEEVIL

This is quite widespread and very difficult to control, being resistant to the chemicals which are currently available through retail outlets; some of the chemicals which are accessible to professional growers are much more effective. The white larvae eat the underground parts – roots, rhizomes, bulbs, corms and tubers, and the adults will eat notches in the edges of the leaves, although this is not serious in the case of bulbous plants; the adults are nocturnal, so a search after dark (whilst on a cutworm/snail hunt, perhaps?!) might help to catch a few; since each female (most are female) can lay up to 1000 eggs, this is perhaps not such a waste of time. It is possible to find them between autumn and early summer; in the case of bulbous plants they can be particularly serious in pots under glass. If an outbreak is suspected (for example, the foliage may wilt on sunny days), the bulbs can be dug up, or the pots tipped out, and inspected. If the grubs are present they should be disposed of, together with the

soil, and the bulbs washed to make sure
there are no grubs or eggs left behind. It is
worth trying a soil drench of a soil pest-
killer (such as those based on pirimiphos-
methyl), or as a dust mixed in with the soil
at repotting or replanting time.

LILY BEETLE
A local problem in some areas in Europe
and Britain is the bright red lily beetle and
its dirty brown larvae, a devastating pest
capable of completely defoliating lilies (also
Fritillaria and *Nomocharis*). These are easily
seen and can be removed by hand-picking
or by insecticide sprays. The larvae, which
encase themselves in their own excreta, can
be washed off the leaves using a jet of water
and, being fairly immobile, do not appear
to be able to climb back up the stems; on a
hot summer's day, if their protective coat of
excreta is washed off, I find that they dry
out and die quite quickly.

RED SPIDER MITES
These tiny red or orange-yellow mites are
well-known to most gardeners, especially
those with a glasshouse or conservatory;
they may not notice the pests, but will certainly know the damage, in the form of
sick-looking pallid finely speckled leaves,
becoming covered with a web of fine
threads and eventually turning brown;
members of the Iridaceae which are in
growth in summer seem to be particularly
vulnerable. Red spider mites thrive in hot,
dry conditions and on a small scale a lot can
be done to control them by spraying the
leaves frequently with water, and by
running a damp sponge along the length of
the leaves. Alternatively, they can be
sprayed (or the whole glasshouse fumi-
gated) with any of the proprietary brands of
insecticide designed for the purpose.

EELWORMS (NEMATODES)
Various eelworms, microscopic eel-like
creatures, attack bulbous plants damaging

the stems, leaves or bulbs, the symptoms
sometimes appearing similar to those of
some viruses – distortion and mottling of
leaves; bulbs may become soft and develop
layers of dead tissue which can be seen
when the bulb is cut open. Control is very
difficult and most amateur enthusiasts just
have to live with the problem; the only
practical way of dealing with the problem is
to destroy the infected bulbs and grow new
stocks from seed in sterilized soil and pots;
commercial growers control them using
hot water treatment (see page 47), or by
soaking the bulbs in chemicals which are
unobtainable on the retail market.

THRIPS
These tiny winged insects feed on leaves,
buds and flowers, sucking out the sap and
causing pallid or silvery areas and distortion; *Gladiolus* is the classical example in
'bulbous' plants but they attack others as
well, especially glasshouse-plants. It is not
only when the plants are in growth that
they are vulnerable, the dry corms/bulbs in
store can also be attacked. They can be controlled by spraying with a proprietary
insecticide when in growth, or by dusting
the corms/bulbs with insecticide when they
are dry-stored at the start of their dormant
period. As with red spider mites, a damp
atmosphere discourages them, so a frequent fine spray with water may help.

Diseases

As with pests, a well-grown plant stands a
better chance of surviving an attack by
disease. It is useless using preventative dips,
drenches and sprays if the cultivation techniques are basically incorrect, so attend to
these and then use chemical controls if all
else has failed. Feeding bulbs with a potash-
rich fertilizer (or sulphate of potash) does
seem to assist in the building up of disease
resistance; high nitrogen feeds, and fresh

organic manures, should be avoided. There are a great many disease problems which the bulb grower can encounter, many of them not necessarily specific to a particular species or genus of bulbs but general problems associated with plants. A few of the more likely ones to be encountered are included here, but for more detailed accounts the reader is advised to refer to specific books on the subject.

Moulds

Moulds can cause damage to any part of the plant and are often a sign of humid conditions with insufficient ventilation, poor hygiene, or perhaps too many plants being crowded together. It is first best to consider what might be causing the problem and take appropriate steps – improve the ventilation, tidy up rotting vegetation etc. – and cut away any diseased parts of the plants. Routine fungicidal smokes can be used (under glass), or one of the systemic fungicides.

DAMPING OFF IN SEEDLINGS
Although a common and very widespread ailment, this does not seem to be quite such a problem with bulbous plants. There is probably no really successful chemical treatment so it is best to pay attention to cultural conditions; use well-drained, sterilized, seed-sowing mixes; sow the seeds thinly, take care not to overwater and use clean water, not from a container which has stood around for a long time; grow the seedlings in a place with plenty of ventilation so that they do not stay in damp soil for long periods after watering.

RUSTS
There are various rust fungus diseases affecting a range of bulbous plants – bluebell (*Hyacinthoides*) rust, erythronium rust, iris rust, leek (*Allium*) rust, lily rust and so on. With a collection of 'specialist bulbs'

these are seldom disastrous in my experience, although the yellowish, orange or brown spots, slits or rings can be unsightly and lead to a loss of vigour, even complete defoliation. Give a fortnightly spray with one of the proprietary fungicides recommended for the purpose, both systemic and non-systemic are available, or try the old Bordeaux Mixture which works on some rusts; trim away infected leaves and burn.

SMUTS
These are fungal diseases related to rusts, often showing up as spots or blisters on the leaves which burst open to release black spores. I have not found these to be serious in the case of bulbous plants, although smuts are recorded on *Gladiolus*, *Allium* (especially the onion, in which it is serious), *Colchicum* and *Anemone*. I have also seen it on the flowers of a wild collected *Bellevalia* from Turkey, presumably 'scilla anther smut', which is known to infect *Muscari* and *Scilla* species. In the case of specialist bulbs it seems that infections are not likely to be serious enough to warrant treatment, but badly diseased plants are probably best destroyed.

Rots of bulbs and corms

There are many diseases causing a range of different rots in bulbous plants, some of them obvious as spots, lesions, variously coloured fungal growths and blackish streaks on dormant bulbs in store; at other times the first signs might be as yellowing or wilting leaves and rotting of the whole aerial shoot; bulbs may simply not grow at all after planting. Diseases which are grouped here include Iris ink disease (especially reticulata irises), various gladiolus problems including scab and dry rot, hyacinth yellows, tulip grey bulb rot, and basal rots in narcissus bulbs; several of these will affect other related genera so the range of bulbs capable of being affected is potentially quite large. A systemic fungicide, made up in liquid form and used as a 30-minute dip whilst the bulbs are dormant, or watered on after the bulbs are growing, is the easiest method of control.

LILY DISEASE (BOTRYTIS ELLIPTICA)
This is a common problem, especially in damp weather in summer when the lilies are in growth; it appears as brown oblong patches and develops until the whole leaf is affected. In severe untreated cases the whole plant may become defoliated with a resulting loss of vigour. As soon as it is noticed, spray with a systemic fungicide, and in areas where it happens frequently spray as a routine at fortnightly intervals; remove and destroy all infected leaves and stems when the plants die down.

TULIP FIRE (BOTRYTIS TULIPAE)
This is one of the worst diseases of tulips. It is not serious with small collections of species tulips growing in cosseted conditions in a bulb frame or in pots in an unheated glasshouse, but potentially very damaging in beds of the large cultivars grown for display purposes. The bulbs fail to develop properly, sending up shoots which rapidly rot off before they produce leaves and flowers; plants which do develop and then become infected have pale or brownish blotches on the leaves and stems. Any infected bulbs should be dug up and destroyed; bulbs in store can be given a 30-minute soak in a systemic fungicide which helps to control a range of bulb disease problems. *Galanthus* species can get a similar disease (*Botrytis galanthina*) and a soil drench of systemic fungicide is recommended in this case.

VIRUSES
Virus diseases are potentially very crippling and there is no cure for an infected plant. Their effects can be quite mild, with perhaps only a loss of vigour, a slight mottling of the leaves or uneven splashes or speckling of darker colour in the flowers. Alternatively they can badly distort the shoots and flowers making them unsightly and, in severe cases, cripple the plant so severely that it is not worth keeping. It is possible for an individual plant to have a range of viruses all at the same time, and one virus can infect a range of different plants; the very common cucumber mosaic virus, for instance, can infect lilies, daffodils and tulips. Some viruses are considered to be acceptable, as in the case of 'broken' tulips (e.g. the Parrot and Rembrandt tulips) and many variegated plants, but, in the case of those which are considered undesirable, the only course of action is to destroy the plants before they pass it on to other healthy ones. Many viruses are transmitted by aphids – probably most creatures which attack plants are capable of doing so – so it is therefore important to keep these under control; others are transmitted by eelworms which are much less easily controlled. It is also possible for the gardener to transfer them when handling the plants, so care should be taken when touching susceptible plants such as lilies. Some viruses are not transmitted from one generation to the next by seed, so new virus-free stocks can be raised in this way. A few nurseries offer stocks of bulbs (e.g. lilies) which have been 'cleaned' of virus by micropropagation techniques, but these can, of course, be re-infected once planted in the garden if preventative care is not taken.

Propagation of bulbs for the amateur

There are several ways of increasing a stock of bulbs: by seed, by division of clumps which have built up by natural increase, either by bulblets or cormlets around the parent or, in the case of rhizomes, by branching; in some cases bulbils (e.g. certain *Lilium*, *Calochortus*) are produced naturally on the stems, usually in the leaf axils. Bulblet production can also be induced artificially by removing bulb scales.

Propagation by seed

The advantage of increasing bulbs from seed is that a large number can be raised from just one parent. Also healthy young stock is obtained (for example, many virus diseases are not transferred to the offspring) and, if stocks are being raised for 'home consumption', the gardener is unwittingly selecting those seedlings that are most suited to their present environment, the unsuitable ones either not germinating at all or not surviving for long

afterwards. On the other hand it takes, in general, much longer to obtain flowering-sized bulbs (on average 3–5 years), and the offspring will not necessarily be the same as the parent bulb (perhaps even hybrids with other species), a fact which may or may not be desirable. On balance, if time is not a critical factor, I would favour starting with seeds, but if a particular clone is required, or if for some reason the plant does not produce seeds, there is really no choice and one of the vegetative methods of increase will be necessary.

Sowing seeds

The simplest method is to sow the seeds thinly in a pot of well-drained soil (the potting mix recommended in Chapter 2 on page 16 is suitable), and cover with a thin layer of grit. The grit is important: it holds down the seeds, stops them from being washed out during heavy rain storms and helps avoid the formation of a pan or crust

25 *Erythronium californicum*. Clumps of bulbs can be divided whilst dormant.

of soil; it helps to prevent mosses and liverworts by providing a sharply drained surface layer; it discourages slugs and snails and provides physical support for the slender seedlings as they push through. After sowing the pots should be kept lightly watered, but the actual treatment after they are sown depends upon which group of bulbous plants they belong to (see below); all of them should be grown on for as long as possible in their first season, only reducing watering and feeding when the leaves begin to die back. Unlike mature bulbs they do not have large reserves of food and water, so care should be taken not to overdo the drying out; in pots, especially, they can easily shrivel and die if dried out too much. In this first year of growth they are best left undisturbed and given liquid (high potash) feeds, although if they grow very strongly the whole pot full of seedlings can be potted on into a larger container or planted out into a prepared seedling bed of good soil.

The following three groupings are only intended as a rough guide since, even within a group, different genera behave very differently in their methods and times of germination.

Tropical and other very tender bulbs

Seeds of these respond primarily to the availability of water and mostly do not require a corresponding cool period in order to germinate; it follows that they should be kept warm after sowing. They are best sown as soon as ripe, using the above basic technique. The fleshy seeds of *Crinum*, *Clivia*, *Nerine*, *Hessea*, etc., will germinate very quickly after ripening and may be sown in a dish of damp tissue covered with a thin polythene film; the flattish black seeds of many South American amaryllids, for example, *Hippeastrum*, *Hieronymiella*, *Habranthus*, *Rhodophiala*, etc., can be germinated successfully in this way, or floated on water in a shallow dish. When small bulbs have been formed they can be 'pricked out' into soil or potted individually.

Temperate 'winter growing' bulbs

Seeds of bulbs which are essentially winter-growers originating from Europe, the Mediterranean region, North Africa, western and central Asia, the south-western part of southern Africa, western USA, western temperate South America and West (and parts of South) Australia behave in much the same way as the parent bulbs which start their root activity in autumn and grow through winter until late spring when they die away for the summer. Fresh seeds should germinate during this period, some of them (mostly those from the milder regions) in autumn in response to watering and falling temperature, others (those from the harsher climatic regions) needing a cold, even frosty, period before they will germinate. The seedlings stay in growth until the following late spring or summer and then die down for a period of rest. As mentioned above, different species behave in different ways; *Calochortus* and many *Allium* species germinate very rapidly after sowing, whereas many *Trillium* species appear to have a 'double

26 Gravel provides a useful topping for seed pots.

dormancy', needing two periods of cold separated by the equivalent of a warm summer. On the whole I find that it is best to follow nature's way and let the seeds germinate as and when conditions are right to do so, and die down when the bulbs normally would; however, for those who like to experiment and speed up the operation, the kitchen refrigerator provides the means by which cold periods can be given to order; I cannot say that I have had any marked success with this, so I have reverted to being patient!

Sowing time will largely depend upon when the seeds are available. Home saved seed can be sown immediately it is ripe, usually in early summer, and this is probably best since it gets its warm spell, followed by a cooler autumn period, just as it would in nature; however, most seed lists do not come out until the autumn or winter, so it is a case of sowing them as soon as they are received. With many 'winter-growers', germination will not take place if the seeds are sown in winter or spring and they are likely to wait until the following autumn/winter before germinating.

After sowing the pots are watered and placed outdoors or in a cold frame or greenhouse to germinate; this depends upon the hardiness of the species concerned. Clearly, seedlings of bulbs which originate from, for example, Australia or South Africa are unlikely to be as frost resistant as those from the mountains of central Asia, so those which are thought to be very hardy are left out to take the frost, while those which are known to be tender are given cool but just-frost-free conditions in a cold frame or glasshouse.

'Summer-growing' bulbs

Seeds of bulbs which occur in the predominantly summer rainfall regions (e.g. Central America, Himalaya and eastern Asia, eastern southern Africa) should be treated almost in the reverse of the winter-growers. They germinate largely in response to rising temperatures and moisture after a winter cold or dry (or both) period and then continue to grow through summer until the following autumn. Those from cold regions – many of the lilies for example – do require a cold period before they will germinate, so these can be sown before or during the winter in order to achieve this, whereas the more tender subjects (e.g. *Tigridia* and other Mexicans) are best left until spring.

Lilies tend to be a special case since there are several methods of germination in the genus. The tender species such as *L. longiflorum* and *L. formosanum* must, of course, be kept under glass after sowing and not placed outside until the threat of frost has passed. The seeds of some species germinate almost immediately while others have what is known as delayed germination, the seeds needing alternating periods of heat and cold before they will germinate. Within these two groups, some lilies produce a thread-like seedling leaf above ground (epigeal germination) and others do not (hypogeal), in the latter case the seed first producing a small bulb which then gives rise to a much broader true leaf above ground. The seeds of all types can be sown and treated conventionally as described above, but for quicker results it is better to treat them in different ways. Those which germinate immediately are sown in early spring and kept growing as vigorously as possible by feeding through to the autumn, then repotted or planted out. The lilies with delayed germination are best sown in autumn and kept warm, at about 18–21 °C (64–70 °F), in a greenhouse or indoors, for the early winter months, then placed outdoors in a cold frame or plunge bed for the rest of the winter and early spring by which time germination should have occurred; they are then treated as above for the rest of the year.

Lilies which have immediate germination include *L. amabile*, *L. candidum* (but some seeds are often also delayed), *L. cernuum*, *L. concolor*, *L. dauricum*, *L. davidii*, *L. duchartrei*, *L. formosanum*, *L. henryi*, *L. langkongense*, *L. leichtlinii*, *L. leucanthum*, *L. longiflorum*, *L. mackliniae*, *L.* × *maculatum*, *L. nepalense*, *L. pumilum*, *L. pyrenaicum*, *L. regale*, *L. sargentiae*, *L. tigrinum*, and most of the Asiatic and Trumpet hybrids. The delayed germination types include *L. auratum*, *L. bulbiferum*, *L. canadense*, *L. carniolicum*, *L. chalcedonicum*, *L. hansonii*, *L. japonicum*, *L. martagon*, *L. monadelphum* and *L. szovtisianum*, *L. pardalinum*, *L. pomponium*, *L. rubellum*, *L. speciosum*, *L. superbum*, and the Oriental hybrids.

Propagation by division of clumps

Some bulbs (and corms and tuberous-rooted plants) increase naturally into clumps by vegetative means, either by splitting or by the production of bulblets, cormlets etc. around the parent; in the case of rhizomes, clumps arise by repeated branching. Propagation is simply a matter of lifting the clumps and dividing, either into several smaller clumps or down to individual bulbs. The best time to do this in most cases is just before the plant would naturally come into growth, so the 'winter-growers' are best divided in late summer or early autumn and the 'summer-growers' in spring. There are a few notable exceptions; *Galanthus* and *Eranthis* are often lifted and divided when in growth, just after flowering, and they do seem to respond well to this. However, they can also be successfully lifted at the conventional time (late summer) providing they are replanted before becoming too dry. In fact many bulbs can be successfully moved whilst in full growth, just before they begin to die down again for their rest period, and this is quite convenient since they have leaves and can be seen; later, when dormant, it is not so easy to find the clumps. The main point, if dividing them when in growth, is to water them in well after replanting to settle the soil before the coming dormant period when they might otherwise become over-dried in the dry loose soil.

Propagation by bulblets, cormlets and bulbils

Tiny bulblets and cormlets are sometimes produced around the parent bulbs (e.g. many *Gladiolus*, *Ixia*, *Iris reticulata* and related species, some *Oxalis*, *Ipheion* and *Nothoscordum* species). Bulblets are sometimes also produced on the underground part of the stem just above the bulb (some *Lilium*), while others (*Lilium*, some *Calochortus*) produce small bulbils on the aerial part of the stem in the leaf axils. These can be removed and treated in the same way as the parent bulbs, planted into pots, or directly into prepared 'nursery beds' of fertile soil until large enough to go into their final positions. These small bulbs or

27 A clump of daffodil bulbs ready for division.

corms can be brought to flowering size rather more quickly than by growing from seed.

Artificially induced bulblet production

Bulblet production can also be induced by removing bulb scales, by damaging the parent bulb, or by cutting up the scales into small pieces. This can be a more rapid method of building up a stock than growing from seed or waiting for clumps to build up naturally.

Scaling

The bulbs which consist of rather loose scales, for example most species and cultivars of *Lilium*, can be propagated by breaking off outer scales without harming the parent bulb, at any time between midsummer and early autumn; if you do not want to disturb a clump of bulbs, it is usually possible to scrape away the soil down to the bulbs to do this. The scales are then dusted with a fungicide (or dipped in a systemic fungicide made up as a liquid) and placed in a polythene bag of slightly damp perlite, vermiculite or clean sharp sand in a warm room (the airing cupboard is a good place) at about 18–20 °C (64–68 °F). In about 3–5 weeks, small bulbs should be seen forming on the broken surfaces and, when roots have been formed, these can be detached and planted in soil in pots, deep boxes or a prepared bed. As with the naturally produced bulblets and bulbils, flowering can be achieved in a matter of 1–2 years, and all the offspring will be identical to the parents. *Fritillaria* species can be propagated in the same way but, since their bulbs have only a few (usually two) scales, the increase is not so great; one of the scales can be broken away leaving the central growing point and the other scale intact; this can be treated in the same way as lily

28 Scales detached from lily bulbs will form new bulblets on the broken surfaces.

scales, but I have also had success by potting up the detached scale in sand and treating it as if it were an adult bulb, a young bulb forming on the scale during the growing season. Both scales can be detached from the central core and, with a bit of luck, the result is at least three new bulbs, although there is also the chance of complete failure!

Scoring and scooping

Another method of propagation of bulbs (true bulbs) which has been mainly used commercially on hyacinths, is to slice a cross pattern deeply into the basal plate during the dormant season; bulblets will often form along the cut surfaces; this is known as 'scoring'. A variation of this, 'scooping', involves scooping out the core of the bulb from the bottom, effectively removing the basal plate and growing point. In both cases this is carried out in late summer or autumn; the treated bulbs should be dipped in a fungicide solution and then planted shallowly on a bed of sand. At the end of the growing season young bulbs should have formed on the cut surfaces; with hyacinths, as many as 20 young bulbs may be formed.

Twin scaling

A more sophisticated technique known as 'twin scaling' is used to bulk up certain bulbs at an amazing rate; the bulbs are chopped vertically into many segments, each segment consisting of two small sections of scale joined together at the bottom by a piece of basal plate (this is most important since it is where the new bulblets form). A razor blade is very suitable, and this should be sterilized or replaced each time a new bulb is chopped up. This operation must be conducted under conditions of great cleanliness or diseases are likely to occur. The bulb itself is first cleaned of any tunics and roots and sliced across the top to get rid of the neck; it is then dipped in a liquid systemic fungicide or industrial spirit to sterilize the outside. After the twin-scales have been prepared they are soaked for 30 minutes in a fungicide solution, then placed in polythene bags with slightly damp perlite, or something similar which is known to be sterile. They are then put in a dark room for about 3 months at about 20 °C (68 °F) during which time bulblets should form. The scales with bulblets can then be removed and grown on in a sandy well-drained potting medium as for the parent bulbs. This technique has been used successfully on *Narcissus*, *Galanthus*, *Nerine*, *Hippeastrum*, *Hyacinthus*, *Hymenocallis*, *Iris* (*Xiphium* group), *Scilla*, *Ornithogalum*, *Sternbergia*, *Chionodoxa*, *Leucojum*, *Pancratium*, *Lachenalia* and *Muscari*. It is likely that it would work for most true bulbs, although it is not very successful with tulips.

The timing of twin-scaling depends upon the bulb: with the winter-growers such as *Narcissus* and *Galanthus* it should be carried out in summer, while with the summer-growers and tropical bulbs, it is best at some time during winter while they are fully dormant.

Chipping

Twin-scaling is sometimes loosely called 'chipping', although this term refers to a slightly different technique; the segments or 'chips' of bulb in this case do not consist of portions of twin-scales but wedge-shaped sections of bulb made up of several scales joined by a piece of basal plate. This results in fewer sections, at most about 16, compared with the 30–60 which can be attained using the twin-scaling method.

Leaf cuttings

Some bulbs, notably members of the Hyacinthaceae such as *Lachenalia* and *Galtonia* will produce small bulbs from leaf cuttings, the leaves being removed and their bases put into sand as for conventional cuttings.

Corm propagation

Corms cannot, on the whole, be induced to produce extra cormlets artificially, at least on a worthwhile scale. However, if the apical bud of a corm (I have tried only with *Crocus*) is removed at the start of the growing season the damaged corm will occasionally call into growth several of the latent buds around its perimeter and at the end of the season there will be several small cormlets instead of the normal one replacement corm. However, this does not always work and the result is sometimes one corm, smaller than the original!

A–Z of genera;
outline of cultivation requirements

CHAPTER 7

Cultivation Guide

The following cultivation notes are adapted from a 'database' (mostly still scraps of paper in a file!) of information which I have been building up, representing a collection of comments about as many 'bulbous monocot' genera as possible. Many of these comments are based on personal observation but in some cases I have relied on the experience of others and, in a few instances, where I could find no records at all, I have made a judgement as to how the plants might be grown bearing in mind their wild origin. I would welcome cultivation tips from any part of the world on any of the less frequently cultivated genera or species as part of this on-going project. If a genus cannot be found in the A–Z sequence, check the index, since some of the less well-known genera are included as comments under others.

Notes
Coverage

I have tried to include as many as possible of the bulbous, cormous and tuberous-rooted monocotyledons that are likely to be encountered in cultivation, wherever I have some information; those rhizomatous ones which are generally treated as herbaceous perennials are mostly excluded, as are the succulents like *Aloe* and *Agave* which are not normally cultivated by bulb enthusiasts. The majority of orchids are not included since there are plenty of books devoted to this vast group and their cultivation; to incorporate those would double the size of this book. However, there are a few comments about the tuberous-rooted Mediterranean species (under the heading 'orchids', not individual genera), since they behave in much the same way as bulbs from that region.

I have almost no cultural information about the large number of fascinating and beautiful monocots from South West (and to a lesser extent south-eastern) Australia – genera such as *Borya, Laxmannia, Johnsonia* and *Thysanotus* – since hardly any of them are obtainable and few have been cultivated, except perhaps in their native country. Most are non-bulbous, many of them having small rhizomes with fibrous root systems, and are more or less 'evergreen'. If the opportunity arises to try them, my inclination is to try them as tender winter-growers; *Patersonia*, for example, seems to respond to being planted directly into a frost-free glasshouse bed in a sandy soil; it is watered through winter, flowers in late winter to spring and then is kept warm and dryish for the rest of the summer.

Seasons and times

Months, dates and festivals have been omitted in favour of seasons so that the comments apply to countries other than Britain; for example, it is of little interest to someone in South Africa that in Britain it is best to start watering sternbergias in September; on the other hand, the statement 'they are best started into growth in early autumn' applies wherever the reader is trying to cultivate the plants.

'Winter-growing': means that the bulbs begin to produce roots in autumn and are in active root and/or shoot growth until after flowering/fruiting the following spring when they then go into a period of dormancy for the warmer summer months.

'Summer-growing': is the reverse; bulbs should be planted or started into growth in spring when they produce roots and begin their period of active growth, continuing through summer until the autumn; they then go into a rest period through the colder winter months.

Soils

Comments about soil conditions and potting mixes should be used in conjunction with the general notes on soils and fertilizers (see pages 15–18, 27–28).

Acidanthera (*Iridaceae*)

Cormous. The species of *Acidanthera*, of which *A. bicolor* (Gladiolus callianthus) is the best-known, are now generally accepted as belonging to the genus *Gladiolus* and require similar methods of cultivation to the summer-rainfall species of that genus (see page 97).

Achimenes (*Gesneriaceae*)

Rhizomatous. Probably around 50 species, native to the warmer parts of South America. They have curious fleshy/scaly elongated rhizomes producing leafy shoots, often with oval, hairy leaves, and elegant flattish 5-petalled flowers which have a long tube; the colours are mostly in the red, blue and violet shades. They are treated as summer-growers, the rhizomes potted and started into growth in spring in a temperature of about 15–18 °C (59–64 °F); full sun should be avoided and they are best given a humid atmosphere and kept well-watered during summer whilst in growth. When they begin to die down in autumn, water can be withheld and the pots dried out and kept at a cooler temperature until the spring repotting; a sandy soil with plenty of humus seems best.

Agapanthus (*Liliaceae/Alliaceae*)

Rhizomatous. A familiar genus of about ten species from southern Africa with strap-like leaves and umbels of blue or white funnel-shaped or tubular flowers. They inhabit both summer rainfall and winter rainfall regions but for cultivation purposes may all be regarded as summer-growers; there are both evergreen species, such as the large stately *A. praecox* and deciduous ones like *A. campanulatus*. The former are rather tender and in cold-winter areas are usually treated as container plants which are moved to frost-free accommodation for the winter. The deciduous species are dormant in winter so they will take much more frost and are often treated as herbaceous perennials for a sunny border. If grown in containers these need to be large so that the plants have plenty of room to increase and fill them completely; it is best to leave them undisturbed for a good number of years and give liquid feeds of a potash-rich fertilizer in summer; less water can be given in winter. In mild-winter areas *Agapanthus* often become naturalized.

Albuca (*Liliaceae/Hyacinthaceae*)

Bulbous. A large genus from tropical and South Africa, also a few species in Arabia. They have white or yellow flowers, with brown, green or yellow stripes along the centre of each outer segment; the three inner segments are held together forming a tube. The tropical and eastern Cape species are best treated as summer-growers, planted or potted in spring and dried off in winter; the South West Cape species are winter-growers so are planted in autumn and dried off in summer; the one Arabian species I have tried, *A. pendula*, behaves as a winter-grower and needs to be grown up on a shelf or in a basket so that its leaves and flowers have room to hang down. Grow albucas in sandy soil in full sun; in cold-winter areas they need frost protection, except for a few higher altitude species from the Drakensberg, such as *A. humilis* which is suitable for an unheated glasshouse.

Allium (*Liliaceae/Alliaceae*)

Bulbous/rhizomatous. A very large genus, perhaps 750 species, widely distributed in the mainly temperate areas of the northern hemisphere with a few in the southern hemisphere (e.g. South Africa); many of them are of little garden value but, on the

30 *Allium nevskii*

other hand, a considerable number are excellent. They all have umbels of flowers, although sometimes the umbels are few-flowered, and nearly all have an onion/leek/garlic smell when leaves or bulbs are crushed. They fall into two broad categories: those from winter rainfall/dry summer areas, that is the Mediterranean region, eastwards through western Asia to central Asia, and the western United States, notably California; these are predominantly bulbous and, after a mid-late summer rest period, start to root in autumn, make their leaf growth through winter and spring and flower right at the end of their growing season, in spring or early summer. There are plenty of examples, such as *A. moly*, *A. ampeloprasum*, *A. karataviense*, *A. giganteum*, and Californian *A. acuminatum*; a few flower in autumn, such as the Cretan *A. callimischon*.

The remainder are predominantly rhizomatous, sometimes with slender poorly developed bulbs attached to a small rhizome; they are more or less winter-dormant, commencing to grow in spring and flowering in summer. These alliums are from the monsoon summer-rainfall areas of the Himalaya and eastern Asia (e.g. *A. sikkimense*, *A. beesianum*, *A. cyathophorum* etc.) and from other mountain areas where there is winter cold and some summer rain, such as the European (e.g. *A. senescens* and its relatives) and western/

central Asiatic mountain ranges; some of the eastern North American species fit in here as well, such as *A. cernuum*.

The bulbous 'winter-growers' are bought and planted in autumn, and mostly need a sunny position in well-drained soil where their bulbs will dry out in summer. In areas with damp summers it may be necessary to lift the bulbs in summer, or grow them in a bulb frame or, in the case of the small species, in pots in an alpine house so that they can be dried out. The summer-growing species will not stand drought and need planting in a situation where there is plenty of moisture available during summer; they are mostly very hardy species and can be left in the ground in their permanent positions.

Alophia (*Iridaceae*)

Bulbous. A small genus of about 5 species from southern USA, Central and South America. *Eustylis* from the southern USA and Mexico is now regarded as belonging to this genus, whereas several South American species, such as *A. lahue*, are classified as *Herbertia* species (see page 101). Alophias have short-lived flowers and are related to *Tigridia*, *Cypella*, *Herbertia*, etc., having similar erect, narrowly sword-shaped leaves, pleated lengthways, and wiry stems carrying one upright flower, or several in succession, lasting only a day or a few hours; in *Alophia* they are usually in shades of purple, violet or blue with a paler or white centre, marked with dark blotches; the three outer segments are large and horizontal, the inner three much smaller and obliquely erect. Those I have tried are summer-growers and could be grown outside in a sunny, well-drained position; in areas which are not frost-free, they need lifting for the winter; otherwise, grow in pots in a slightly heated glasshouse and reduce watering in winter, although not to the point of dessication.

Alrawia (*Liliaceae/Hyacinthaceae*)

Bulbous. Two or three species from Iraq and Iran, spring-flowering, rather *Muscari*-like with racemes of blue flowers becoming brown with age. Plant in autumn, dry off in summer when dormant. Well-drained soil in sun. In damp-summer areas grow in a bulb frame or pots in an alpine house.

Alstroemeria (*Alstroemeriaceae*)

Fleshy tubers. Although these South American monocots are perhaps considered to be rather more herbaceous perennials than 'bulbs', many bulb enthusiasts are now taking an interest in these exciting plants, especially the more dwarf of the wild species, since so many have now been introduced into cultivation in recent years by seed collectors such as John Watson and Anita Flores and Jim and Jenny Archibald. Alstroemerias have clusters of fleshy tubers, giving rise to leafy stems, the non-flowering ones often much more compact than the flowering shoots; the leaves are very variable from short and almost scale-like, sheathing the stem, to long and narrow, often grey-green and sometimes hairy. The flowers are carried in a cluster (rarely one) at the apex of the stems and come in a very wide range of colours, normally with differently-coloured 'signal patches' on at least two of the six segments; these are not arranged equally and are usually differently shaped, the inner upper two often being narrower and prominently spotted, streaked or stained with a contrasting colour, and the lower inner one sometimes also narrower than the outers and occasionally marked in the same way as the uppers; the three outers are normally unmarked and broader.

Alstroemerias are widely distributed in both the warmer regions (mainly Brazil) and more temperate areas (especially Chile) of South America. Only a few of the former group of species are cultivated and I have not tried them; they can be treated as summer-growers, but even so need to be cultivated under heated glass in temperate areas with frosty winters since their rootstocks will not survive. The complex hybrid cultivars which are grown for the cut-flower market are also mostly, if not all, grown under glass.

The more temperate species, on the other hand, mainly from the Andes and especially Chile, appear to be primarily winter-spring growers (those which I tried many years ago from an early expedition of John Watson's definitely were); these flowered in early to mid-summer before dying down for the rest of the summer and autumn; it would perhaps be wrong to think of them as strictly 'winter-growers' in the sense that many bulbs are, but they did tend to produce non-flowering shoots in winter if mild enough; however, the main thrust of growth took place as the soil warmed up in spring. The conditions they appeared to hate more than any were cold and wet in winter, hence the reason for some growers recommending protecting the 'dormant' rhizomes in winter using some loose material such as bracken; others grow them in sheltered positions, alongside sunny walls for example. A well-drained, sandy loam seems to suit them well; our natural wet, cold clay is definitely not to their liking! The smaller species – I have tried *A. pygmaea* (*Schickendantzia pygmaea*) and *A. hookeri* – are suitable for pot cultivation in a gritty soil mix in a just-frost-free glasshouse or bulb frame, grown with as much light and ventilation as possible in the winter and spring to keep them dwarf. During the dormant season in late summer the tubers should not be overdried – it is easy to do this in pots, so a little water should be supplied from time to time. Probably many of the higher altitude variants are frost-hardy, but in areas such as southern Britain where temperatures can

alternate rapidly between about +12 (53 °F) and -6 °C (21 °F) in mid-winter, coupled with much rain, many plants which are essentially winter-spring growers try to come into growth too early and get severely damaged; colder, drier climates would induce them to stay dormant longer until spring proper arrived; also areas with slightly milder winters would probably meet with more success. Doubtless with the new introductions much will be learned in the near future about the requirements of these lovely plants.

Amana (*Liliaceae*)

Bulbous. Three or four species from China, Japan and Korea. Spring-flowering, related to *Tulipa*, looking like small white tulips, striped red-brown on the outside. Plant in autumn, dry off in summer. Well-drained soil, sunny position. In damp-summer areas grow in a bulb frame or in pots in the alpine house.

Amaryllis, × Amarcrinum, × Amarine, × Amarygia (*Amaryllidaceae*)

Bulbous. A well-known genus of one species, *A. belladonna*, from the winter rainfall part of South Africa. It has an umbel of large, pink flowers on a stout bare, often purplish, stem in autumn, followed by a cluster of broad, strap-shaped leaves in winter-spring. The Cape Belladonna requires a sheltered position away from serious frosts where its large bulbs will receive plenty of hot sun to warm the soil during its resting period in summer; in cold-winter, cool-summer areas the foliage can be damaged in winter, resulting in loss of vigour, and the bulbs will not form flower buds if they do not get warm enough in summer. In such places (our garden is one such!) it is necessary to choose a site against a sunny wall; in other more favourable areas with mild winters and hot summers it flourishes, increasing into huge clumps and even becoming naturalized. Since the bulbs have perennial roots they are best left undisturbed for as long as they are flowering well but may eventually require lifting and dividing; they sometimes take a year or so to settle in again after disturbance. Bulbs which are shy-flowering can sometimes be induced to flower by feeding with a potash-rich fertilizer, or sulphate of potash itself, in autumn. The hybrids with *Crinum*, *Nerine* and *Brunsvigia* require similar growing conditions.

Ammocharis (*Amaryllidaceae*)

Bulbous. A small genus of perhaps five species from South Africa and the drier parts of south tropical Africa, seldom cultivated. Large bulbs produce up to 10 basal strap-shaped leaves, lying more or less flat on the ground; the flower head is carried on a short leafless stem and appears before the leaves, usually in autumn; it develops into large umbel of pink to red flowers which are tubular in the lower part with six recurved segments. *Ammocharis* are summer-growers; they should be given warm growing conditions in spring and summer, then a cooler dry period through winter; try growing in large pots, or planted directly into a glasshouse bed, in a sandy, well-drained soil mix.

Amphisiphon (*Liliaceae/Hyacinthaceae*)

Bulbous. Only one very rare species is known from South Africa, *A. stylosa*; this is rather like a *Massonia* (see page 118), with two leaves, nearly flat or suberect, produced at ground level with a stemless 'head' of yellow flowers which have conspicuous stamens, appearing in winter. Cultivation, if you are lucky enough to acquire this fascinating plant, is as described for *Massonia*.

Anapalina (*Iridaceae*)

Cormous. Peter Goldblatt now recommends including this genus in *Tritoniopsis* but at present I imagine that most bulb enthusiasts will look for *Anapalina* in literature, and still have their plants labelled as such. About 7 species from South Africa, tall, slender plants with erect, narrow, prominently veined leaves and spikes of irregular, red, reddish-pink or purple-red flowers with a large upper hooded segment and the other five smaller and reflexed. These are from a winter rainfall area and should be planted in autumn and watered through winter and spring until after flowering in spring or early summer, then dried off for the rest of the summer; the corms need planting deeply in a sandy soil mix.

Androcymbium (*Liliaceae/Colchicaceae*)

Cormous. A few species in the Mediterranean region and several more in tropical and South Africa. The *Colchicum*-like corms produce rosettes of lanceolate leaves and a cluster of small, funnel-shaped white or pinkish flowers, often surrounded by wide, leaf-like bracts which may be white, conspicuously veined green, sometimes pink- or purple-tinged. The species from the Mediterranean and the South West

31 *Androcymbium pulchrum*

Cape are winter-growers, flowering in winter-spring and should be planted in autumn after a warm, dry, summer rest period; those from tropical Africa and the East Cape can be treated as summer-growers and are dried off for the winter. In cold-winter areas all require frost-free cultivation, with plenty of light to prevent etiolation. Corms of the summer-dormant ones sometimes stay dormant for several years; if this happens, try a summer baking, then break open the outer tough black-brown corm tunics just before watering in autumn.

Androsiphon
(Liliaceae/Hyacinthaceae)

Bulbous. There is only one, rather rare species in the South West Cape region of South Africa, *A. capense*; it is rather like a *Massonia* (see page 118); it has two broad, green, dark-spotted leaves, nearly flat on the ground, and a stemless 'head' of yellow flowers with conspicuous stamens, appearing in winter. I have not yet had the fun of trying this, but cultivation should be the same as for *Massonia*.

Anemone (Ranunculaceae)

Tuberous/rhizomatous. A large genus but few species can be described as 'bulbous'. They have flattish flowers in a wide range of colours, often many-petalled and, unlike *Ranunculus* species, lacking a green calyx; their leaves are usually attractively divided, sometimes into many lobes. The rhizomatous ones like *A. nemorosa*, *A. trifolia* and *A. ranunculoides* are often traded by 'bulb' nurseries although their stick-like rhizomes should never be dried out; if they are moved it is best to store them in damp peat until replanting time. Planting or dividing of clumps can take place in autumn or early spring since these are spring-early summer-growers. The tuberous species fall into

32 *Anemone blanda*

groups: the essentially Mediterranean species *A. coronaria* (from which the florists St Brigid and De Caen anemones have been selected), *A. pavonina*, *A. fulgens* and *A. hortensis* are naturally winter-growers for planting in autumn in well-drained, sunny sheltered positions since, although they will take light frosts, they do not perform very well in cold, damp positions; alkaline soils seem to give the best results. Tubers of the highly developed florists anemones (St Brigid etc.) are usually available for spring planting, having been kept dry over winter; they tolerate this treatment and will flower in summer. *A. blanda*, *A. caucasica* and *A. apennina* are much hardier and are best in dappled shade in leafmould-rich soil where they may well seed about and become naturalized. The lovely Iranian *A. biflora* and its central Asiatic relatives such as *A. petiolulosa*, *A. tschernjaewii* and *A. bucharica* are very frost-hardy but require a warm, dry, summer rest period; in areas with relatively cool, damp summers they are definitely plants for a bulb frame or unheated glasshouse in well-drained gritty soils.

Anoiganthus See *Cyrtanthus*

Anomalesia (Iridaceae)

Cormous. Only two or three species from South Africa, looking rather like some

Gladiolus species in overall growth, but with curiously shaped orange to red flowers which have one long-hooded segment, two large ones which stand up like wings, and three tiny insignificant ones underneath. Drs. Peter Goldblatt and Miriam de Vos have merged this with *Gladiolus*. For those who receive plants under the old name, these are winter-growers, not frost-hardy, so in cold-winter areas require cultivation in a frost-free glasshouse; they can be grown in pots or planted directly into a bed, and they seem to respond best to a sandy soil mix. After flowering in late spring, the corms should be dried out for the summer months.

Anomatheca (*Iridaceae*)

Cormous. Four species from South Africa and south tropical Africa with erect fans of leaves and short spikes of red, white, blue or green long-tubed flowers, mainly in summer. Plant in spring, dry off in winter when dormant. Sunny position in well-drained soil which does not dry out excessively in summer. In cold-winter areas lift corms and store frost-free. Exceptions are the blue *A. laxa* subsp. *azurea* and green *A. viridis,* both winter-growers. *Anomatheca* has now been united with *Freesia*, except for *A. fistulosa* which is placed in a new (winter-growing) genus, *Xenoscapa*.

Anthericum (*Liliaceae/Anthericaceae*)

Rhizomatous/fleshy or tuberous roots. A large genus, mainly distributed in the Mediterranean region, Africa and America, although most of the African ones have been transferred to the related genus *Chlorophytum*. Anthericums have tufts of long, narrow leaves and usually loosely branched stems bearing starry white (rarely yellow) flowers. Apart from the European/Mediterranean *A. liliago* and

A. ramosum few are cultivated; these two are easily grown in an open, sunny position, flowering in summer. Probably all species can be treated as summer-growers but the African and Central American species will be much more tender. The similar-looking *Chlorophytum* (hundreds of species, mainly in the warmer regions of Africa, South America and India) is a familiar name because of the variegated form of one species, the spider plant, *C. comosum*. They are mostly rather uninteresting as ornamentals and require warm growing conditions; the same comments may be made of the African *Trachyandra*, hardly any species of which are cultivated (these often look rather like anthericums, although they are placed in the family Asphodelaceae). The Mexican *Echeandia* (C. 14 spp. with yellow flowers which have stamens with serrated filaments) need similar conditions to *Anthericum* but are a little tender; if container-grown they can be stored frost-free for winter. *Hemiphylacus* (1 sp. Mexico, with white flowers) is very similar in appearance to *Anthericum*, although it is placed in the Asphodelaceae; it can be grown as for *Echeandia*.

Antholyza (*Iridaceae*)

Cormous. The two species from the South West Cape area of South Africa, *A. plicata* and *A. ringens*, are now considered by the Iridaceae expert Peter Goldblatt to belong to *Babiana*, but I mention the genus here since it will still be found in most 'bulbous' literature under *Antholyza*. These have strongly pleated sword-shaped leaves and dense spikes of tubular red flowers, the branches of the inflorescence curved almost to the horizontal, but the flowers held erect. They are winter-growers so the corms should be planted in autumn and kept in growth through flowering time in late winter/early spring to the summer when water can be withheld until autumn; a sandy soil is best; if growing in pots under glass, these need to be deep to accommodate the long corms. In mild-winter areas they could be tried outdoors in a sunny position.

Apodolirion (Amaryllidaceae)

Bulbous. This South African genus of about six species is closely related and similar to *Gethyllis*; I have not tried to grow any but I would expect them to require similar conditions to *Gethyllis* (see page 96).

Argyropsis (Amaryllidaceae)

A synonym of *Zephyranthes*.

Arisaema (Araceae)

Tuberous. Large genus in Asia, India, Africa and Americas. Mostly summer-flowering, with cylindrical green to dark purple or pinkish spathes, widening out at the mouth, and often with a protruding spadix. Plant in spring; in mild-winter areas they can be left in the ground but where the ground freezes to a considerable depth it is necessary to lift and store the tender species away from frost. Most species are best in semi-shade, with plenty of moisture available in the summer growing period. Some of the Japanese species (e.g. *A. sikokianum*) come into growth very early and the young shoots may be frosted; on the other hand *A. candidissimum* rarely appears above ground before early to mid-summer. Species from the tropics are, of course, subjects for a heated glasshouse.

Arisarum (Araceae)

Tuberous. A small group of arum-like plants from the Mediterranean region with hooded green or dark brown spathes and arrow-shaped leaves. They are winter-growers, so plant or divide clumps in autumn before growth commences. *A. vulgare* and the related *Ambrosina bassii* are slightly tender and require a sheltered, well-drained spot, or cool glasshouse treatment. The mouse plant, *A. proboscideum*, grows well in semi-shade in humus-rich soil or in rock crevices.

Aristea (Iridaceae)

Rhizomatous. A genus of about 50 species, mainly in southern Africa but also in tropical Africa and Madagascar. They make evergreen tufts of tough, long, narrow leaves and have spike-like clusters of flattish, short-lived flowers, mostly blue; few are cultivated, but one or two, such as *A. ecklonii* and *A. ensifolia* are occasionally to be seen and are naturalized in some countries outside Africa. They have no swollen storage organ, so cannot be dried like bulbs and corms. The species I have tried behave as summer-growers and flower in summer, and this is what one would expect of those from tropical areas

33 *Arisaema sikokianum*

and the eastern (summer rainfall) Cape; however, some species occur in the South West Cape (winter rainfall) area and should presumably be given more water in autumn-winter-spring. A sandy soil rich in humus seems to suit them well; they are not frost-hardy and in cold-winter areas need container cultivation in a just-frost-free glasshouse; in mild areas they can be grown outdoors in sunny or semi-shady positions where there is a plentiful supply of moisture in summer. The most beautiful is *A. lugens* (*Cleanthe bicolor*) which I grew for many years, planted directly into a sandy bed in a cool glasshouse, although it was not free-flowering; it has large flowers, bicoloured pale and dark blue.

Arum (*Araceae*)

Tuberous. A genus of about 25 species of aroids distributed from Europe eastwards to central Asia; they have a cowl-like to sail-shaped spathe enclosing a pencil-like spadix. Most species have green to purple spathes but some are white or yellow. They are winter-growers so should be planted in late summer or autumn, the sooner the better as they start new root growth earlier than most of the winter-growing bulbs. The frost-tender species such as *A. pictum* (not to be confused with *A. italicum* 'Pictum' [='Marmoratum'] which is very hardy) will need protection in cold-winter areas, in a bulb frame or cool glasshouse; if grown in pots it must be remembered that the tubers pull themselves down very deeply, and are very strong rooting, and therefore require large deep pots.

Asphodeline (*Liliaceae/Asphodelaceae*)

Rhizomatous/fleshy-rooted. These are primarily Mediterranean plants, distributed widely through southern Europe, North Africa and western Asia; there are approximately 12 species which have a small rhizome with radiating fleshy roots, dense tufts of many very narrow, often grey-green leaves, sometimes mostly at the base of the plant, sometimes spread more diffusely up the stems. The starry flowers are yellow, white or pink, carried in long spike-like inflorescences, each one short-lived but produced successively over the whole length of the spike, not in succession from base to apex or vice versa. These are all autumn/winter/spring growers, flowering towards the end of the growing season in late spring/early summer. The commonly cultivated *A. lutea* is not a difficult plant given very well-drained soil and a sunny position, but it and the other species that I have tried are not very tolerant of a combination of winter wet and cold. In places where that is the normal climate, cultivation in a sandy/gritty raised bed or a bulb frame gives the best chance of success, although they are too tall for the average bulb frame; plant with rhizome crown just below soil level.

34 *Arum dioscoridis*, with spathe cut open to show interior.

Asphodelus
(*Liliaceae/Asphodelaceae*)

Rhizomatous/fleshy or tuberous roots. A primarily Mediterranean genus of about 20 species from southern Europe, North Africa and western Asia. They have a small rhizomatous crown and thick, fleshy roots, often swollen and somewhat dahlia-like, giving rise to a basal tuft of tough long, narrow leaves which are deeply channelled in cross-section. The tall, stout flower stem is branched in most species but usually unbranched in one of the commonest species, *A. albus*. The many flowers are produced in succession and are white or pink and starry, usually with a darker stripe along the centre of each perianth segment. *A. acaulis* from North Africa differs from the rest in being very dwarf, with the short-stemmed pink flowers nestling amid the very narrow leaves. These are all winter-growers, flowering in late winter to late spring or early summer. Most are not very

35 *Asphodelus microcarpus*

frost-hardy, coming from low altitudes, and I find that they seldom survive for more than a winter or two here in Surrey, but *A. acaulis* is hardier and makes a fine alpine house or bulb frame plant; like many Mediterranean bulbs it needs to be dried out in summer whilst dormant, otherwise it may rot off in a damp summer; some growers have found it satisfactory in a very well-drained, raised bed outdoors. *A. fistulosus* is short-lived, sometimes only an annual, so it is best to allow it to self-sow; it is, however, not very striking and could well be weedy in mild areas; plant with crowns just below soil level. *Simethis* (1 sp. from Mediterranean region with loosely-branched stems bearing white, purple-tinted flowers) has similar requirements. The related *Paradisea* (2 spp. from Europe, with spikes of funnel-shaped white flowers) is hardier; an open, sunny place is suitable.

Babiana (*Iridaceae*)

Cormous. A genus of approximately 60 species, now including *Antholyza*; they are nearly all from southern Africa but with one outlying species on the island of Socotra (*B. socotrana*). They have elongated corms, often rather bottle-shaped, covered with tough fibrous tunics; the leaves are frequently narrowly lance-shaped, pleated or strongly veined and hairy, sometimes spirally twisted or wavy at the margins. The flowers have a long tube and six segments which form a funnel-shape, or spread out more widely often forming an irregular-shaped flower; the colours range from white to yellow, pink, red, purple and blue, sometimes with contrasting basal blotches on some of the segments. Most species inhabit the south-western parts of southern Africa, thus receiving winter rainfall, and are winter-growers, flowering in late winter to spring. In cultivation they should be started into growth in autumn after a summer rest period; in mild-winter areas they can be grown outside in well-drained, sunny positions, but in countries with cold winters they need frost-free conditions and so are best grown in pots under glass where there is a slight amount of heat to keep the temperature just above freezing; they need deep pots since the corms pull themselves down in the soil and will not flower if they are placed too near the surface; large containers allowing at least a 15 cm (6 in) planting depth are best. A rather sandy soil mix seems to suit them best. In summer they should be kept warm and almost dry; the foliage will turn brown but is very tough, and unlike most other bulbs, cannot be easily removed without pulling up the corms as well and so, in the case of babianas, it may be necessary to use scissors when tidying up in late summer.

There are few summer-growing species; *B. hypogea* has a wide distribution and occurs in both winter and summer rainfall regions, so cultivation will depend upon the origin of particular plants.

B. socotrana, if it is at some time introduced into cultivation, will presumably be rather tender and might be best treated as a summer-grower.

Baeometra (*Liliaceae/Colchicaceae*)

Cormous. A South African genus of one species, *B. uniflora*, which has channelled leaves up the stem and, in early spring, a raceme of starry, yellow flowers, suffused red on the outside. I have not yet grown this to flowering but it is a winter-grower and is likely to need frost-free conditions, so in cold-winter areas pot cultivation in a slightly heated glasshouse seems to offer the best chance of success; when growth has finished in late spring, dry off for the summer months. The related *Iphigenia* (about 13 spp. in Africa, Madagascar, India and Australia; most spp. have racemes

or cymes of small 'spidery' flowers with very narrow, green, brown or reddish segments) should probably be given similar treatment, although those from the more tropical regions could be tried as summer-growers. *Hexacyrtis* (1 sp. from South West Africa) is also related, and is somewhat similar to *Iphigenia*; this will be almost certainly a winter-grower, and frost-tender. I have not tried either of the two species of *Camptorrhiza* but, given the chance, I would try *C. indica* (which has pink flowers like a small colchicum but with reflexed segments) as a summer-grower, drying off the corms in winter; the South African *C. strumosa* is probably a winter-grower, summer-dormant, but it has insignificant flowers and is scarcely worth trying.

Begonia (*Begoniaceae*)

Tuberous/rhizomatous. A large genus, widely distributed, mainly in the tropics; the tuberous types are well-known for their flamboyant flowers, much-used for summer bedding displays, in containers and as house-plants. The tuberous hybrids, collectively known as *B.* x *tuberhybrida*, are available in a wide range of colours, single and double, and may be erect or pendent in habit; these are all very frost-tender. They are summer-growers, so plant tubers in spring; in areas with late frosts it is best to start them into growth under glass or indoors and then plant out when the soil has warmed up; they need a fertile soil with a plentiful supply of water in summer; in autumn, lift and store for the winter in frost-free conditions. Two species from temperate areas are hardy enough to be worth trying in the open ground: *B. sutherlandii* and *B. grandis* (*evansiana*) are summer-growers, dying down for the winter; choose a sheltered position in dappled shade in humus-rich soil. Both produce small stem bulblets which provide a useful method of propagation.

36 *Begonia grandis*

37 *Bellevalia hyacinthoides*

Belamcanda (*Iridaceae*)

Rhizomatous. An eastern Asiatic genus of two species, allied to *Iris* and similar in growth to the rhizomatous species in having flat fans of erect sword-shaped leaves; the flowers are carried on loosely branched stems and are flattish when fully open, with six spreading almost equal segments which are orange (*B. chinensis*) or yellow (*B. flabellata*), spotted darker inside. Although frost-hardy, this sometimes succumbs to winter wet, so requires a position where there is good drainage; much lower temperatures are endured where they experience dry cold, as in the more continental climates of parts of Europe and North America. During the summer growing and flowering season it does need plenty of moisture and will not succeed in warm, dry positions. Young plants are best planted out in spring and then left undisturbed.

Bellevalia (*Liliaceae/Hyacinthaceae*)

Bulbous. About 50 species, from Mediterranean region, western and central Asia, spring-flowering, with racemes of mostly rather dull with white, greenish or blue flowers becoming brown with age. Plant in autumn, dry off in summer when dormant. Well-drained soil in sun. In damp-summer areas grow in bulb frame or pots in alpine house.

Bessera (*Alliaceae*)

Cormous. This should be cultivated in a similar way to the related *Milla* (see page 119).

Biarum (*Araceae*)

Tuberous. Genus of about 15 species from Mediterranean region and western Asia. Mostly autumn-flowering with smelly purple spathes (*B. davisii* has creamy-yellow sweet-smelling spathes) produced at ground level, before the leaves appear; leaves emerge in autumn-winter and last until late spring. Plant in late summer/early autumn, dry off in summer when dormant. Well-drained soil in full sun. In damp-summer and cold areas grow in bulb frame or alpine house.

Bloomeria *(Liliaceae/Alliaceae)*

Cormous. About 3 species, western USA, late spring-flowering with umbels of starry, yellow flowers, leaves dying off by flowering time. Plant in autumn, dry off in summer when dormant. Well-drained soil in full sun. In damp-summer areas grow in raised beds, bulb frames or alpine house.

Bobartia *(Iridaceae)*

Rhizomatous. These South African plants are very seldom cultivated; there are about 15 species, mainly from the winter rainfall South West Cape area. All are evergreen perennials, often forming dense clumps of rush-like or narrowly lance-shaped leaves with yellow (rarely blue) flowers in heads carried on leafless stems; the flowers are short-lived, flattish with six more or less equal segments. I have tried to cultivate only one or two of these so cannot give precise details; they appear to be primarily winter-growers but they do not die down for an obvious dormant season so should never be dried out completely, although watering can be reduced in summer. The most successful was planted directly into a glasshouse border of very sandy soil and kept frost-free in winter; like other members of the family which have perennial fibrous root systems and no swollen storage organ (such as *Orthrosanthus* and

Patersonia) they cannot be moved very easily so it is best to plant out young seedlings and leave them undisturbed to grow on to maturity. In mild-winter areas they could be planted directly into an open, sunny position, but their ornamental value is limited by the very short life of the flowers.

Bomarea *(Alstroemeriaceae)*

Tuberous-rooted. This Central and South American genus is related to *Alstroemeria* (see page 60); there are many species, very few of which are in cultivation although they are very striking and would be worthwhile subjects for a conservatory in cold-winter areas or for the outdoor garden in milder regions. The more vigorous taller species are climbers, or rather twiners, with long, slender, leafy stems, but there are also shorter species with self-supporting stems, some of them stiffly erect and densely covered with narrow leaves. The flowers are more tubular than those of alstromerias, mostly orange or reddish, and produced in dense heads. I have tried only a few of these, the most successful being a Mexican one, probably *B. hirtella*, sent by Sally Walker many years ago. This is a summer-grower, dying away for the winter months; it grew most successfully planted directly into a frost-free glasshouse bed and given sticks for support whilst in growth. One of the higher altitude, smaller non-climbing species from the Andes, introduced by Robert Rolfe, is evergreen and is growing well in a pot of a peaty-gritty soil mix, also under slightly heated glass.

Bongardia *(Berberidaceae)*

Tuberous. One species with ornamental pinnate, grey, red-zoned leaves and loose heads of *Berberis*-like yellow flowers. Plant

38 *Bomarea multiflora* subsp. *caldasii*

in autumn, dry off in summer when dormant. Well-drained soil in full sun. In damp-summer areas grow in raised beds, bulb frames or alpine house.

Boophane (*Amaryllidaceae*)

Bulbous. About 5 species, from the south-western part of southern Africa, extending into eastern tropical Africa. These are spectacular plants, flowering in autumn, or at the start of the rainy season in the tropics; large round umbels of pink, red, purplish, cream or yellow short-tubed flowers with 6 spreading segments; leaves either spreading on the ground or, in the most frequently cultivated species, *B. disticha*, radiating in a beautifully symmetrical fan-like fashion, each one wavy at the margins and grey-green. The bulbs can grow to an enormous size. Most of the species are winter-growers, coming from the predominantly winter rainfall areas, and should therefore be kept warm and dry through the summer, then encouraged into growth by watering in the early autumn; I have, unfortunately, not had the opportunity to try any of the interesting species such as *B. haemanthoides* and the wine-red *B. pulchra*, but I have grown *B. disticha* with a certain amount of success; this occurs over a very wide area from South Africa north to Kenya and can behave as a winter- or a summer-grower, probably largely depending upon the origin of the bulbs. For those gardening in cold-winter areas it would be more convenient to have the summer growing version, keeping the dormant bulbs reasonably warm and dry for the winter months. A sandy soil mix appears to suit them best, either planted directly into a glasshouse bed or in deep containers; they should be left undisturbed for as long as possible, feeding with a potash-rich fertilizer just after starting them into growth; plant with the large bulbs half-exposed.

Bowiea (*Liliaceae/Hyacinthaceae*)

Bulbous. A genus of three species from tropical and South Africa, the most frequently cultivated of which is *B. volubilis*; this is really a curiosity plant, having a huge spherical bulb and long, much-branched, twining, leafless stems bearing green fleshy flowers in summer. This is a summer-grower and is suitable for pot cultivation in a slightly heated glasshouse or conservatory; the bulb should be half-exposed; it seems to flourish on neglect and the bulbs will expand to totally fill the container and continue to perform well without feeding for years on end. In winter the stems die away and water can be withheld until the following spring; a winter minimum temperature of about 5 °C (41 °F) is sufficient; in summer it can be placed outside as soon as the warmer weather has arrived (about 15 °C [59 °F] min. at night) but some means of support for the climbing stems is required.

Bravoa (*Agavaceae*)

This is usually included in *Polianthes* and I have given cultivation notes under that genus.

Brevoortia (*Liliaceae/Alliaceae*)

Cormous. A synonym of *Dichelostemma*.

Brimeura (*Liliaceae/Hyacinthaceae*)

Bulbous. Two spring-flowering species from the Pyrenees and western Mediterranean islands. Plant in autumn. *B. amethystina* has racemes of blue (or white) pendent tubular flowers; this can be planted in sun or partial shade in a moisture-retentive soil. *B. fastigiata* has much shorter racemes of pale pinkish-lilac or white starry, short-tubed flowers facing upwards; this needs well-drained soil which dries out in summer, so grow in raised beds, bulb frames or in pots in an alpine house.

Brodiaea (*Liliaceae/Alliaceae*)

Cormous. About 15 species, western USA, late spring-flowering with umbels of funnel-shaped blue, violet, purple or pink flowers, leaves dying off by flowering time. Plant in autumn, dry off in summer when dormant. Well-drained soil in full sun. In damp-summer areas grow in raised beds, bulb frames or alpine house.

39 *Brodiaea californica*

Brunsvigia, and × Brunsdonna (*Amaryllidaceae*)

Bulbous. About ten species from southern Africa, striking for their huge umbels of pink or red funnel-shaped flowers produced in late summer or early autumn before the leaves emerge; the large, oval or strap-like leaves are either flat on the ground or semi-erect. The large bulbs are given a warm, dry rest period in summer, followed by a watering in late summer to stimulate growth, although sometimes they will flower without this. Continue to water sparingly through winter then more copiously in spring until the leaves show signs of dying back. They are not frost-hardy so in cold-winter areas need planting in a frost-free (about 8 °C [46 °F] min. in winter) glasshouse, preferably directly into a bed of sandy soil, although I have also flowered them in large pots – these must be deep since the bulbs get to a very large size and have long, perennial roots; in mild areas they can be tried outdoors in sunny positions which dry out and become warm in summer. The hybrids beween *Brunsvigia* and *Amaryllis* (× *Amarygia*, or × *Brunsdonna*) should be given similar treatment; plant with the neck of the bulbs at soil level.

Bulbine (*Liliaceae/Asphodelaceae*)

Rhizomatous/fleshy roots. A genus from South and East Africa and Australia of possibly up to 35 species, many of them with very succulent leaves in compact rosettes and perhaps better grown with collections of cacti and succulents than bulbs. They have fleshy roots from small rhizomes (a few are annuals), short, thick to long cylindrical leaves and dense spikes of small yellow, orange or white flowers which have conspicuously hairy stamens (the filaments); some species are sub-shrubby, while others have rosettes like those of aloes. Bulbines require a sandy, well-drained soil which is not too rich or they will develop out of character. The species from the South West Cape area are winter-growers, flowering in spring, so should be watered through autumn and winter then at least partially dried out during summer; they are not frost-hardy so in cold-winter areas are best grown in a slightly heated glasshouse. The related and similar genus *Jodrellia* should probably be treated in the same way. I have not tried the bulbines from Australia (e.g. *B. bulbosa* and *B. semi-barbata* [these are sometimes treated as *Bulbinopsis*]); they appear to be variable in behaviour, in some areas winter-growers and flowering in spring while in others they seem to flower in summer, emerging after rain has fallen or staying dormant if there is insufficient moisture. The East Cape and tropical African species could probably be treated as summer-growers but I have not had access to these either.

Bulbinella
(*Liliaceae/Asphodelaceae*)

Rhizomatous/fleshy roots. About 20 species from South Africa and New Zealand with rather fleshy leaves in basal tufts and long, densely-flowered spikes of small orange, yellow or white flowers; these do not have hairy filaments like those of *Bulbine*. The South African species are from the south-west winter rainfall region so are winter-growers, requiring water from autumn through to spring and flowering at any time from late winter to early summer. They are not very frost-hardy so in cold areas need glasshouse cultivation, but in mild-winter regions they are grown out-doors in sunny positions in well-drained soils; wherever they are grown, they need to dry out to some extent in summer whilst dormant. The New Zealand species (I have tried only *B. hookeri*) are hardier and will tolerate some frost, although not if combined with excessive wet; they are spring-flowering and require a rather more moisture retentive, although still well-drained soil, so a gritty/peaty mix has proved suitable.

Bulbocodium
(*Liliaceae/Colchicaceae*)

Cormous. A small genus from southern, central and eastern Europe, related and similar to *Colchicum*, with erect purple, funnel-shaped flowers in spring. Plant in autumn in a well-drained position in full sun where they will dry out in summer; also suitable for pots in an unheated glasshouse.

Calochortus (*Liliaceae*)

Bulbous. A large genus from western North America, usually including a group of Mexican species which have been treated as a genus, *Cyclobothra*, or as section *Cyclobothra* of *Calochortus*. *Calochortus* have slender stems carrying showy flowers which are pendent and bell- or globe-shaped (the globe lilies or fairy lanterns such as *C. albus*, *C. amabilis*, *C. amoenus* and *C. pulchellus*) or upright and bowl- or saucer-shaped (the Mariposa tulips such as *C. clavatus*, *C. gunnisonii*, *C. kennedyi*, *C. luteus*, *C. superbus*, *C. vestae* and *C. venustus*); the colours range from white to yellow, lilac, pink, purple and red, often strikingly blotched and zoned in the centre, and usually with hairs on the inside, sometimes almost filling the whole centre (the cats' ears group such as *C. caeruleus*, *C. elegans* and *C. tolmiei*). For cultivation purposes they fall into two basic groups, the North American winter/spring growers which are summer dormant and the Mexican summer-growers which are winter-dormant.

In the case of the North American species, in view of the fact that the habitat, soil and climates differ widely, it is surprising that most of them can be cultivated using a fairly standard soil mix and uniform growing conditions. However, I must not give the impression that they are all easy plants, for *C. kennedyi* is very difficult to please in the conditions I have to offer! They should be planted or potted in autumn in well-drained, gritty or sandy soil and grown with as much light as possible when the leaves emerge through to flowering time in spring/early summer, after which water can be withheld and the bulbs dried out until the following autumn. Although the majority are fairly frost-hardy they are often not very successful in areas with a combination of wet and cold in winter, so are best treated as bulb frame plants; Wim de Goede, in Holland, has however shown that they can be grown in a colder more continental type of climate if the bulbs are lifted and dried in summer; they are also good in pots in an unheated glasshouse, although many are rather tall and inclined to be untidy unless supported by sticks. Anyone gardening in a Mediter-ranean-type (winter wet/summer dry) climate should be able to grow quite a range of them in the open garden.

The Mexican species (such as *C. barbatus*, *C. ghiesbrechtii* and *C. hartwegii*) are summer-growers and, on the whole, less hardy; the bulbs should be planted in spring in a sunny position in well-drained soil which is well-supplied with moisture; in autumn, after flowering, they are best lifted and dried off for the winter and kept frost-free; otherwise grow in pots where watering can be controlled more easily. Some species of both types produce tiny bulblets in the leaf axils; these can be detached (usually ready at about or just after flowering time) and 'sown' like seeds at the appropriate time: spring for summer-growers and autumn for winter-growers.

Caloscordum (*Liliaceae/Alliaceae*)

Bulbous. A genus of one species which has loose umbels of starry, rose-pink flowers in mid-late summer, related to *Allium*. Plant bulbs in spring in a sunny position in soil which is well-drained but well-supplied with moisture in summer; in areas with cold, wet winters, lift bulbs and store nearly dry in winter whilst dormant; alternatively grow in pots in alpine house or frame and dry out when dormant in winter.

Calostemma (*Amaryllidaceae*)

Bulbous. A genus endemic to south-eastern Australia consisting of two species, *C. pur-pureum* and *C. luteum,* which differ mainly in flower colour. The bulbs each produce several narrowly linear, basal leaves and a leafless flower stem carrying an umbel of up to 30 purple, pink, white or yellow, funnel-shaped flowers; these have a short tube, six spreading segments and a small cup in the centre, somewhat like a *Narcissus*. They are essentially winter-growers, dormant in early to mid-summer and flowering in late summer before the leaves emerge in autumn; these elongate through winter and spring then die down, after which the bulbs are given a warm, dry rest period. In cold-winter areas it is only possible to grow them under glass, with a minimum winter night temperature of about 8 °C (46 °F). In fact I find that *C. pur-pureum* only just survives if given this treat-ment and I now bring the pot into the house and stand it on a shelf over a slightly warm radiator. A glasshouse bench with pots plunged in sand with soil-warming cables would seem to be a good idea for many of these tender amaryllids. A sandy soil mix seems to suit them best, in deep pots. In very mild-winter areas they could be planted out in a sunny position.

40 *Calochortus luteus*

Camassia
(Liliaceae/Hyacinthaceae)

Bulbous. A North American genus of 5 species having long, narrow basal leaves and racemes of white, pale to deep blue or violet starry flowers, comparatively large for a member of the Hyacinthaceae. They have great garden value, mostly making large clumps which flower freely in early summer, and they are very hardy, not requiring a hot, dry, dormant period in summer like so many of the bulbous plants. In fact, they thrive in moist soils and can be treated as border perennials. The bulbs should be planted in autumn since they start to make active root growth at this time.

41 Camassia cusickii

Canna (Cannaceae)

Rhizomatous. A small genus of about 10 species, mainly from subtropical and tropical Central and South America but extending into the warmer parts of southern USA; they are widely naturalized in tropical countries and many cultivars (C. x generalis) are used worldwide as ornamentals. They have stout rhizomes producing robust, leafy stems with bold leaves, often selected for their bright green or bronze-purple colouring; the large showy flowers arise at the apex of the stems and appear in succession over a long period, almost orchid-like and in a range of brilliant shades of yellow, orange, pink or white, sometimes prominently spotted darker. Cannas are more or less evergreen and flower almost continuously in the tropics but in cooler countries are treated as summer-growers, lifting the rhizomes for the winter and storing them away from frost, preferably at about 10 °C (50 °F), in a shed or glasshouse. In spring they are potted up and started into growth again by watering and raising the temperature to a minimum of 15 °C (59 °F); they can be divided up at this time and then planted out when the soil has warmed up in early summer. They need a rich, deep soil which is well-supplied with moisture in summer. They also make impressive plants for large containers which, in cold areas, can be moved under cover for the winter. In areas where there are only superficial light frosts, they will sometimes survive outdoors in sheltered positions if given a mulch of loose dry material.

Cardiocrinum (Liliaceae)

Bulbous. Sometimes included in Lilium. There are three species in the Himalaya, Burma, China and Japan and the Kurile Islands, differing from the true lilies in having large, heart-shaped leaves and monocarpic bulbs (dying after flowering), although small offsets are produced which will grow on in time to flowering size. They have huge, trumpet-shaped white flowers in late summer, in some species tinted green or with purple spots inside.

If rapid results are required, large bulbs should be purchased as it may take seven years to flower them from seed and three or four years from the offset bulbs. Cardiocrinums, like most lilies, are summer-growers, dying down for the winter months, although they have perennial roots and should never be dried out. They thrive best in areas with a cool, humid atmosphere, planted in deep humus-rich soil in dappled shade and kept well-supplied with moisture through summer, preferably on a slight slope so that excess water drains away in winter. Although fairly hardy the bulbs may start to grow in spring before frosts are past and the young shoots may be damaged; in areas where this is a possibility, provide a loose covering such as bracken, or try one of the modern fleece materials. They also require a lot of space! Plant the bulbs with their tips only just below the surface.

Carpolyza (*Amaryllidaceae*)

Bulbous. The one species, *C. tenella* (*C. spiralis*) from the South West Cape region of South Africa, has thread-like, coiled, basal leaves and wiry stems carrying a few-flowered umbel of small, upright, flat white flowers. It is a winter-grower, flowering soon after watering in autumn; in summer it is given a drier period, but not completely dried out since the leaves are present through the year. The soil mix is a sandy loam; the pots are kept in a light position in a just-frost-free glasshouse. Although in mild-winter areas it would be hardy, it is so small and delicate that it would be lost in the open ground; plant the bulbs just below soil level.

Chasmanthe (*Iridaceae*)

Cormous. A genus of three species from the South West Cape region of South Africa having fans of erect, sword-shaped leaves and many-flowered simple to branched

spikes of orange, red or bicoloured flowers (there is also a yellow variant of *C. floribunda*, var. *duckittii*); these are tubular in the lower part and strongly curved with an elongated, hooded upper segment. They are winter-growers, dying down in summer when they can be kept drier. The corms should be planted or potted in early autumn in a well-drained, humus-rich soil and kept well-watered through winter, flowering in late winter/early spring; in mild-winter areas they can be planted outside in full sun or dappled shade but are not tolerant of frost so in colder climates require frost-free glasshouse cultivation; if grown in pots these need to be large since they are vigorous plants, increasing quite rapidly vegetatively into clumps. Unless repotted each year in autumn, regular feeding in winter/spring with a potash-rich fertilizer is essential.

Chionodoxa (*Liliaceae/ Hyacinthaceae*)

Bulbous. About 7 species, native to western Turkey, Crete and Cyprus, with two basal leaves and short racemes of flattish

42 *Chionodoxa siehei*

blue or lavender (pink and white forms also) flowers in spring; related to *Scilla*. Plant bulbs in autumn in semi-shade or a sunny position which will not become too hot and dry in summer when the bulbs are dormant as they can be killed by desiccation. Good for naturalizing under deciduous shrubs.

Chionoscilla (Chionodoxa × Scilla) (*Liliaceae/Hyacinthaceae*)

Bulbous. Cultivation as for *Chionodoxa*.

Chlidanthus (*Amaryllidaceae*)

Bulbous. A small genus of perhaps six or seven species, mainly from South America but with one species reputedly reaching Central America, in Mexico. They have narrow basal leaves and a leafless flower stem bearing a few-flowered umbel of widely funnel-shaped to flattish flowers, yellow, pink or red. Only the Peruvian *C. fragrans* is at all well-known in cultivation and this is rather shy-flowering in my experience. It is a summer-grower (as are the others, I imagine) for planting in spring; water lightly until growth is obvious, then increase watering and feeding (potash-rich) for the summer months; dry off and keep frost-free in winter. In cold areas it should be grown in pots in a conservatory or glasshouse, either permanently or they can be started in pots under glass and planted out as soon as the soil has warmed up; choose a sheltered, sunny position where there is plenty of moisture available in summer.

Chlorogalum (*Liliaceae/?Anthericaceae*)

Bulbous. A seldom-cultivated genus of 5 species, mainly from California. They have fibrous-coated bulbs producing long, tough, basal leaves, often greyish and wavy at the edges; the tall, loosely branched flower stems carry many flattish, starry white, pinkish, blue or purple flowers which mostly open only in the evening (2 spp. open in the day). I have cultivated only *C. pomeridianum* and this is a very easy plant in an open, sunny position in reasonably well-drained soil; it is in active growth for much of the winter, spring and summer, flowering in mid-summer and then dying back in the late summer and autumn.

Clivia (*Amaryllidaceae*)

Rhizomatous. A South African genus of four species, all evergreens with stout rhizomes and tufts of thick leathery, strap-shaped leaves arranged in two ranks; the funnel-shaped to tubular flowers are carried in umbels and are orange, red, pinkish or yellow, the six segments often tipped yellow or green; the most frequently cultivated species is *C. miniata*, of which yellow variants have been selected, and there are also some hybrids. Being evergreen, clivias should never be dried out completely, but given a rest period with less water in winter before flowering in late winter/spring. In mild-winter areas they can be grown outside in partial shade, but where there are cold, frosty winters it is

43 *Clivia miniata*

necessary to plant them in glasshouse borders or in containers in an open, loose soil mix containing leafmould; they appear to flower best when 'pot bound'. During winter a minimum of about 10 °C (50 °F) should be maintained, although they will stand lower temperatures for short spells. In the summer growing period, regular, weak liquid feeds are beneficial, otherwise the leaves can become very yellow, possibly also caused by using alkaline tap water; plant with the crowns only just below soil level.

Codonopsis (*Campanulaceae*)

Tuberous/fleshy roots. A large genus from central to eastern Asia, including the Himalaya, notable for their attractive saucer- to bell-shaped flowers in various shades of blue, green and pinkish-white, often conspicuously veined, or zoned inside with contrasting colours; they may be short, erect plants to twining-stemmed climbers or scramblers. *Codonopsis* are summer-growers, dying down to tubers or clusters of thick, fleshy roots in the winter; they require a soil which is moisture-retentive since they do not thrive in hot, dry conditions in summer; most can be grown outside but the climbers need an adjacent shrub for support, although they can also be grown up twiggy sticks in containers. Some of the tuberous-rooted species do seem to survive better if grown in this way so that they can be moved to a frost-free glasshouse for the winter where the tubers can be partially dried off, otherwise, if left in the open ground, they sometimes rot during cold, wet winters.

Colchicum (*Liliaceae/ Colchicaceae*)

Cormous. A large genus from Europe, North Africa and western to central Asia with goblet-shaped flowers in white or

44 *Colchicum cilicicum*

shades of lilac-pink to purple (one yellow-flowered, *C. luteum*), sometimes strongly chequered darker; there are autumn- and spring-flowering species, some of the former flowering without leaves. They are all winter-growers and should be planted or potted in late summer to early autumn (the earlier the better for the autumn-flowering ones) in a well-drained, sunny position; dappled shade is acceptable for some of the more robust such as *C. speciosum*. They remain in growth until the following late spring/early summer when the corms need to be fairly warm and dry if they are to thrive and flower well; some produce very large leaves in spring so need careful placing where they will not swamp other smaller plants. The small-flowered species such as *C. cupanii*, *C. triphyllum*, *C. cretense*, *C. luteum* and *C. kesselringii* are best in a bulb frame or in pots in an unheated glasshouse as they do not stand up well to bad weather outdoors and their corms need to be dried out in summer. Some of the low-altitude Mediterranean species are not very hardy and their corms can be killed in areas where frost penetrates the soil to more than the surface layer. *C. variegatum* and *C. macrophyllum* will not thrive unless given a hot, sunny position.

Commelina (*Commelinaceae*)

Tuberous-rooted. This is a large, widespread, mainly tropical, genus, most species of which are fibrous-rooted. Commelinas are characterized by their 'Mickey Mouse' flowers, mostly bright blue (also white, yellow and orange), with two large ear-like upper petals. There are some tuberous-rooted species from Mexico, for example *C. coelestis*, *C. dianthifolia* and *C. tuberosa* which are well worth growing; these are summer-growers and should be planted in an open, sunny position in a free-draining, non-alkaline soil, well-supplied with moisture through the summer; they die down for the winter months to a cluster of tubers.

Conanthera (*Tecophilaeaceae*)

Cormous. A few species from Chile having loosely branched inflorescences of small blue, purple or white-and-purple blotched

45 *Conanthera bifolia*

bell-shaped flowers, sometimes with the segments reflexed in cyclamen fashion. Plant bulbs in autumn in sandy soil and keep watered until leaves die down in early-mid-summer, then dry off until autumn. In cold-winter areas they need protection in a frame or greenhouse, just-frost-free.

Cooperia (*Amaryllidaceae*)

Now included in *Zephyranthes*.

Corydalis
(*Papaveraceae/Fumariaceae*)

Tuberous. A large genus widespread in the temperate northern hemisphere with many tuberous and non-tuberous species, the latter perennial, monocarpic or annual. They are spring- or summer-flowering with attractively dissected leaves and 4-petalled flowers, the upper and lower enlarged to give a 2-lipped appearance, and the upper extended at the back of the flower into a conspicuous spur. The tuberous species are very popular, mostly fairly dwarf but with relatively large spikes of flowers in a wide range of colours. Botanically, and for cultivation purposes, they fall into several distinct groups. (1) The mainly European *C. bulbosa* (*cava*) and *C. marschalliana* start to root in autumn and flower in spring; they need cool-growing conditions in dappled shade in humus-rich soil; the misshapen tubers should not be allowed to dry out, even in their dormant period in summer. Plant the tubers in autumn. (2) The Eurasian spring-flowering group containing *C. solida*, *C. caucasica*, *C. ambigua*, *C. bracteata* and their many relatives have rounded, often yellowish tubers; these grow well in semi-shade or full sun in well-drained humus-rich soil and will tolerate more drought during their summer dormancy, although a combination of extreme heat and drought will cause them to desiccate and possibly die; the Siberian *C. bracteata* requires very cool growing conditions and appears above ground much later than the rest. Plant the tubers of this group in autumn. The unrelated eastern Asiatic *C. buschii* and *C. decumbens* seem to require similar treatment. (3) The mainly Middle Eastern/Central Asiatic group comprising *C. rutifolia*, *C. ledebouriana*, *C. sewerzowii*, *C. afghanica*, *C. aitchisonii*, *C. macrocentra*, *C. popovii* and their relatives are from open rocky areas which dry out in summer; in cultivation they need full sun in well-drained gritty/sandy soil; in areas with unreliably dry summers, plant in a bulb frame or grow in pots in an unheated glasshouse, otherwise the dormant tubers may rot off in summer. If growing in pots, plant one tuber in a wide pot (half pot or deep pan probably better) since these species have stems which spread widely underground before emerging. Plant tubers of this group in autumn. (4) The many Himalayan/Chinese species which are summer-growing and have clusters of fleshy roots (sometimes also with small scaly 'bulbs') such as *C. cashmeriana*, *C. juncea*, *C. flexuosa*, *C. polygalina* etc. should never be dried out; these are

46 *Corydalis bracteata*

winter-dormant and require cool-growing conditions in humus-rich soil in semi-shade of deciduous trees and shrubs. These are usually sold as growing plants in pots so can be planted in spring or summer. (5) *C. conorhiza*, *C. alpestris*, *C. pauciflora* and their relatives are mountain plants, dormant in winter (beneath snow) and flowering in spring/summer. The have elongated, forked tubers and are rare and difficult in cultivation, requiring cold winters and cool summer growing conditions, although in full sun or they become etiolated and out-of-character. A sharply drained soil consisting mainly of grit and humus seems to offer the best chance of success.

Crinum and × *Crinodonna* (*Amaryllidaceae*)

Bulbous. A large genus of well over 100 species, widespread in tropical, subtropical and warm, temperate regions in Asia, Australia, Africa and the Americas. They range from small bulbous deciduous species to huge evergreen ones with the leaf bases sheathed together to form a false stem, scarcely bulbous at all at the base; the flowers are carried in an umbel (or sometimes solitary) and have their six segments arranged so that they form a narrow to broad funnel-shape, or they spread more widely giving a rather 'spidery', less substantial appearance; they are often fragrant and mostly white or pale pink, some of them with darker red or purple stripes on the outside. Nearly all species can be regarded as summer-growers, although there are two from the winter rainfall region of South Africa (*C. lineare* and *C. variabile* which will behave as winter-growers and require a dry summer while dormant. Few crinums are frost-hardy, and the only ones which may be regarded as at all hardy are those from the higher ground in the eastern summer rainfall region

47 *Crinum kirkii*

Crocosmia (*Iridaceae*)

Cormous. A genus of about 7 species from
tropical and eastern South Africa, familiar
because of the frequently cultivated 'montbretia', *C.* ×*crocosmiiflora*, which is a hybrid
between *C. pottsii* and *C. aurea*. They have
erect, sword-shaped leaves and simple or
branched spikes of tubular or funnel-
shaped orange to red flowers, held in a
slightly pendent, horizontal or upright
position on the inflorecence branches.
The largest species, *C. masonorum* and *C.
paniculata* (*Antholyza paniculata*, *Curtonus
paniculatus*) are often cultivated for their
statuesque habit, bold pleated foliage and
brilliant flowers. These are all summer-
growers, usually dying down in winter but
sometimes nearly evergreen. They do
better in light, well-drained soils than in
heavy, wet clay, often succumbing to winter
wet in the latter conditions, although the
old 'montbretia' is almost indestructable
and has become a pest in some mild-winter
areas of the world. The species are better
behaved and they, and the modern hybrids,
of which there are many named cultivars,
are excellent plants for a perennial border.
They require plenty of moisture during the
summer growing season and, once established, are best left undisturbed to form
clumps; the initial planting is best undertaken in spring. In areas where the ground
freezes solid to some depth they can be
killed off, so it is necessary to cover them in
autumn with a thick mulch or lift them for
the winter and store in a frost-free place.

Crocus (*Iridaceae*)

Cormous. A large genus of about 80 species
from Europe, North Africa and western to
central Asia, very familiar with their
upright, wineglass-shaped flowers in
spring or autumn, in white, yellow or
shades of blue, lilac-blue or purple. They
begin root growth in autumn after a

of southern Africa; *C. bulbispermum*,
C. moorei and their frequently cultivated
hybrid, *C.* ×*powellii*, are the best-known
and can be cultivated in sheltered, sunny
positions which are well-supplied with
moisture during the summer growing
season. *C. powellii* is almost evergreen in
mild winters; the foliage may be severely
damaged during frosty periods in winter
but this does not seem to affect performance the next year. These, and many
other crinums, make good container plants
and appear to flower better when they have
increased and filled the space; liquid feeds
with a potash-rich fertilizer (tomato type)
are probably beneficial once they have
become too large to repot. In cold-winter
areas the containers can be moved into a
frost-free glasshouse or conservatory.
The more tropical species such as *C. asi-
aticum* do not really have a dormant period
and if kept warm enough (min. 16–20 °C
[60–68 °F]) will grow and flower most of
the year. Unfortunately very few of the
C. 130 species are in cultivation and even
fewer are available through nurseries; plant
the larger species, which have bulbs up to
30 cm (12 in) long, with their necks
reaching up to soil level.

48 *Crocus cartwrightianus*

summer dormancy and mostly require a sunny, well-drained position which dries out in summer; if this is not possible a raised bed, bulb frame or pot cultivation in an unheated glasshouse may be necessary. *C. scardicus* and *C. pelistericus* should never be dried out and are best with cool-growing conditions in a gritty/peaty soil mix; try similar conditions for *C. scharojanii*. *C. banaticus* will grow well in partial shade or full sun providing that the soil does not become both hot and dry at any time. *C. nudiflorus* grows well in damp grassland, its natural habitat.

Curculigo (*Hypoxidaceae*)

Cormous/tuberous. A mainly tropical and subtropical southern hemisphere genus of about 10-20 species, quite widespread in south-east Asia, Australia, the Seychelles and Southern Africa, with a few in South America. They have evergreen tufts of linear to lance-shaped or oblong leaves, often strongly pleated and bright glossy green, so are attractive as foliage plants; they may be as much as a 1 m (3 ft) in length but the inflorescences are usually much shorter, sometimes only just above ground

level. The flowers are sometimes solitary, or in few-flowered to dense head-like racemes, yellow and flattish when fully open; some species are quite small and look more like *Hypoxis* (see page 106). I have not grown any of these but, since they are mainly tropical/subtropical, in cooler climates they will require heated glasshouse cultivation, certainly frost-free and probably a minimum of about 10 °C (50 °F) in winter would be better; treat as summer-growers, with plenty of moisture in a humus-rich soil and humid atmosphere in partial shade, with less water in winter; planted directly into a bed would be best but a large container would probably also suffice; I suggest covering the corms with about 5 cm (2 in) of leafy soil.

Cyanella (*Tecophilaeaceae*)

Cormous. About 8 species, all from the south-western winter rainfall part of southern Africa. They have long, narrow leaves in rosettes or tufts, sometimes undulate-margined, and unbranched or loosely branched flower stems bearing small white, yellow or blue to lilac flowers; these have 6 segments which tend to reflex, leaving the stamens protruding. The corms should be planted in a well-drained, sandy/gritty soil in autumn and watered through the winter-spring growing season until after flowering in spring/early summer, then dried off for the rest of the summer. Plant outside in a sunny position or, in cold-winter areas, in a frost-free glasshouse in pots or directly into a bed.

Cybistetes (*Amaryllidaceae*)

Bulbous. There is only one species, *C. longifolia*, from the South West Cape region of South Africa. It has large umbels of flowers in summer, each of which has six reflexed segments, changing from white to pale pink as they age; the strap-shaped leaves appear later and elongate through the winter, dying away the following spring/early summer. I have not tried to grow this plant but the recommendations are that it is given a sandy, free-draining soil in full sun and dried off after the leaves have died down in spring. In cold-winter areas it will need frost-free conditions so could be either planted into a glasshouse border or grown in a large pot or container. Thus, its needs are similar to those of *Brunsvigia*; plant the bulbs with their necks at ground level.

49 *Cyclamen purpurascens*

Cyclamen (*Primulaceae*)

Tuberous. About 19 species from central and southern Europe, the Mediterranean region, western Asia and Somalia. Some flower in autumn before their leaves, others with their leaves in late summer, autumn, winter and spring; the flowers are white, pink or carmine, scented or unscented, with characteristic reflexed petals. The leaves are heart-shaped or rounded, often beautifully marked with light and dark or silvery zones. Start tubers into growth by watering in early autumn after a summer rest period and keep watered until leaves die down in summer. They need well-drained soil and most prefer alkaline soil with some leafmould added. Most species tolerate light shade and *C. hederi-folium* and *C. repandum* are best with dappled sunlight. They are ideal alpine house-plants for pots or deep pans; the tubers are normally planted just below soil level, but the cultivars of *C. persicum* are usually grown with the top exposed. Exceptions to general rules: *C. purpur-ascens*, *C. fratrense* and *C. parviflorum* are almost evergreen and should not be dried out completely; *C. coum* can be dried but should be kept fairly cool; *C. graecum* and *C. rohlfsianum* need a warm, dry period when dormant if they are to flower well; *C. somalense*, no information yet.

Cyclobothra (*Liliaceae*)

Bulbous. See under *Calochortus*.

Cypella (*Iridaceae*)

Bulbous. A South American genus having loose scaly bulbs and erect, pleated, sword-shaped leaves; the yellow, blue or purple flowers are somewhat *Iris*-like with three large outer segments and three smaller inner ones. The relatively commonly-culti-vated *C. herbertii* and *C. plumbea* (*Phallo-callis coelestis*) behave as summer-growers, dying down somewhat in winter; they need a sheltered, sunny situation in well-drained soil but with plenty of moisture available during the growing period; they are not very frost-hardy but will survive in mild areas. Other species are rare in cultivation but *C. peruviana* and *C. herrerae* are occa-sionally seen; these are sometimes treated, with some other cypellas, as species of *Hesperoxiphion*; it is best if these, and *C. osteniana*, *C. huilense*, *C. hauthalii* and *C. armosa* are also given a rest period (not too dry) in winter and encouraged to behave as summer-growers since they are not very hardy; *C. aquatilis* needs much water so I grow it in a pot of peaty soil, standing in a dish of water in summer.

Cyrtanthus (*Amaryllidaceae*)

Bulbous. A genus of about 50 species, mainly from South Africa but also in south tropical and East Africa; they have narrow to broad strap-shaped, basal leaves and umbels of tubular to widely funnel-shaped red, pink, yellow or white flowers. Cultivation depends upon the wild origin of the species; the majority occur in areas where they receive rain for much of the year and are more or less evergreen, flowering in spring or summer, for example, *C. mackenii*, *C. obrienii*, *C. macowanii* and the frequently cultivated *C. elatus* (*C. purpureus*, *Vallota speciosa*); these should be given a rest period in winter, when watering is reduced but not stopped altogether; *C. obliquus* and *C. falcatus* are spring-flowering after a winter rest period during which time they are kept dry; those from the eastern parts of southern Africa and tropical Africa receive summer rainfall and are primarily summer-growers, for example, *C. breviflorus* and *C. sanguineus*); there are also a few species, seldom cultivated, from the winter rainfall area of the South West Cape; as such, these are predominantly winter-growers. Most species perform best when grown in containers in a

50 *Cyrtanthus elatus*

well-drained, sandy compost, even the hardiest needing frost-free conditions; they are said to respond well to high potash fertilizers; most are grown with their bulbs below ground but in the case of *C. obliquus* and *C. falcatus* they should be half-exposed. Graham Duncan of Kirstenbosch recommends allowing the potting compost to dry out between waterings in summer.

Dahlia (*Compositae*)

Tuberous roots. Although dahlias are familiar garden plants it is mainly the highly developed hybrid cultivars which are seen, the species seldom being cultivated. There are about 12 species in Central and South America, mainly Mexico, with small flower heads compared with their hybrid offspring, consisting of a single whorl of ray florets. They are all tuberous-rooted summer-growers and most require some frost protection in winter whilst they are dormant, although *D. merckii* will stand a few degrees as long as the soil does not freeze solid; in cold areas it is safer to lift and store them dry for the winter, then start them off in slight heat in spring before planting out. It is a common practice to encourage top growth in spring and take cuttings from this, discarding the old rootstocks; this works with the species as well, although planting out the existing rootstock is quite satisfactory unless extra plants are required.

Daubenya (*Liliaceae/ Hyacinthaceae*)

Bulbous. Only one rare species is known from the winter rainfall region of South Africa, *D. aurea*; this is rather like a *Massonia* (see page 118) in having two broad leaves, smooth in this case, nearly flat on the ground with a stemless 'head' of red, yellow or orange flowers appearing in winter; the outermost flowers in the head have a curious structure, each one with three large segments on the side of the flower away from the central axis of the plant; these larger segments thus form a showy 'ring' around the circumference of the head, creating a very striking display. Cultivation is as described for *Massonia*; my experience is that in the poor light of an English winter the plant very easily becomes drawn up, tending to lose the very flat rosette habit, so it should be grown as cool as possible, without actually being frozen, and in as light a spot as can be found.

Dicentra (*Papaveraceae/Fumariaceae*)

Tuberous/Rhizomatous. Most of the species of this eastern Asiatic/North American genus are herbaceous perennials but there are a few with small, swollen, tuber-like rootstocks; they have attractively dissected, often grey-green foliage and pendent 2-spurred flowers in spring; these have been likened in shape to a Dutchman's traditional breeches, hence the common name. *D. canadensis* and *D. cucullaria* have small, rounded tubers which are planted in autumn in a cool position in partial shade in a humus-rich soil; they are also suitable for growing in pots in an alpine house, shaded from any hot sun. The beautiful Japanese *D. peregrina* is not an easy plant to cultivate; the best chance of success seems to be in pots in a well-aired unheated glasshouse in an extremely sharply drained gritty soil mix, watered frequently during its summer growing period.

Dichelostemma (*Liliaceae/Alliaceae*)

Cormous. About 7 species, western USA, related to and sometimes merged with *Brodiaea*. Late spring-flowering with umbels of tubular blue, purple, crimson or pink

51 *Dichelostemma ida-maia*

flowers, leaves dying off by flowering time. Plant in autumn, dry off in summer when dormant. Well-drained soil in full sun. In damp-summer areas grow in raised beds, bulb frames or alpine house. The twining *D. volubile* requires support from neighbouring plants.

Dierama (*Iridaceae*)

Cormous. A beautiful group of plants consisting of over 40 species, mainly from the eastern parts of southern Africa and tropical Africa. They have tough, long, narrow, erect or arching basal leaves and wiry flower stems bearing spikes of several bell-shaped flowers on slender pendent stalks, in a range of colours but mostly shades of pink to purple-red. These are all summer-growers but, at least those I have tried, do not die down completely in winter unless frosted. I am not really the best person to advise on what are the best conditions since they do not thrive in our current garden! However, in a garden not far away where I planted them they naturalized and seeded almost too freely. They appear to require plenty of moisture during the growing season, in fact they are often planted near to water, but the positions should certainly not be waterlogged. The gardens where I have seen them doing well have been on sandy or stony soils, never on heavy clay unless this has been modified to improve the drainage. It is best to plant them out in spring, while still as young seedlings, into their permanent positions and then leave them undisturbed for as long as they are doing well since they appear to dislike being transplanted.

52 *Dierama pulcherrimum*

Dietes (*Iridaceae*)

Rhizomatous. A small genus with about 5 species in tropical and South Africa and one, *D. robinsoniana*, on Lord Howe Island. They are most attractive evergreen, tuft-forming plants with fans of long, narrowly sword-shaped leaves and *Moraea-* or *Iris*-like white or yellow flowers with three large outer segments. They are not frost-hardy so need to be grown in a glasshouse or conservatory, and preferably planted directly into a bed since they are mostly rather too vigorous for pots; they can, however, be grown in large containers. Although evergreen they make most of their new growth in summer. A light, sandy, humus-rich mix seems to suit them best. *D. iridioides* (*vegeta*) has a very

spreading habit and eventually needs a considerable amount of room; its flower stems last for a very long time and often produce more flowers in their second year, so should not be pruned off too quickly. In mild-winter areas *Dietes* can be grown outside in partially shaded positions; plant with the rhizomes on surface.

Dipcadi (*Liliaceae/ Hyacinthaceae*)

Bulbous. A sizeable genus of perhaps 50 species, widespread from the Canary Islands, south-west Europe and North Africa, south to tropical and South Africa and east to Saudi Arabia and India. These are not exciting garden plants and will be seldom encountered; they have narrow, basal leaves and racemes of bell-shaped, usually slightly pendent flowers which tend to have the inner three segments held together to form a tube and the very narrow outer three curving outwards; the colours are on the whole rather dull – green, whitish-green, yellowish, brown, orange or pinkish-brown. The species most frequently seen is the Mediterranean *D. serotinum* which is very variable in colour. This is a winter-grower and is suitable for a sandy soil in a bulb frame or unheated glasshouse, with a hot, dry rest period; it is scarcely showy enough for the open garden. The Saudi Arabian species I have grown also behave as winter-growers whereas those from tropical Africa (I have tried only a Malawi species) are dormant in winter, flowering in summer.

Dipidax (*Liliaceae/Colchicaceae*)

Cormous. Should now be known as *Onixotis*.

Drimia (*Liliaceae/ Hyacinthaceae*)

Bulbous. A small genus of perhaps 15 species, predominantly from tropical and South Africa but now including the

Mediterranean, North African and western Asiatic species formerly in the genus *Urginea*. They have lance-shaped basal leaves, sometimes undulate at the margins, and these are often produced after the flowers. The flowers are in spikes or racemes, sometimes very long, as in the Mediterranean *D. maritima* (*Urginea maritima*) and have six spreading segments giving a starry shape, usually white with a darker vein along the centre of each segment. The Mediterranean species are, as one would expect, winter-growers after a hot, dry summer dormancy; they are not very hardy and in areas which are likely to receive even light frosts they are only suitable for a sheltered, sunny position, for example, against a sunny wall; otherwise they require bulb frame or frost-free glasshouse cultivation, although whether they are worth the space, from the display point of view, is debatable. I have not tried the tropical African species; it is likely that they could be treated as summer-growers, with a warm, dry winter rest period.

Drimiopsis
(*Liliaceae/ Hyacinthaceae*)

Bulbous. About 7 species from tropical and South Africa, mostly having oval basal leaves with conspicuous dark blotches, and dense muscari-like spikes of small, rounded, white or greenish flowers. The only species I have cultivated, *D. maculata,* is a summer-grower, suitable for a frost-free glasshouse; in mild-winter areas it could probably be grown outside in a semi-shaded position. It makes a good foliage pot plant, grown in slight shade as the leaves have a tendency to scorch in full sun; it grows well in a sandy potting soil, watered through the summer months and then dried out in winter; the bulbs are planted with the tips just above soil level. I would expect the other species to behave in much the same way in cultivation.

Duthiastrum (*Iridaceae*)

Cormous. There is only one species, *D. linifolium*, from South Africa. It has narrow basal leaves and a very short flower stem bearing 1-several yellow flowers; these have a very long, slender tube and six equal spreading segments forming a flattish flower when fully open. It is a winter-grower, needing frost-free conditions and a warm, dry, summer rest period.

Elisena (*Amaryllidaceae*)

Bulbous. The one species which is sometimes encountered, in literature if not in cultivation, is now treated as a *Hymenocallis* (see page 105).

Eminium (*Araceae*)

Tuberous. Genus of about 7 species from western to central Asia. Mostly autumn-flowering with smelly, purple spathes produced at ground level, before the leaves appear; leaves emerge in autumn-winter and last until late spring. Plant in late summer/early autumn, dry off in summer when dormant. Well-drained soil in full sun. In damp-summer and cold areas grow in bulb frame or alpine house.

Empodium (*Hypoxidaceae*)

Cormous. A genus of about 10 species from South Africa, related and similar to *Hypoxis* and *Spiloxene*; those I have seen have erect, flat, starry flowers, not unlike large gageas, yellow inside and green on the outside; the lance-shaped leaves, usually quite broad and varying from one to several per corm, are conspicuously pleated lengthways, and are either present at flowering time or are produced later. I have not tried to grow these but, if given the opportunity, would treat the South West Cape species in the same way as *Spiloxene* (see page 141) and the East Cape species like *Rhodohypoxis* (see page 134).

Engysiphon (*Iridaceae*)

Cormous. Now included in the genus *Geissorhiza* (see page 95).

Eranthis (*Ranunculaceae*)

Tuberous. Small genus of about 8 species from Europe and Asia, all dwarf plants well-known for their yellow or white cup-shaped flowers over a ruff-like whorl of dissected leaves, produced in spring. They are all woodland or mountain plants needing cool growing conditions. Plant in autumn in dappled shade, never allowing the tubers to dry out completely. Purchased tubers which have been dried should be soaked overnight before planting. The eastern Asiatic species such as *E. pinnatifida* need good drainage in humus-rich soil; a gritty, leafmould mix is suitable. *E. cilicica* and the hybrid *E.* × *tubergenii* will take more sun than *E. hyemalis*.

53 *Eranthis cilicica*

Eremurus (*Liliaceae/Asphodelaceae*)

Rhizomatous/fleshy roots. A large genus, mainly from the Middle East and Central Asia, extending westwards just into south-

54 *Eremurus lactiflorus*

eastern Europe and eastwards to the western Himalaya. They have compact crowns with radiating stout, fleshy roots, producing tufts of very long, narrow-channelled leaves and long, stout, many-flowered racemes of starry flowers in a range of colours: mostly white, yellow, orange or pink. These, the foxtail lilies, are distributed through the drier parts of Asia where they receive autumn/winter/spring rainfall (snow at higher altitudes), cold winters and warm moist growing conditions in spring before a long hot, dry summer; they flower towards the end of the growing period in early summer when the leaves are beginning to die back (tatty leaves are therefore not necessarily a sign of poor cultivation). The rootstocks should be planted in autumn in a fertile, well-drained, gritty/sandy loam with the crowns just below soil level. In areas with cold, wet winters with no snow cover, the crowns are best protected with a mulch of straw or similar material, or even a cloche; in soils which are not naturally free-draining it is best to construct a raised bed for them so that they dry out in summer after flowering. They appear to be better on alkaline soils and also respond to potash feeds in autumn and spring (wood ash is suitable). An open, sunny position is essential but in windy sites it may be necessary to provide support for the long inflorescences. Their size really prevents them being grown in a bulb frame, although this does supply the ideal conditions in areas with poor summers; they could be grown in this way, with the frame lights removed at flowering time and then replaced for the summer rest period; plant with the crowns just below soil level.

Eriospermum
(Liliaceae/Eriospermaceae)

Tuberous. A large genus of perhaps up to 100 species from tropical and southern Africa, barely known in cultivation. They have slender spikes of small, starry, white or yellow flowers, not unlike small scillas or ornithogalums, often with a darker stripe along the centre of each of the six segments; the seeds are hairy, hence the name; the foliage may appear with the flowers or separately, and varies from a solitary oval leaf flat on the ground to several narrow ones in a tuft. I have little experience with these; the few I have seen are from the predominantly winter rainfall region of the South West Cape and these, of course, are winter-growers needing to be kept warm and dry in summer and watered in autumn and winter; they are not frost-hardy and in cold-winter areas will need to be grown in a slightly heated glasshouse; a sandy potting soil would seem appropriate. The species from the East Cape (predominantly summer rainfall) region and those from tropical Africa should be treated as summer-growers, drying them off in a warm, dry place for the winter.

Erythronium (Liliaceae)

Bulbous. A genus of about 20 species, mostly from western North America but also a few in eastern North America and Eurasia. They are all spring-flowering, with two basal leaves and slender flower stems carrying 1-several pendent flowers with reflexed segments in white, yellow, pink, lavender and purple. These are all woodland or mountain meadow plants and need cool-growing conditions in a humus-rich but well-drained soil which does not become hot and dry; the bulbs will take drought whilst dormant in summer as long as it is not hot as well. If lifted, keep bulbs in slightly damp peat in a shady place. The high altitude species are tricky to grow and are best in cold-winter areas where they stay firmly dormant until spring. Plant bulbs in autumn in dappled shade.

Eucharis (Amaryllidaceae)

Bulbous. A genus of about 17 species from Central America south to Colombia, Peru, Bolivia and Ecuador; few have been seen in cultivation, the hybrid E. x grandiflora ('E. amazonica') (E. sanderi x E. moorei) being the most frequently encountered. They have deep green, broadly oval, basal leaves and umbels of white fragrant flowers

55 Erythronium caucasicum

which have six spreading segments with a large cup in the centre. Since these are predominantly rain forest plants they require warm growing conditions with high humidity. As with other bulbs from tropical latitudes, their flowering season is not as fixed as in the more temperate ones, so they are likely to flower at almost any time depending upon the temperature and humidity; winter flowering is possible if a temperature of at least 22–25 °C (71–77 °F) is maintained. In the cooler climates they will need glasshouse cultivation so it may be preferable to treat them as summer-growers, keeping them at about 18–20 °C (64–68 °F) and slightly drier (but never dried out completely) in winter; they require plenty of water in the growing season and overhead sprays during hot, dry weather. A rather loose open potting soil consisting of loam, peat, leafmould and sand is recommended, and some growers suggest adding old crumbly manure.

56 *Eucomis humilis*

Eucomis
(*Liliaceae/ Hyacinthaceae*)

Bulbous. About 11 species, all from southern Africa and mostly from the Eastern Cape region, Natal and Lesotho. They have rosettes of rather fleshy leaves and stout dense spikes of green, white or purple starry, flat or cup-shaped flowers, mostly in summer or early autumn; the top of the spike bears a characteristic tuft of leaf-like bracts. These are mainly summer-growers (one winter-grower, *E. regia*) so should be planted in spring after a winter dormancy. In mild-winter countries with warm summers they can be grown in partial shade beneath trees, but in cold-winter regions plant in a sunny, sheltered position, in well-drained soil but with a plentiful supply of water in summer. They are also good container plants but are very strong-rooting, so allow plenty of space and feed regularly.

Eucrosia (*Amaryllidaceae*)

Bulbous. A South American genus of about 7 species, mainly from Ecuador and Peru. They have large bulbs producing oval or elliptical leaves after the flowers. The latter are produced in umbels and are tubular or funnel-shaped with a cluster of six protruding stamens, sometimes bent downwards and out of the axis of the flower; the flower colour may be red, pink, orange or yellow, often bicoloured and partly green. Eucrosias are very tender and in all but warm temperate and subtropical areas are best treated as pot or container plants in a glasshouse or conservatory, although they can also be planted directly into a bed under glass. I have had the opportunity to try only *E. bicolor* but the other species are likely to behave in much the same way in cultivation. They would flower at almost any time of year, at the end of a warm, dry, dormant period (min. 10 °C [50 °F]) at least eight weeks long; however, it makes sense in cold-winter areas to treat them as summer-growers, drying them off in a warm place until spring, then starting them off by light watering and maintaining them in active growth through summer, in slight shade; in warm summers the containers can be placed outside. I have tried only *E. bicolor* but the other species are likely to require similar treatment. The potting soil should be well-drained, a loam-sand-peat mix probably the best.

Eurycles (*Amaryllidaceae*)

Bulbous. There are only three species of *Eurycles*, in south-east Asia and north-east Australia; they should now, for nomenclatural reasons, be called *Proiphys* and will be found under that name on page 133; however, in most books they will be found under the more familiar name.

Eustephia (*Amaryllidaceae*)

Bulbous. A small South American genus, only one species of which, *E. coccinea* from Peru, is at all well-known and even that is rather rare in cultivation. It has narrowly strap-shaped basal leaves and leafless flower stems, usually produced before the leaves appear, with umbels of up to 10 pendent tubular/funnel-shaped red flowers tipped with green, thus resembling *Phaedranassa* (see page 130). I have not had the opportunity to try this but I would suggest deep pots of an open, sandy, loam-based soil mix, kept nearly dry and warm (min. 10 °C [50 °F]) in winter, then watered in spring to encourage flowering before placing outside for the summer during the growing season.

Ferraria (*Iridaceae*)

Cormous. A genus of about 10 species from South Africa and the drier parts of south tropical Africa having flat fans of narrowly sword-shaped leaves and short-lived flowers with the three outer segments larger than the three inner, all of them with crisped edges; the colours are usually subdued, brown, dull yellow, cream or dull blue, often spotted and blotched in the central cupped area. Those I have tried are winter-growers, so should be started into growth in autumn after a long summer dormancy and watered until the foliage dies back in early summer after flowering time in late winter/spring. Most of them inhabitat the winter rainfall regions so are likely to behave in this way in cultivation, but it is possible that those from the more tropical regions might not be as fixed in their pattern of growth, in which case they might be induced into growing and flowering in summer. They appear to grow best in a sandy soil mix, planted deeply or they will not flower; they are, in fact rather shy-flowering anyway. In cold-winter areas they require frost-free growing conditions, so plant in a bed or grow in deep containers.

Fortunatia (*Liliaceae/Hyacinthaceae*)

Bulbous. This small genus from South America has been incorporated into *Camassia* although I am not convinced of the wisdom of this. There are two species in cultivation, *F. biflora* and *F. arida*, which have long, narrow, basal leaves and starry, white flowers in racemes, looking more like ornithogalums than camassias. In cultivation they behave as winter-growers, dormant in summer and flowering at any time during the autumn-winter-early spring period. I have not tried them outdoors but I would not expect success; they have been grown in a just frost-free glasshouse in long pots of a sandy soil mix, dried off in summer.

Freesia (*Iridaceae*)

Cormous. A small genus of about 11 species from southern Africa, mainly the South West Cape winter rainfall region, familiar because of the wide range of colourful, fragrant, large-flowered hybrid cultivars which are grown as cut-flowers for the winter months. They mostly have fans of erect (sometimes prostrate) narrowly sword-shaped leaves and short spikes of widely funnel-shaped flowers; the stem is bent almost horizontally just below the lowest flower. Most species are white- or yellow-flowered but they may be pink or tinged with purple or green; the hybrids are available in a huge range of colours. Freesias are naturally winter-growers, starting into growth in autumn and continuing through to late spring; however, corms can be stored dry through winter and then planted in spring for later flowering, and seeds of the hybrids can be sown at almost any time for flowering later in the same year, hence the availability of cut-flowers almost year-round. They are not frost-hardy, so in cold-winter areas they need to be cultivated in a glasshouse which is just kept above freezing; the corms are started into growth in early autumn in pots (or deep boxes or directly into a bed) of a sandy soil mix; plenty of light and air is necessary to keep them as stocky as possible

but, even so, they often require sticks for support. After flowering, when the leaves begin to die back, they can be dried off and stacked away under the bench for the summer months. In mild-winter countries they can be grown outside in a well-drained, sunny position which will dry out in summer. Corms which are offered for spring planting will behave as summer-growers only for the first season, after which they will try to revert unless they are lifted in autumn and stored warm and dry for winter.

Fritillaria (*Liliaceae*)

Bulbous. A northern hemisphere genus, very widespread in temperate Eurasia and (mainly) western North America, consisting of well over 100 species. They have leafy stems carrying one to many alternate, opposite or whorled leaves, and one to several more or less pendent, bell-shaped flowers in a wide range of colours; most are in plain, chequered or striped shades of green and purple-brown, but there are species with yellow, white, pink, red and orange flowers. They are predominantly winter-growers, producing new roots in autumn and winter, and flowering in spring to early summer before dying down for a summer dormancy. The bulbs should be planted in late summer/early autumn. Most species require sunny positions, although a few will do well in dappled shade, for instance *F. pontica*, *F. camtschatcensis*, *F. meleagris* and *F. verticillata*. They do need plenty of moisture in the growing season but with good drainage so that the soil dries out in summer, but not to the extent that it becomes dust dry or they will shrivel. *F. meleagris* and *F. pyrenaica* can do well in damp grassland, again if it dries out somewhat in summer. *F. camtschatcensis* will grow in a humus-rich soil, such as a

57 *Fritillaria pudica*

peat garden, but it is tolerant of a wide range of conditions and others find it a good plant for a sunny position on a rock garden, although this should not be too hot and dry. The smaller species like *F. conica*, *F. minima*, *F. pinardii*, *F. pudica* and *F. japonica* are best grown in a bulb frame or in pots in an unheated glasshouse where the conditions can be controlled. Also, those from habitats which dry out and become sunbaked in summer are not suitable for outdoor cultivation in countries which cannot rely on hot, dry summers; the Rhinopetalum group, *F. gibbosa*, *F. karelinei*, *F. stenanthera* and their allies fall into this category and appear to do best in a sandy/gritty potting soil. The more robust species such as *F. imperialis*, *F. persica*, *F. pyrenaica*, *F. verticillata* and *F. thunbergii* are sometimes very successful in the open garden, and the first, *F. imperialis*, has even become more or less naturalized in a few suitable places in the western USA; others find it very unsatisfactory, dwindling away after the first year following purchase. Unfortunately this is how they behave in our garden! The best results seem to be associated with deep, rich, well-drained alkaline soils which dry out in summer.

Most of the central and eastern Asiatic species start to root quite soon after their summer dormancy so should be potted or planted in early autumn, and those lucky enough to acquire the Chinese *F. davidii* should not be surprised to see it in full leaf in autumn for this seems to be its normal behaviour in cultivation. Some of the higher mountain species, not surprisingly, require cool-growing conditions; in mild-winter areas, if they grow at all, they start too early and their flowers tend to open as they push through the ground; they are much better in places where there is a fairly consistently cold, frosty winter followed by a 'proper' spring, rather than alternating warm and cold spells such as we have in southern England.

Gagea (*Liliaceae*)

Bulbous. A large genus from Eurasia, very little cultivated; many are attractive but very small. They are dwarf plants with narrow, basal, and stem leaves and small clusters of starry, yellow flowers in spring, usually striped green or brown on the exterior; *G. graeca* (*Lloydia graeca*) differs in having white flowers. They are winter-spring growers, many of them mountain plants requiring cool-growing conditions in full sun or dappled shade but some, for example, *G. reticulata*, inhabit stony areas which become hot and dry in summer; these are better with rock garden or bulb frame treatment.

Galanthus (*Amaryllidaceae*)

Bulbous. About 20 species, distributed in Europe and western Asia to the Caspian Sea. Mostly winter or spring-flowering but two, *G. reginae-olgae* and *G. peshmenii*, flower in autumn, just before leaves emerge. All species have 2–3 basal leaves and solitary white flowers with three large outer segments and three much smaller inner ones, marked with green at the apex of the inner and sometimes also at the base;

58 *Galanthus lagodechianus*

there are many cultivars, variously marked, single and double. *Galanthus* are all winter-growers, dormant in summer; they can be planted in autumn while still dormant but if dug up and moved in this state should be kept cool and preferably not over-dried. Alternatively they can be planted, or clumps dug up and split, in spring, at or just after flowering time. The site should be slightly shaded, the soil enriched with humus (leaf litter rather than peat) and well-supplied with moisture in the growing season; they are particularly good on alkaline soils. *Galanthus* require cool winters in order to thrive and may be very difficult to cultivate in areas which have very mild winters.

Galaxia (*Iridaceae*)

Cormous. A small genus of about 15 species from the South West Cape region of South Africa. They are beautiful miniature plants with relatively large but short-lived flowers. Tiny corms produce short, narrow, leaves and upright, stemless flowers which have a slender tube and six equal-spreading segments forming a flattish to cup-shaped flower; the colours are yellow, red, pink or purple, often with contrasting yellow or darker purple zones in the centre. I have tried several of these, for example *G. fugacissima*, *G. versicolor* and *G. ovata* and, if these are representative, they are very easily cultivated plants for a frost-free glasshouse or conservatory. Even in mild-winter areas they are really too small to plant outside, so pot cultivation is preferable, in a sandy soil mix. The corms should be repotted and started into growth by watering in early autumn; just frost-free conditions are all that is required, with as much light and air as possible to keep them dwarf. After flowering in winter they are kept growing until late spring, then dried off and kept warm through the summer-dormant period.

Galtonia
(*Liliaceae/ Hyacinthaceae*)

Bulbous. Four species from the eastern summer rainfall part of southern Africa. They are vigorous bulbs, each producing several long, fleshy, channelled basal leaves and a raceme of white or green pendent, funnel-shaped or bell-shaped flowers. They are summer-growers, dormant in winter, and are best grown outside in the open ground in deep soil which is moisture-retentive since they need copious amounts whilst in growth. In areas with reasonably mild winters they can be left in the ground but where the winters are likely to be severe the bulbs must be lifted and stored dry away from frost; in places where the soil warms up slowly in spring, rather than planting the bulbs out into the cold, wet ground, it is better to pot them up individually in small pots and start them into growth in the warmth of a glasshouse and then plant them out when conditions are better and the roots have begun to fill the

59 *Galtonia candicans*

pots; this gets them off to a much better start. In spite of its name, *Pseudogaltonia* is not very similar to *Galtonia*. There is only one species, *P. clavata*, from dry regions in Namibia, Angola and Botswana; it has a basal tuft of erect, grey-green leaves and a dense, almost head-like raceme of tubular white flowers in spring; in very mild climates it can be grown outside, but in areas with cool winters it needs a minimum of about 8 °C (46 °F) and is probably best planted directly into frost-free glasshouse border in a sandy soil; the bulb should be partly exposed and needs to be kept dry when dormant in mid- to late summer or early autumn and then watered sparingly to stimulate growth.

Geissorhiza (*Iridaceae*)

Cormous. A large genus of over 80 species from the South West Cape region of South Africa, very few of which are known in cultivation. They have small corms producing a few narrow leaves which often have strong ribs, sometimes hairy, sometimes coiled on the ground and flat or almost cylindrical in cross section. The few to several flowers are produced in a spike, usually flattish or saucer-shaped when fully open, with six equal segments, sometimes slightly unequal giving an irregular flower; although fairly small they have a good range of colour, often very bright, in shades of violet, red, blue or yellow, or white, and often have contrasting zones in the centre. I have tried a few of these and they seem to be fairly easy to cultivate, given that they are winter-growers and not hardy, so require frost-free glasshouse cultivation in cold areas. They should be potted in a sandy potting soil in autumn and watered through winter and spring, during which time they will flower, and then dried off for the summer months. In mild areas where there is no danger of frost they can be planted out in the open ground but, unless a dryish rest period in summer can be guaranteed, they are probably best in containers where watering can be controlled.

Gelasine (*Iridaceae*)

Bulbous. A small genus of perhaps four species from South America, now including *Sphenostigma*. It belongs to a group of related genera from the Americas with narrowly sword-shaped leaves which are pleated lengthways. The upright flowers have six spreading segments, usually with the outer three slightly larger than the inner three, but sometimes almost equal; they are blue or violet with a paler, dark-spotted centre. I have tried only *G. azurea* and this behaves as a summer-grower but is not frost-hardy so in cold-winter areas must be either lifted and stored frost-free or grown in large pots in a slightly heated glasshouse. It should be given plenty of water during the growing season and then partially dried out in winter; in mild areas it could be grown outside in a sunny, well-drained position. Other South American genera in this group of 'plicate-leaved' (=pleated-leaved) irids which appear to be best treated similarly as summer-growers include: *Calydorea* (flowers with 6 equal segments, yellow, blue or white), *Eleutherine* (probably 1 sp., *E. plicata*, with white flowers with 6 equal segments); also grouped here, but with flowers shaped more like those of tigridias or cypellas with three large outer segments and three small inner ones, are *Mastigostyla* (c. 15 spp., mostly blue- or violet-flowered), *Ennealophus* (3 spp. with white, blue or purple flowers: *E. euryandrus* is occasionally cultivated), *Cardenanthus* (c. 8 spp. from the high Andes with blue, violet or white flowers) and *Cipura* (c. 5 spp. from the warmer parts of C. and S. America and the West Indies; yellow, blue or white flowers with the three larger outer segments curving upwards and inwards).

Gemmaria (*Amaryllidaceae*)

Bulbous. A small genus from South Africa, similar to, and requiring much the same cultivation as *Hessea* (see page 103).

Geranium (*Geraniaceae*)

Tuberous. There are a few tuberous-rooted geranium species which are grown by bulb enthusiasts and offered by the bulb nurserymen. *G. tuberosum* is the commonly cultivated one, but there are several other similar species from the Mediterranean region and western Asia. These have nicely dissected foliage and mostly blue to lilac-blue flowers in loose heads. These behave like winter-growing bulbs so should be planted in autumn in a warm, sunny spot in well-drained soil which will partially dry out in mid- to late summer after they have flowered. In some areas with cold, wet winters they do not thrive and are better when planted in a raised bed or even a bulb frame with some overhead protection.

Gethyllis (*Amaryllidaceae*)

Bulbous. A genus of over 30 species from the south-west part of southern Africa, very few of which are in cultivation. They have near stemless, funnel-shaped or flattish white or pink-flushed erect flowers in summer, produced before the leaves appear in autumn; these are in a basal tuft, usually very narrow and spiralled, and have an attractively spotted sheath; the fruits stick up out of the ground like yellow clubs, fleshy and fragrant, but sadly these are seldom produced in cultivation – with me, at least. *Gethyllis* are winter-growers, although their flowers appear in summer out of the bare earth. I grow mine in pots in sandy soil in a frost-free glasshouse, dry until September, then watered through autumn, winter and spring until they die down. Most of my South West Cape bulbs are stacked away under the bench whilst dry in summer but *Gethyllis* should be kept out since it will suddenly produce its crocus-like flowers at the height of summer, without any apparent stimulus; since they only last a day or so one needs to be vigilant or there is no point in growing the plant! I have seen mine in flower only once in about five years. In mild-winter areas *Gethyllis* could be grown outside but it would not really be worthwhile since they are not impressive plants, just fascinating.

Gladiolus (*Iridaceae*)

Cormous. A very large genus, perhaps as many as 150 species, and now including the species which were formerly in *Acidanthera*, *Anomalesia*, *Homoglossum* and *Oenostachys*; in cultivation and in catalogues these genera are still referred to, so are cross-referenced here. This is a very widespread genus, mainly African (tropical and southern Africa) but also with several species in the Mediterranean region eastwards to the Middle East, and there are a few in Madagascar and the Mascarene Islands. Gladiolus have erect, often rather tough and strongly ribbed, sword-shaped leaves and spikes (rarely branched) of irregularly shaped flowers, characteristically with a hooded upper segment, a curved tube and often with contrasting marking on the lower three segments. Those species which were in *Acidanthera* tend to have very long-tubed regular flowers with almost equal segments; those which were in the other genera mentioned above have rather bizarre flower shapes with one large very conspicuous upper segment and three tiny insignificant ones underneath; in some species the two lateral segments stand up like wings above the upper segment. *Gladiolus* species fall into three groups:

a) The Mediterranean, North African and Asiatic ones are winter-growers and are frost-hardy to varying degrees; these can be cultivated in the open ground in a well-drained, sunny position where the soil will at least partially dry out after their early summer-flowering period. In areas where the summers are cool and wet they may require a raised bed or even some protection to prevent the corms from rotting whilst dormant; the shorter species such as *G. triphyllus* are suitable for a bulb frame or unheated glasshouse, while the more vigorous species like *G. italicus* and *G. communis* subsp. *byzantinus* are easy garden plants requiring only a reasonably well-drained soil in full sun.

60 *Gladiolus communis* subsp. *byzantinus*

b) The second group, those from the South West Cape region, are also winter-growers but these are not frost-hardy and, in cold-winter areas, require a slightly heated glasshouse; they are started into growth by watering in early autumn, kept in growth with as much light and air as possible through winter, then dried off in summer; they mostly flower during winter or early spring but a few flower soon after watering in autumn and before the leaves emerge, for example *G. carmineus*. A sandy potting soil suits these very well, although I have grown some of them quite well in a loamless peat-based compost. Together with these, we can place the so-called 'Nanus' gladioli, *G. × colvillei*, a race of fairly small hybrids with far fewer flowers on the spike than the tall summer-flowering hybrids (see below), but attractively coloured with large contrasting splashes on the lower segments; these are winter-growers, flowering in late spring or early summer after growing through the winter/spring, but they are hardier than most of the South West Cape

species and will perform quite well if planted in sheltered, sunny positions in autumn, perhaps with a little protection from straw or bracken during very frosty weather; some nurseries keep the corms dry over winter, offering them for sale for a spring planting, and this also works reasonably well. In cold areas where the ground freezes deeply these Nanus cultivars require glasshouse protection but they can make attractive container plants for the conservatory; conversely, in mild areas they can be planted out permanently; we have some plantings here in Surrey about five years old, whereas the large-flowered hybrids seldom survive the winter.

c) The third group comprises those from the Eastern Cape summer rainfall area; with these we can include the species from tropical Africa (including those formerly in *Acidanthera*), and most of the hundreds of hybrid cultivars; all of these can be treated as summer-growers. In the case of the vigorous species such as *G. dalenii*, *G. saundersii* and *G. papilio* the corms can be planted out into the open ground in spring as soon as the soil has begun to warm up; in cold areas it may be preferable to start them off in pots under glass and then plant them out, thus giving them a better start; the corms are then lifted in autumn for dry storage in a frost-free place for the winter; *G. papilio* is, in fact, very hardy and the corms will stand up to being frozen in the soil. In some areas where the frosts are superficial and do not freeze the ground deeply, the large-flowered cultivars can also be left in for the winter.

It should be mentioned that the winter-growers have been crossed with the summer-growers; the resulting hybrids are said to be less fixed in their behaviour and can be dried off or started into growth at almost any time of year, thus being very useful for the cut flower trade; there is also the possibility that more than one crop of flowers per year could be produced.

Gloriosa (*Liliaceae/Colchicaceae*)

Cormous. A tropical or subtropical genus from Africa and India, possibly consisting of only one very variable species, *G. superba*. It has curious, elongated corms which divide into finger-like branches; these produce slender erect stems which, in the shorter form are self-supporting but in the taller ones, up to 2 m (7 ft) or more, cling on to neighbouring plants by means of leaf-tip tendrils; the leaves are normally oval or lance-shaped and the upper ones bear in their axils large, pendent red, orange, yellow or bicoloured flowers with six reflexed, wavy-margined segments, the wavy margins of the red forms often coloured yellow. Some plants, such as the tiny narrow-leaved *G. minor* from northern Kenya must surely represent separate species!

61 *Gloriosa superba*

Gloriosas are summer-growers, suitable for planting permanently outside only in warm temperate to subtropical areas; in cooler countries they must be treated as glasshouse or conservatory subjects where the dormant corms can be dried off and kept warm for the winter; alternatively they can be container-grown and placed outside for the warmer summer months, but even then are only successful in regions with reliably warm summers. When culti-vated under glass, some form of support must be given; the potting soil needs to be a well-drained, sandy mix in deep pots, with liquid feeds (tomato fertilizer) given at approximately fortnightly intervals during the growing/flowering period. In the case of the tall vigorous gloriosas I have found that proprietary loamless potting mixes work quite well, with a good rate of increase of corms in one season.

Gymnospermium (*Berberidaceae*)

Tuberous. A few species from central Asia with ornamental, dissected grey leaves and dense heads of Berberis-like yellow flowers, often bronze-tinted on the exterior. Plant in autumn, dry off in summer when dormant. Well-drained soil in full sun. In damp-summer areas grow in raised beds, bulb frames or alpine house.

62 *Gymnospermium altaicum*

Gynandriris (*Iridaceae*)

Cormous. A small genus of 2 or 3 species in the Mediterranean region and western to central Asia and 7 more in South Africa. They have small, Iris-like blue, violet or white flowers, each one open for only a few hours. The northern hemisphere species, *G. sisyrinchium* (*Iris sisyrinchium*) and its relatives, are from winter rainfall regions, rooting and growing through autumn and winter, then flowering in spring, as are six of the South African species; the other one, *G. simulans*, is from a summer rainfall area and, although I have not tried to cultivate this, it should be a summer-grower, dormant in winter. In my experience the winter-growers require a warm, dry, dormant period in summer and are therefore not suitable for outdoor cultivation in countries which cannot guarantee this; the northern species can be grown in a bulb frame or in pots in an unheated glasshouse; the southern species are less hardy and require a just frost-free house. A very sandy soil mix suits them best.

Habranthus (*Amaryllidaceae*)

Bulbous. A sizeable genus of perhaps 20–30 species from Central and South America, just extending into southern North America. They have narrow, linear or strap-shaped leaves and solitary, funnel-shaped flowers, mostly pink or yellow, which are inclined upwards at an angle and have unequal stamens, unlike the very similar *Zephyranthes* in which the flowers are usually erect with equal stamens. Flowering is stimulated by rain after a period of warm dormancy; most of those in cultivation flower in mid- to late summer and are capable of sending up several flowers intermittently over a period of time after each watering; the leaves appear soon after the flowers and some species are almost evergreen. The commonest species in cultivation, *H. tubispathus* (*H. andersonii*, *Zephyranthes andersonii*) can become quite weedy in mild-winter areas, and in bulb frames, since it seeds very freely, and the young bulbs rapidly reach flowering size in about 2 years. *H. martinezii* (and several other species from Argentina/Uruguay) is most definitely a winter-grower and will flower well in autumn only after a

63 *Habranthus martinezii*

good baking in summer; the leaves are then produced and stay green until the following late spring.

Haemanthus (*Amaryllidaceae*)

Bulbous. This striking South African genus has over twenty species but unfortunately only a few are in general cultivation. Some species (for example *H. multiflorus* and *H. puniceus*) have been moved to the genus *Scadoxus* and will be found on page 138. *Haemanthus* mostly have just two leaves which are often broad and almost prostrate on the ground, sometimes hairy, especially on the margins, sometimes wavy-margined and occasionally dark-blotched. The small white or pink flowers are produced in a shaving-brush shaped umbel which is surrounded by broad bracts which may be white, pink or bright red, and it is these which give the whole flower head its striking appearance, contrasting with the very prominent yellow stamens. *Haemanthus* species occur in both the winter rainfall (south-western) and the summer rainfall (eastern) parts of southern Africa. Cultivation methods depend upon where the species originates from.

The winter rainfall species (such as *H. coccineus*, *H. pubescens* and *H. sanguineus*) flower in summer or autumn before the leaves appear, are in leaf through autumn, winter and spring then die down for a warm, dry summer rest.

The summer rainfall species vary in their behaviour depending upon whether they are coastal species (e.g. the most commonly cultivated species, *H. albiflos*, and *H. deformis*) or inland, higher altitude ones (rarely cultivated species such as *H. humilis*). Coastal species are more or less evergreen, flowering in autumn and winter and producing a new pair of leaves with or soon after the flowers; these should never be dried out completely but possibly benefit from a slightly drier rest period in late

summer. Inland group species produce their flowers with or before the leaves in late spring to mid-summer after a winter dormancy, the leaves then last until autumn or early winter. All of the species are frost-tender so, in all but mild-winter areas, they need to be grown in containers in a frost-free glasshouse; they make excellent conservatory plants. The species I have tried appear to grow well in a sandy, loam-based potting soil with a minimum temperature of about 5 °C (41 °F) in winter.

Haylockia (*Amaryllidaceae*)

Bulbous. A small genus from South America with about six species in Bolivia, Argentina and Uruguay. They are charming plants, with white, yellow, orange, lilac or red stemless flowers which look like crocuses, although it would be more accurate to think of them as stemless *Zephyranthes*; the narrowly strap-shaped leaves appear with or after the flowers. Few of these fascinating plants are in cultivation, and I have grown only *H. andina* and *H. pusilla*. The former starts to grow in spring and flowers just before the leaves are produced, whereas the latter makes its leaf growth in winter, dying down in late spring and flowering without leaves in summer. Although they should be fairly frost-hardy (as far as I know they are untested outside), they are really best suited to pot cultivation in an unheated glasshouse or frame where their small flowers can be appreciated. A sandy/gritty, loam-based soil seems to suit them, given plenty of water in the growing season, reducing this during dormancy.

Hedychium (*Zingiberaceae*)

Rhizomatous. A large, mainly tropical genus of about 50 species from south-east Asia, southern China, the Himalaya, India and Madagascar. These are large, striking plants with tall, leafy stems and dense,

64 *Hedychium gardnerianum*

more tropical species such as the lovely *H. coronarium* need heated glasshouse conditions with a minimum winter temperature of about 18–20 °C (64–68 °F). Plant with the upper side of the rhizomes at soil level.

Herbertia (*Iridaceae*)

Bulbous. A small genus of South American irids with short-lived, iris-shaped flowers, related to *Tigridia, Cypella, Alophia*, etc. A few species are cultivated, notably *H. lahue* (*Alophia lahue*). They have erect, narrowly sword-shaped leaves, pleated lengthways, and wiry stems carrying one upright flower, or several in succession, lasting only a day or a few hours, usually in shades of violet or blue with a paler or white centre, marked with dark blotches; the three outer segments are large and horizontal, the inner three much smaller and obliquely erect. These are winter-growers, flowering in late winter or spring and dormant in summer; they could be grown outside in a sunny, well-drained position in frost-free areas; they are not hardy here in Surrey and need to be pot-grown in a frost-free glasshouse, along with bulbs from the South West Cape. *Kelisa* (1 sp. from Brazil, *K. brasiliensis*, with very conspicuously blue-blotched flowers) can be treated in much the same way in cultivation. Probably the rather similar *Onira* (1 species from

terminal spikes of orchid-like flowers, mostly white or in shades of yellow, orange and red and often fragrant; each has a long tube, a large, 2-lobed lip and a long-protruding stamen. These are strong-growing, tall plants mostly needing warm growing conditions and so are often cultivated for display in tropical and subtropical countries world-wide; in temperate regions they are suitable for planting directly into a bed in a heated glasshouse, or for growing in large containers. The hardier Himalayan ones (such as *H. gardnerianum, H. densiflorum, H. coccineum, H. spicatum*) are good container plants, treated as summer-growers, keeping them nearly dry and frost-free in winter and then standing them outside as soon as the weather has warmed up; use an open, humus-rich potting soil (loamless proprietary mixes are suitable), with regular liquid feeds since these are robust plants; after they have flowered, in the autumn the old flowering shoots can be pruned down to ground level since they will not flower again, new shoots being produced for that purpose during the next growing season. These Himalayan species and their cultivars can be grown outside in mild areas and in sheltered positions where the ground does not freeze. The

65 *Herbertia lahue* subsp. *amoena*

Brasil and Uruguay) and *Catila* (1 species from S. Brasil, Uruguay and Argentina) also need much the same treatment.

Hermodactylus (*Iridaceae*)

Tuberous? Only one species, *H. tuberosus* (*Iris tuberosa*) from the Mediterranean region. It has misshapen 'tubers' giving rise to long, grey leaves, square in cross-section, and solitary, fragrant, *Iris*-shaped flowers in shades of yellowish green with a dark velvety brown to black blotch at the tips of the outer segments. It is a winter-grower, flowering in spring. The tubers should be planted in autumn in a warm, sunny situation which is well-supplied with moisture through winter and spring but dries out and gets hot in summer, otherwise it will not flower well; a site against a sunny wall is best in areas with cold winters and poor summers; otherwise plant in a bulb frame where the tubers can be covered in summer when dormant; it is not suitable for pot cultivation or areas where there is little room to spare since it increases vegetatively quite rapidly and soon uses up its space. The soil should be well-drained, preferably alkaline.

Hesperantha (*Iridaceae*)

Cormous. An entirely African genus of over 50 species, mainly from South Africa, where they grow in both summer and winter rainfall regions, but also on the mountains of tropical Africa.

They mostly have narrow, erect, flat to cylindrical basal leaves and a spike of flowers (sometimes only one flower) which are saucer-shaped to flattish when fully open, some of them only in the evenings, hence the name. The colours range from white to yellow, pink and purple; some of them are very striking, such as *H. vaginata* which has yellow flowers with black centres and tips to the segments, while others are small-flowered and scarcely worth cultivating.

Cultivation differs according to the origin of the species; the tropical and summer rainfall species (I have tried only *H. petitiana* from the tropical African mountains and *H. baurii* from the Drakensberg) need to be treated as summer-growers, the corms kept dry and frost-free for winter then started into growth in spring to grow and flower in the summer; these can be planted outside as soon as the soil has warmed up and then lifted again in autumn. Mrs McConnel used to grow *H. baurii* in the same way as her *Rhodohypoxis*; it is hardy as long as the frosts do not penetrate deeply for long periods. I suspect that several of these summer-growers from the mountains of Natal and Lesotho would be hardy enough to be grown outside in mild areas.

The winter rainfall hesperanthas can be treated in the same way as other South West Cape bulbs, planted in autumn, outside in the open garden in a sunny, well-drained position in mild-winter areas but under frost-free glasshouse conditions in colder regions; I grow them in pots of a sandy soil mix but they could be planted directly into a glasshouse border. In summer the corms are dried out.

Hesperocallis (*Liliaceae/?Hyacinthaceae*)

Bulbous. A genus of one beautiful species from California and western Arizona. It has a rosette of blue-green, wavy-edged leaves and a raceme of white, funnel-shaped flowers. I have not succeeded with this plant beyond the young seedling stage so cannot really recommend what to try! It is a winter-grower from sandy areas; my very limited success was achieved by sowing the seeds directly into large pots of a very sandy/gritty soil mix in autumn, keeping them in growth through winter and spring in a frost-free glasshouse and then drying the small bulbs off for the summer, still in their pots; they reappeared in autumn but rotted off during their second winter.

Hessea (*Amaryllidaceae*)

Bulbous. A small genus of dwarf amaryllids from South Africa with very narrow, sometimes thread-like, and occasionally hairy, basal leaves and slender, bare flower stems carrying loose umbels of small, starry, white to pinkish flowers which often have wavy-margined segments. They are not showy plants so, even in countries where they are hardy, are really best in pots where their delicate charm can be better appreciated. Those I have tried are winter-growers, flowering in autumn or winter after a dry summer dormancy. They grow well in a sandy soil mix in a just frost-free glasshouse with as much light and ventilation as possible. Other related genera from southern Africa which can be treated in much the same way include *Carpolyza*, *Strumaria* and *Gemmaria*, and probably *Bokkeveldia*, *Namaquanula* and *Teddingea* but I have not yet tried these.

Hexaglottis (*Iridaceae*)

Cormous. A small genus of about five species from the winter rainfall region of southern Africa with a few (sometimes one) long, narrow, basal leaves and a branched flower stem carrying yellow, short-lived, flattish flowers facing upwards. They are little-cultivated, mainly by Iridaceae enthusiasts. The corms should be planted in autumn and grown through winter and spring, when the plants flower, and then dried off for the summer. They would probably be hardy enough to be grown outdoors in areas with mild winters, but in southern England I grow them in pots along with other South West Cape 'bulbs'

in a just frost-free glasshouse in a sandy soil mix.

Hippeastrum (*Amaryllidaceae*)

Bulbous. A South American, mainly tropical genus of between 40 and 60 species; a sizeable number of species have been removed to other genera, notably some of the smaller-flowered ones occurring in more temperate regions, especially Chile, which form the genus *Rhodophiala*; the blue-flowered Brasilian *H. procerum* is now treated as a monotypic genus, *Worsleya*. Hippeastrums have large bulbs producing several basal, usually strap-shaped leaves, either present at flowering time or produced after the flowers; the stout, leafless stems bear umbels of 2–8 large white, pink or red (sometimes conspicuously striped) flowers, these normally short-tubed and widely funnel-shaped with the tips of the six segments tending to reflex; a few species have long-tubed flowers; the stamens are bunched together and are curved down to the lower side of the flower. There are many large-flowered hybrid cultivars, often marketed as 'Amaryllis', although not to be confused with the true *Amaryllis*, *A. belladonna*, from South Africa.

Hippeastrums appear mainly to behave as summer-growers; some flower in late winter or early spring, almost before leaf growth commences (some flower with their leaves), the leaves then lasting through much of the summer before dying away; others flower with the leaves in summer. Since they occur mostly in tropical latitudes it is probable that their dormant/growth periods are related mainly to dry/wet seasons rather than a combination of temperature and moisture availability, this accounting for the fact that they can be flowered at almost any time of the year; the colourful hybrids which are sold in pre-pack boxes will flower in response to watering, whenever it happens

66 *Hippeastrum machupichense*

to be. This is in marked contrast to most 'temperate bulbs' which are much more fixed in their ways and tend to fall into winter- or summer-growing categories. Hippeastrums are much more tender than their temperate cousins such as *Rhodophiala*; in warm, subtropical or tropical countries they can be grown outside in the garden but elsewhere they require glasshouse cultivation, or a windowsill indoors if it is not too hot and dry; after flowering and when the weather has warmed up in late spring or early summer they can be placed outside for the summer, giving them liquid feeds of a tomato fertilizer (i.e., potash-rich). When the leaves show signs of yellowing – or if not, in late summer anyway – they should be encouraged to die down by witholding water and drying them off for the rest of summer and autumn in warm, dry conditions (min. 15 °C [59 °F]); they can then be started off again by giving water and light as required during late winter or early spring. Although they could be planted out into a bed in a glasshouse, they are mostly grown in large pots, using a well-drained potting soil; the various loamless mixes on the market seem to work quite well for these strong-growing bulbs. Repotting takes place in winter just before starting them into growth again. *Griffinia*, a small genus from Brazil, requires similar treatment.

Homeria (*Iridaceae*)

Cormous. South African plants, occurring wild in southern Africa, mainly in the winter rainfall South West Cape region but a few, notably *H. collina*, can be rather weedy and are naturalized elsewhere; since it is poisonous it is not welcome. They have long, narrow, basal leaves, often only one per corm, and simple to branched stems bearing fairly large, yellow, pink or orange flowers; these have six more or less equal segments forming a bowl-shaped to flattish flower. Homerias are winter-growers. The corms should be planted in autumn in a sunny, well-drained situation and will stay in growth through to the following late spring/early summer after they have flowered. In mild-winter areas they are hardy (it is these areas where they should be treated with caution since they may increase too rapidly: take advice from the local appropriate government body) but in regions with cold, frosty winters they do not thrive and may even need to be grown under glass with frost protection. In southern England I find that they do survive some winters if planted outdoors but do not make an attractive sight, so it is not worthwhile; a just frost-free glasshouse is suitable, grown in pots of a sandy soil mix, where they flower in early spring; in summer the corms are dried off. I have not tried the related South African *Roggeveldia* (1sp., *R. fistulosa*) and *Barnardiella* (1 sp., *B. spiralis*), both of which have short-lived, violet-blue flowers, but if given the chance would try treating them in a similar way, as winter-growers in a frost-free glasshouse in a sandy soil mix.

Homoglossum [syn. Petamenes] (*Iridaceae*)

Cormous. This African genus has now been merged with *Gladiolus* by Drs. Peter Goldblatt and Miriam de Vos. For those who receive plants under the name

Homoglossum, cultivation is as for *Anomalesia* (see page 63) which is also now included within *Gladiolus*.

Hyacinthella
(Liliaceae/ Hyacinthaceae)

Bulbous. About 16 species, from south-eastern Europe and western Asia, spring-flowering, with 2 or 3 short, basal leaves and compact racemes of small, bell-shaped purple or blue flowers. These are winter-growers, so plant in autumn and dry off in summer when dormant. They need well-drained soil in full sun. In damp-summer areas, grow in a sandy or gritty soil mix in a bulb frame or in pots in an unheated glasshouse.

Hyacinthoides
(Liliaceae/ Hyacinthaceae)

Bulbous. This is a small genus containing about 5 species which have been included in *Scilla* and have also been called *Endymion*. The most well-known species are *H. non-scripta* and *H. hispanica*, the English and Spanish bluebells. Cultivation is as for *Scilla* species.

Hyacinthus
(Liliaceae/ Hyacinthaceae)

Bulbous. About 3 species from Turkey to central Asia, well-known because of one species, *H. orientalis*, which has given rise by selection to the familiar large-flowered cultivars, far exceeding the wild species in size and range of colours. All the species have a cluster of strap-like or narrowly lance-shaped basal leaves and rather tubular flowers with reflexed tips to the six segments. They are all winter-growers so should be planted in autumn and dried off in summer when the leaves have died away. They are suitable for sunny situations in well-drained soil where the resting bulbs will become reasonably dry and warm in summer, otherwise they may not flower. The wild species are suitable for bulb frame cultivation in areas with unreliably dry summers. The very fragrant large-flow-ered cultivars are excellent pot plants for growing indoors for an early display, and 'prepared' bulbs will flower even earlier, in mid-winter (see page 37).

Hymenocallis (Amaryllidaceae)

Bulbous. Some authorities include *Ismene* and *Elisena*, others separate them. However, as this is primarily a cultivation book I will not delve further into this but place them all here, since their cultural requirements are similar. In this wide sense, *Hymenocallis* comprises about 60–65 species, all from the Americas, from south-eastern USA and the West Indies, south through Central America to the Andes and tropical South America. They have a cluster of basal leaves which range from strap-like to oval or elliptic, sometimes sheathed together at the base to form a false stem; many species are deciduous but some are evergreen. The flowers are carried in an umbel and have six spreading to reflexed

67 *Hymenocallis longipetala* (also called *Ismene longipetala*, *Elisena longipetala*)

segments, often very narrow and ribbon-like, surrounding a central cup which varies from a shallow disk to a rather deeper funnel shape; the species which was in the genus *Elisena*, *H. longipetala*, has rather irregular-shaped flowers with a narrowly tubular cup. Many species have white flowers but some are creamy, yellow or greenish, and many are fragrant.

The more tropical, evergreen species such as *H. speciosa* appear to require much the same treatment as *Eucharis* (see page 89) but I have no personal experience. Those which die down for a dormant period, such as *H. narcissiflora*, *H. harrisiana*, *H. amancaes* and *H. ×festalis* are hardier and are best treated as summer-growers, keeping them dry and warm (min. about 15 °C [60 °F]) in winter and then bringing them into growth by watering, with increasing warmth, in spring. The potting medium needs to be open and well-drained; a sandy/gritty loam-based mix with granular peat or old leafmould seems to suit the few species which I grow. In summer the pots can be stood outdoors; some growers recommend planting the bulbs out in the open ground, as soon as the soil has warmed up, in a sheltered position where they will receive partial sun and plenty of moisture, then lifting and drying them off for winter storage in a warm place (12–15 °C [55–60 °F]). In areas with mild winters these deciduous species can be grown permanently outside. *Paramongaia*, a genus of one species from Peru, *P. weberbaueri*, needs similar treatment to the deciduous species of *Hymenocallis*, with a warm, dry, dormant period in winter (although it will grow and flower at any time, depending upon the watering/drying regime adopted); it has large yellow flowers.

Hypoxis (*Hypoxidaceae*)

Cormous. A large genus of perhaps as many as 150 species, many in tropical and

68 *Hypoxis parvula*

southern Africa but with representatives in the Americas, south-east Asia and Australia. They are mostly rather small plants with rosettes or tufts of very narrowly linear to lanceolate, often hairy leaves and flat, starry, yellow (more rarely white) flowers, usually green on the outside and solitary or with a few on branched stems. The majority of species are from tropical Africa and in cultivation need to be treated as summer-growers, drying them off in winter whilst dormant. One of the most attractive species is the white- or yellow-flowered *H. parvula* from southern Africa, a native of the eastern, summer-rainfall regions, so this is naturally a summer-grower and is also frost-hardy; it hybridizes with *Rhodohypoxis baurii* to give a range of attractive intermediates, in white and pink. The North American *H. hirsuta* can be cultivated outdoors on a sunny part of a peat garden; *H. hygrometrica* from eastern Australia and Tasmania grows well in pots in an unheated glasshouse.

Ipheion (*Liliaceae/Alliaceae*)

Bulbous. A small genus, mainly from Argentina and Uruguay, perhaps also Chile, known mainly for the excellent *I. uniflorum*; they have narrow leaves smelling of onions when crushed and, in spring, one or rarely two large, flat, starry flowers per stem, pale to deep blue or white, mostly with a darker central stripe on each segment. The yellow-flowered species, *I. sellowianum*, *I. hirtellum* and *I. dialystemon*, which are very similar in outward appearance except for the colour, are now considered to belong to the genus *Nothoscordum*. Ipheions are winter-growers so should be planted in autumn; they require only an open site in well-drained soil which becomes drier (though not dust-dry) and warm in summer when the bulbs are dormant; if the summer is cold and damp the bulbs sometimes stay dormant for more than one year. They also make good plants for an unheated glasshouse and can be grown in large pans for a mass effect in spring.

69 *Ipheion uniflorum* 'Alberto Castillo'

Iris (*Iridaceae*)

Bulbous/rhizomatous. A large, well-known genus consisting of about 250 species, widespread in the temperate northern hemisphere and varying from the dwarf, early spring bulbous 'reticulata' irises to the tall, summer-flowering rhizomatous types. Obviously they differ widely in their cultural requirements, so I have divided them very roughly into 9 groups:

a) Juno (subgenus Scorpiris). The 40-plus species of Juno iris are autumn/winter/spring-growers, mostly from the dry-summer regions of western and central Asia, so the bulbs should be started into growth in autumn. Much has been said about avoiding damage to the thick, fleshy roots which are attached to the basal plate of the bulb and it is true that it is better to keep them intact but, if the roots do become detached it will not normally kill the bulb, perhaps just weaken it a little; the detached roots are useless for propagation purposes in my experience, unless they have a piece of basal plate and a bud attached, and normally when a root breaks off it has neither of these. However, using a scalpel, it is possible to detach roots with these attached and this can be used as a method of vegetative propagation, albeit rather slow and nerve-racking if it is a solitary rare bulb! The junos are on the whole very hardy plants and in cultivation can be grown without artificial heat. However, they do need protection from excess wet in winter, and also in summer whilst they are dormant, otherwise they may well rot off. They are really best in climates with cold, dry winters and warm, dry summers. In areas such as Britain, with relatively mild winters, these, and many other bulbs, come into growth very much earlier than they would in nature and are subjected to very moist air; condensation collects on the leaves and is funnelled down by the channelled leaves into the neck of the bulb, causing it to rot. In such areas the majority of these lovely irises are best grown in a well-aired (with electric fans is ideal) unheated glasshouse or bulb frame in a sharply-drained soil mix; if in pots, the deepest ones possible should be used since they have very long roots; some growers even use clay chimney pots. However, some of the junos are excellent and easy garden plants, notably *I. magnifica* and *I. bucharica*. The Mediterranean *I. planifolia* and *I. palaestina* are rather more tender than most and need protection from severe frosts.

70 *Iris narbutii* (a Juno Iris)

b) The Reticulata (Hermodactyloides) group of about nine species are also autumn/winter/spring growers from a similar area to the junos and are equally hardy, except perhaps for the most southerly-occurring *I. vartanii* and *I. histrio*; in areas with bad winters and damp summers these need bulb frame or unheated glasshouse cultivation for protection, both from frost and damage from inclement weather in winter, and from rain in summer when the bulbs should be warm and dry; in Mediterranean-type climates they could be cultivated outdoors. The rest of the species are hardy and can be grown outside in a sunny situation in a sharply drained soil which dries out in summer. *I. danfordiae* is notorious for splitting up after flowering into many small 'rice grain' bulblets; this can be discouraged to some extent by planting the bulbs at least 10 cm (4 in) deep and feeding with a potash-rich fertilizer, or sulphate of potash, two or three times during the growing season. *I. kolpakowskiana* is not very persistent with me, outside, in pots or in a bulb frame, so I am not in a position to make recommendations! It grows wild in heavy soil which is buried in snow in winter, soggy in spring and dry in summer, much the same as several of the others which do thrive in the garden. Most of the reticulatas also make excellent plants for the bulb frame or in pots in an unheated glasshouse but, in the latter case, should be given deep pots and repotted each autumn; a sandy/gritty soil mix is suitable, neutral to slightly alkaline, with liquid feeds of a potash-rich (tomato-type) fertilizer during the growing season.

c) The bulbous Xiphium group – the Spanish, English and Dutch irises from south western Europe and North Africa – are also autumn/winter/spring-growers, although they do not reach their maximum growth and flowering period until the following late spring or early summer; the odd *I. serotina* does not flower until mid- to late summer when the leaves are nearly dead. However, their roots begin to grow soon after planting in autumn and will continue to do so until the following spring. These are relatively easy bulbs, suitable for an open, sunny position in reasonably well-drained soil which dries out, at least partially, in summer, although *I. latifolia* (*I. xiphioides*) prefers a rather more moist, but not stagnant, situation.

d) Nepalensis group: these species – *I. decora* is the most likely one to be encountered – are from the monsoon summer rainfall regions of eastern Asia with cool, dry winters; they have thick, fleshy roots from a compact rhizome. Cultivation is relatively simple in deep pots of gritty, well-drained potting soil in an unheated glasshouse; the plants are kept cool and dry through winter whilst dormant and then repotted and watered in spring. In summer they need plenty of moiture with occasional overhead spraying to keep the atmosphere cool and humid; if too hot and dry they will go prematurely dormant. Outdoor cultivation is not successful in Britain since the winters are too wet for the resting rootstocks but these irises would be worth trying in areas with colder, drier winters, preferably with snow cover.

e) Bearded, rhizomatous irises (Pogon irises, Oncocyclus, Regelia, etc.): these are primarily winter-spring-growing irises, making their active root growth through this period and flowering at the end of the season before the dry heat of summer. They need open, sunny conditions with deep, fairly rich, preferably alkaline soil which dries out to some extent in summer, although they should never be dried out completely, especially when in pots. The Pogon irises are fairly tolerant of some summer rain, so are relatively easy plants to grow in most temperate climates; the Regelias are rather less tolerant and the Oncocyclus barely at all, so it follows that in areas with reasonably dry summers it is possible to grow the Regelias outside, though Oncocyclus irises are likley to need at least some glass protection during wet periods.

f) Lophiris (Evansia) irises: The North American species *I. cristata* and *I. lacustris* are tough little plants needing cool-growing conditions in a gritty/leafy soil mix in dappled shade; they are more likely to succumb to winter wet in the milder areas than to frost. *I. tenuis* from Oregon prefers a protected position in dappled shade in a loose leafy soil. The Chinese *I. japonica*, *I confusa* and *I. wattii* are fairly tender and are best in a frost-free glasshouse; although the first is fairly hardy, even in southern England, it tends to look so battered by the end of the winter that it is unattractive; they need a light, open, humus-rich soil mix. The Himalayan/Chinese *I. milesii* and *I. tectorum* are hardier and relatively easy to cultivate in an open, sunny situation in well-drained soil.

g) Beardless irises of the following groups: Chinenses, Tenuifoliae, Ensatae, Syriacae, Longipetalae, Unguiculares, taller species of Spuriae: an open, sunny, well-drained position which dries out a little in summer but does not become dusty-dry.

h) Beardless irises of the following groups: smaller species of Spuriae, Foetidissimae, Vernae, Californicae, Ruthenicae, Tripetalae: well-drained gritty/peaty or gritty/leafy soil mix in semi-shade to full sun if not too dry.

i) Beardless irises of the following groups: Sibiricae, Hexagonae, Laevigatae, Prismaticae: deep, rich soil in full sun or partial shade, moist all summer during growth period; Hexagonae and Laevigatae do well in shallow water.

Ismene (*Amaryllidaceae*)

Bulbous. This South American genus of
10–15 species is treated as distinct by some
authors and as a synonym of *Hymenocallis*
by others. The latter course has been followed here and notes on cultivation will be
found on page 105.

Ixia (*Iridaceae*)

Cormous. A large South African genus of
nearly 50 species, nearly all confined to the
south western winter rainfall region. They
mostly have long, narrow, erect, rather
tough leaves and wiry stems bearing simple
or branched spikes (occasionally single-
flowered) of flat, starry or sometimes
cupped flowers in almost any colour, blue,
green, red, pink, purple, yellow, orange or
white, often with a contrasting eye in the
centre. They are all winter-growers so the
corms should be planted in early autumn
and watered to start them into growth. In
mild areas they may be grown outside in
well-drained, sunny positions but in cold-
winter areas they need frost protection;
they are suitable for planting directly into a
bed in a cool glasshouse or conservatory
which is kept just-frost-free, or for growing
in pots, although many of them are a little
tall for this purpose; a sandy soil mix suits
them very well. Under glass they need
plenty of light if they are to grow well and
open their flowers properly. After flowering in winter/spring and reaching the end
of their growing season in late spring they
can be dried off for the summer months. As
with *Babiana* and *Sparaxis*, bulb nurserymen sometimes offer corms of mixed
hybrid ixias for spring planting to flower in
summer; these are corms which have been
stored through winter to prevent them
growing. For the first flowering season
after planting they will grow in summer,
but after that they will try to revert to their
normal autumn/winter growing habit

71 *Ixia viridiflora*

unless they are dug up at the end of that first
season and dried off again for the winter.
On the whole this is not very satisfactory
and, as they are fairly cheap, it is probably
best to regard them as summer bedding for
one season only, then discard them.

Ixiolirion (*Liliaceae/ Amaryllidaceae/Ixioliriaceae*)

Bulbous/cormous? A genus of 2 or 3 species
from western to Central Asia having long,
narrow leaves and branching stems bearing
funnel-shaped blue flowers. They are
winter-growers so should be planted in
autumn in an open, sunny situation in well-
drained, sandy or gritty soil; after flowering
in spring/early summer the soil should dry
out and become quite warm if they are to
succeed; if such conditions cannot be supplied the bulbs should be planted in a bulb
frame where water can be withheld in
summer, or grown in deep pots in an
unheated glasshouse.

Kniphofia (*Liliaceae/Asphodelaceae*)

Rhizomatous/fleshy roots. A large genus
from tropical and South Africa, Madagascar and Yemen, familiar garden plants

because of the many colourful cultivars which are probably all hybrids of the hardier South African species. They have tufts of long-channelled basal leaves and, mostly, dense spikes of yellow, orange, red, pinkish, greenish, brownish or white tubular to funnel-shaped flowers. These can all be treated as summer-growers (some are evergreen) for open, sunny positions in well-drained soils; they seem to do well on the warmer sandier soils, often rotting off in winter when grown on heavier, wet clay soils. Many of the species from the more tropical areas are, of course, frost-tender and in cold-winter areas will require cultivation in a frost-free glasshouse or conservatory.

Korolkowia (*Liliaceae*)

Bulbous. The one species, *K. sewerzowii*, from Central Asia should probably be regarded as a *Fritillaria* and has similar cultivation requirements. It has waxy, green, broad leaves and several elegant, bell-shaped flowers of a gun-metal colour with the tips of the six segments turned outwards showing a hint of the green or yellow interior. Although it is a very hardy plant, in relatively mild-winter countries like England it sometimes starts to grow too early in spring and the young shoots become caught by the late frosts; in such places it is better in a bulb frame or in deep pots in an unheated glasshouse.

Lachenalia
(*Liliaceae/Hyacinthaceae*)

Bulbous. A large and horticulturally valuable genus but only a few of the 100 or more species are in general cultivation and even those are not commonly grown. They are mostly from the South West Cape region of South Africa; they have basal leaves which are extremely varied, from one to several per bulb, flat on the ground to erect, narrow

to broad, plain green or dark-blotched, smooth or covered with warts or blister-like protuberances. The flowers are borne in dense spikes, ranging from pendent to horizontal or erect and from long and tubular to a shorter bell-shape, often rather irregular in shape; almost all colours of the rainbow are represented, the individual flowers often bi-, tri- or even quadri-coloured. These are mostly, or all, winter-growers and should be started into growth in early autumn after a dry summer dormancy. During winter they can easily get 'drawn up' if the light intensity is poor, or if they are grown too wet and warm, so I grow them, with other Cape bulbs, in a just frost-free glasshouse in a light position with a fan to circulate the air; the potting soil is a sandy-loam mix, so it is well-drained and not too rich. Many of them are very easy to grow, and, since most flower in mid to late winter or early spring, they deserve to be much more widely grown than they are. On the other hand there are some tricky,

72 Lachenalia pustulata

seldom-seen, species to challenge the more specialist growers. In mild-winter, frost-free areas the easy ones can be grown permanently in the open ground and make very striking garden plants for the cooler months.

Lapeirousia (*Iridaceae*)

Cormous. A sizeable African genus of over 30 species, mainly in the winter rainfall region of southern Africa but also widespread in tropical Africa. They have small, bell-shaped, flat-bottomed corms and tough, narrow leaves, erect to sickle-shaped, often strongly ribbed. The wiry flower stems are usually much-branched but sometimes the whole inflorescence is short-stemmed so that the flowers are carried in a bunch just above ground level. Each flower has a funnel-shaped tube, sometimes long and slender, and six segments which are either nearly equal or are unequal, forming a two-lipped flower with conspicuous markings on the three segments which form the lower lip. There is a wide colour range, in shades of blue, violet, purple or red, or yellow or white. I have tried only a few of these and their treatment depends upon origin. The tropical African species, such as *L. sandersonii* and *L. erythrantha* can be treated as summer-growers, dried out and kept frost-free in winter, while those from the western and south-western part of southern Africa, such as *L. oreogena*, *L. silenoides*, *L. jacquinii* and *L. fabricii* are definitely winter-growing and, in cold-winter areas, need a slightly heated glasshouse; they should be started into growth in early autumn and kept growing, with as much light and air as possible through winter; after flowering in late winter/early spring they can be progressively dried out as they die down, then given a warm, dry, summer rest. They appear to prefer a sandy potting medium. The related genus *Savannosiphon* (1 sp., *S.*

euryphylla, from south tropical Africa) has broad, pleated leaves and large, long-tubed white flowers; it could be tried in the same way as the summer-growing lapeirousias.

Lapiedra (*Amaryllidaceae*)

Bulbous. A genus of one species, *L. martinezii*, from Spain and North Africa. It has dark green leaves with a pale stripe along the centre and an umbel of small, white flowers. Commence watering in autumn after a summer rest period; grow in full sun in a warm situation; in cold areas plant in a bulb frame or deep pot in a frost-free glasshouse using well-drained soil. The small genus *Hannonia* from North Africa needs much the same treatment.

Ledebouria (*Liliaceae/Hyacinthaceae*)

Bulbous. These were once included in *Scilla* but have long ago been separated; the number of species is not clear, perhaps only about 20 or maybe as many as 30–40, from South Africa, tropical Africa north to Socotra and possibly in India also. They have basal, lance-shaped to oval leaves, usually marked with conspicuous blotches or stripes, and short spikes of small, bell-shaped flowers, brownish, green, purplish or pink. Most of those I have cultivated are evergreen and make good windowsill plants for their foliage (e.g. the *L. socialis* forms, such as 'Scilla violacea'); in cold-winter areas they need to be kept frost-free in winter but can be placed outside for the summer. In order to get the best leaf colours they need plenty of light and not too much water, just enough to keep them from shrivelling; the bulbs should be planted at or only just below soil level. The plant in cultivation as *Scilla adlamii* dies down in winter, but is also excellent for its longitudinally purple-striped leaves.

Leontice (*Berberidaceae*)

Tuberous. A few species from the eastern Mediterranean and western Asia, having ornamental, dissected, grey leaves and loose to dense heads of *Berberis*-like yellow flowers. Plant in autumn, dry off in summer when dormant. Well-drained soil in full sun. In damp-summer areas grow in raised beds, bulb frames or alpine house.

Leontochir (*Alstroemeriaceae*)

Tuberous/fleshy rooted. There is only one species from Chile, *L. ovallei*, which is very rare in cultivation. It is a robust plant, related and similar to *Bomarea* and *Alstroemeria* with leafy stems and large bunches of orange flowers; in cultivation it probably needs to be treated as a tender Andean *Alstroemeria* (see page 60).

Leucocoryne (*Liliaceae/Alliaceae*)

Bulbous. A small genus of about 12 species from Chile. The rounded bulbs produce a few long, narrow basal leaves and a tall, wiry, leafless flower stem carrying a few-flowered umbel of short-tubed, often fragrant flowers with six spreading segments; they are white, blue or purple, sometimes yellow or purple in the centre, and usually with three protruding yellow or white sterile stamens. These are winter-growers so the bulbs should be potted or planted and started into growth in autumn and kept in growth in full light through the winter. After flowering time in spring, water can be withheld as the foliage dies away and they go into summer dormancy; in cold-winter areas they need to be grown under glass, just with frost protection, and are suitable for deep pots or containers in a conservatory. A sandy soil mix seems to suit them best. They are excellent for picking as

they last for a very long time. *Stemmatium narcissoides*, also Chilean, is in general very similar, but its white flowers have a small, yellow or green corona so that it looks just like a *Narcissus* (but with a superior, not inferior, ovary); it is now thought that this would be better classified as a *Leucocoryne*; cultivation is the same. There are several other small genera in the Alliaceae from the Andes, mainly Chilean, which are rare in cultivation; they seem to require much the same treatment as *Leucocoryne*. They include: *Gilliesia*, *Ancrumia*, *Gethyum*, *Trichlora*, *Miersia*, *Solaria*, *Garaventia* and *Latace*.

Leucocrinum (*Liliaceae/Anthericaceae*)

Rhizomatous/fleshy roots. A small North American genus of only one species, *L. montanum*, from rather dry situations in California, Oregon, Nevada and Utah. It has long, fleshy roots radiating from a compact rhizomatous crown, producing a basal tuft of narrow, grey-green leaves and, in spring, short-stemmed, white flowers which resemble those of some *Anthericum* species; in fact the whole plant is rather like a very compact stemless *Anthericum*. I have found this not difficult to cultivate in a deep pot of very gritty/sandy soil with the crown covered by about 5 cm (2 in) of pure, sharp

73 *Leucocoryne purpurea*

sand; the pots are dried out completely in the summer, then watered in autumn to start the plants into growth; they are kept just frost-free in a glasshouse in winter, then given plenty of water in spring. The plants need as much light as possible in winter or the flowers become elongated and weak and fall over. It would probably do well planted in a sandy bulb frame where the very long, vigorous roots would have almost unlimited space.

74 *Leucojum autumnale*

Leucojum (*Amaryllidaceae*)

Bulbous. There are about 9 species of snowflake from Europe and North Africa, producing thread-like to strap-shaped leaves and pendent, bell-shaped white or pale pink flowers, either solitary or in an umbel, in autumn or spring. They are all winter-growing, so plant or pot the bulbs in autumn and keep in growth until late spring or early summer. *L. aestivum* and *L. vernum* are very hardy and need plenty of moisture so plant in sun or semi-shade in a site which does not dry out excessively in summer; they do well in clayey soils but are equally good on sandy soils if plenty of humus is worked in. Although the leaves die down in summer the roots are present through the year; clumps can be lifted and divided in early autumn or in spring, after flowering. The rest are small-flowered species, most of which are best grown in sandy soil mix in a bulb frame or in pots in a cool glasshouse, although *L. autumnale* can be very successful in an open, sunny, well-drained position where it will become warm and dry in summer. *L. nicaeense*, *L. valentinum* and *L. tingitanum* (*L. fontianum*) appear to need rather more moisture in the growing season than *L. roseum*, *L. longifolium* and *L. trichophyllum* and less of a 'baking' in summer. *L. trichophyllum* tends to produce tiny bulblets at the neck of the bulb, probably quite naturally, not as a fault of cultivation.

Lilium (*Liliaceae*)

Bulbous. A large genus of around 100 species, widespread in the northern hemisphere and found mainly in the temperate regions; there are also countless hybrid cultivars which are, on the whole, much better garden plants than the wild species, although they often lack the subtle beauty of the species. Lilies have bulbs with loosely packed scales compared with many of the scaly bulbs such as hyacinths, onions and daffodils; their leaves, which vary in shape enormously, are all carried on the stem (i.e. not basal as they are in the Liliaceae/Hyacinthaceae) and the relatively large flowers are carried in loose racemes, sometimes reduced to a single flower. The flowers may be trumpet- or funnel-shaped, upright and bowl-shaped, flattish with reflexed tips or pendent with the segments rolled backwards giving the 'turk's cap' shape; the range of colours is quite wide, although predominantly white or shades of yellow, orange, red and pink.

Lilies are mainly summer-growers, dying down for the winter months; they are, however, not dry during their dormant season – many are under snow or frozen – and thus in cultivation should never be dried out completely or they will die. In the wild, lilies mostly do not occur in regions which have a dry season, for example, the Middle East and Central Asia, and are to be found mainly in those areas which have a monsoon, summer rainfall, climate (e.g., Himalaya to China and other parts of eastern Asia), or in mountainous areas with cool weather and some rain through the summer (e.g., the European Alps, parts of North America), or in damp situations (some of the 'swamp lilies' of North America). There are a few exceptions, notably *L. candidum*, from the Mediterranean region which is a winter rainfall area; this, the Madonna lily, does make a lot of root growth and some foliage in the autumn and winter before flowering in spring/early summer, rather earlier than the majority of lilies which have their main growth period in late spring building up to flowering time in mid- to late summer. It follows that *L. candidum* must be planted rather earlier than the rest; this also applies, but to a lesser extent, to the other southern European lilies such as *L. carniolicum*, *L. pomponium* and *L. chalcedonicum*.

The ideal time to plant the bulbs is as soon as possible after they have been lifted from the nursery in autumn. This ensures that there is no time for the roots and bulbs to dry out and shrivel, and they have the maximum amount of time in which to become established before the winter sets in. Some nurserymen do sell their bulbs in autumn, while others lift them and put them in controlled cold storage until the spring. It is best to obtain the bulbs as soon as they are on the market, be it autumn or spring, and plant them immediately for they are much better in the ground than left to dry out. With autumn planting, in cold-winter areas where the ground freezes it may be necessary to pot up the bulbs and keep them in a cool place, just frost-free and slightly watered, until spring when they can be planted out. The pots need not be much larger than the bulbs since this is only a temporary situation.

Most lilies do well if given a site where their bulbs will be shaded by low-growing shrubs or perennials, with the stems poking through into the sunlight, or dappled shade of taller trees and shrubs. A deep, well-worked, rich soil is best, so dig in a liberal amount of well-rotted organic matter, preferably containing a good proportion of leafmould. If the drainage is poor, add sharp sand or a coarser grit or gravel; it may be necessary to raise the planting area slightly above the surrounding soil to improve drainage. Also work in some general (NPK balanced) fertilizer. The top layer of soil should also be enriched with organic matter and the same fertilizer, and sand if necessary, before filling in on top of the lily bulbs. The larger-growing lilies need a space of about 30 cm (1 ft) across for one bulb; three bulbs planted in a triangle need a 60 cm (2 ft) diameter hole. Smaller species such as *L. pumilum* could be planted much closer, at 10–15 cm (4–6 in) apart. In a well-prepared site with good drainage it should not be necessary to place more sand around the bulb, but if there is any doubt it might be beneficial to encase the bulb in a thin layer of gritty sand.

Most of the lilies can be grown on alkaline soils, providing a liberal amount of humus is worked in at planting time, with further top-dressings later on. Some species, however, are much more tolerant than others and include *L. amabile*, *L. candidum*, *L. henryi*, *L. pardalinum*, *L. cernuum*, *L. chalcedonicum* and *L. pomponium*. When preparation has been thorough, lilies can be very long-lived; they will require a regular supply of moisture during the growing season, so watering may be necessary during dry periods, and also a top dressing of old, well-rotted organic matter, especially in the case of the stem-rooting lilies. Weak liquid feeds of tomato formula fertilizer are beneficial; after flowering, if seeds are not required, cut off the stems just below the flowers and continue to water and feed until the leaves begin to turn colour in late summer or autumn. When the stems and their leaves have died back

75 *Lilium chalcedonicum*

they can be cut off at soil level, and this is a good time to lift and divide any congested clumps, usually every 2–3 years if the lilies are growing well. The swamp lily, *L. superbum*, and its relatives from North America will do well in gardens if given a moisture-retentive soil rich in humus; it is certainly not necessary to create a bog or swamp for them to thrive. The small Himalayan and Chinese species related to *L. nanum*, *L. flavidum*, *L. oxypetalum* and *L. lophophorum*, and *L. mackliniae*, all require a climate which has cool, damp atmospheric conditions in summer; they are very unsuited to, for example, the south-east of England where in some places we have only 625 mm (25 in) of rain per year, often with very dry air. The best chance of success lies in a semi-shaded 'peat bed' or cold frame with a misting system.

Growing lilies in containers is often a very good method of cultivation in gardens where they do not normally thrive (we have such a garden!), and it is a way in which the frost-tender species (such as *L. formosanum* and *L. longiflorum*) can be grown in cold areas under glass; even the hardy ones can be pot-grown to encourage them to flower earlier for decorative use. Also, when grown in containers, the lilies can be placed in a prominent position in the garden when in flower and afterwards moved away again to make room for something else. As a guide to pot size, one bulb of a large lily such as

L. regale or one of the trumpet hybrids would need a 20 cm (8 in) diameter pot, whereas the same pot would take three to five bulbs of the smaller types, for example, *L. pumilum* and the many quick-growing Asiatic hybrids of the group to which 'Enchantment' and 'Connecticut King' belong. The potting soil needs to be an open, well-drained mix; a loam-based 1:1:1 (loam:leafmould:sharp sand) is usually successful, with a balanced fertilizer. A good gap should be left between the soil surface and top of the pot to allow for top dressings in summer; this is particularly important for those lilies which produce stem roots. After planting, water and place the containers in a cool place for the rest of the winter and early spring, preferably plunged up to the rims in sand or similar medium to keep them at a uniform temperature and frost-free; a loose covering of straw will also help. As the top growth commences they need to be given more water and light, finally moving them to their flowering positions when there is no danger of frost at night. With regard to watering, Patrick Synge once told me to allow the containers to dry out in between waterings, rather than keeping them permanently damp, and I have found this very sound advice, especially with non-porous (such as plastic) pots. When the lilies die down in autumn the stems can be cut off and the bulbs repotted, or top-dressed if in large containers; remove the old soil down to bulb level and replace with fresh; most lilies can be grown in pots and most of those generally available produce stem roots. However, those which have a wandering habit (by means of stolons), such as *L. wardii* and *L. duchartrei*, are not so well suited to pot cultivation.

Litanthus
(*Liliaceae/Hyacinthaceae*)

Bulbous. There is only one species, *L. pusillus*, from South Africa. This is a real collector's plant, a miniature with thread-like leaves and stems and tiny, white tubular flowers. I have tried it, thanks to Chris Lovell, and find that it needs similar conditions as described for *Carpolyza* (see page 76); although not related it has much the same ornamental value.

Littonia (*Liliaceae/Colchicaceae*)

Cormous. A small genus of about 6-7 species from Arabia, tropical Africa and South Africa; they are similar to *Gloriosa* (see page 98) in the misshapen corms and growth habit but have orange flowers which are pendent and bell-shaped. The only species cultivated to any extent is *L. modesta*. This is a summer-grower with cultivation needs similar to those of *Gloriosa*; it makes a superb conservatory subject for the summer months.

Lloydia (*Liliaceae*)

Bulbous. A small genus of diminutive plants, very widespread around the temperate northern hemisphere, Himalaya and China. They have tiny bulbs producing thread-like leaves and bell- or funnel-shaped yellow or white (often veined purple) flowers, usually pendent. They are mostly mountain plants, never drying out completely and needing cool growing conditions in a gritty-peaty soil mix; they succeed best in areas with a cool, moist summer atmosphere and are nearly impossible in low rainfall regions; a misting system might provide the necessary humidity.

Lycoris (*Amaryllidaceae*)

Bulbous. An interesting genus of amaryllids in eastern Asia, mainly China and Japan, where the family is otherwise poorly represented; there are perhaps about 20 species, resembling nerines in that they are autumn-flowering with umbels of brightly coloured flowers with reflexed, wavy segments and long-protruding stamens, although the colour range is greater in white, yellow and shades of pink, red to blue; *L. squamigera* has flowers more funnel-shaped like those of *Amaryllis belladonna*. The leaves are basal and strap-shaped, sometimes with a pale stripe along the centre. Some species produce their leaves in autumn soon after flowering time (e.g. *L. radiata*) while others do not push up leaves until late winter or early spring (e.g. *L. sprengeri*). *Lycoris* are active in autumn, winter and spring and dormant in summer, during which time the bulbs need to kept warm if they are to thrive and flower; in areas where the summers are not hot and dry enough to ripen the bulbs it is unlikely that they will flower unless grown under glass. The best success I have had, with *L. aurea* and *L. albiflora* was when they were planted directly into a sandy bed in a glasshouse; they were left hot and dry through summer and then given a good watering in early autumn to encourage root growth and flowering. In mild areas they can be grown successfully outside in a warm, sunny position against a wall – *L. squamigera* can be quite successful, even in Britain. Hardiness is often questioned but, at least in the case of those which produce leaves in spring, it is probably the lack of warmth in summer that precludes success rather than winter cold; however, as with the hardiest of the nerines, *N. bowdenii*,

76 *Lycoris albiflora*

lycoris are not hardy where the ground freezes deeply for any length of time. Deep containers can also be used but so far I have not flowered them well under these conditions. The soil should be well-drained and it seems that a sandy, loam-based mix is best; some bulbs which I 'parked' temporarily in some calcareous sand have grown extremely well, so this may be another clue to success; as with nerines, a high-potash liquid tomato fertilizer is helpful; plant with the neck of the bulb reaching soil level.

Massonia
(Liliaceae/Hyacinthaceae)

Bulbous. A small genus of dwarf, rather striking plants from South Africa which have been gaining in popularity in recent years with 'alpine' plant enthusiasts. They are compact and attractive, and hardy enough to be grown in a glasshouse which has frost protection on cold nights. There are about eight species, mainly from the South West Cape; they usually have a pair of broad leaves lying flat on the ground, sometimes smooth and sometimes covered in pointed protuberances ('pustules') or bristles. The white, green, yellowish, brownish or pink flowers are produced in a tight head (actually a very compact raceme) nestling down in between the leaves, their most conspicuous feature being the long-

77 *Massonia pustulata*

protruding stamens since the segments are quite small. All those I have tried are winter-growers; they are kept in a just frost-free glasshouse with as much light and ventilation as possible to prevent them becoming 'drawn up' in the dull English winters. The potting medium is a gritty/sandy loam mix, not too rich or it encourages lush growth; only one bulb is placed in a wide pot or pan since the leaf rosette develops to about 15 cm (6 in) across and is not shown off to full advantage if it overlaps with another. Most flower during the late autumn to late winter and should be kept in growth by light watering until late spring when they begin to die down; the pots are then dried off for the summer, although not in too hot and sunny a place or the fleshy bulbs can become desiccated and die (personal experience!). In mild-winter areas they could be grown outside, although their very dwarf stature does make them ideal for display in pots on a raised bench. The following related South African genera can be treated in exactly the same way: *Amphisiphon*, *Androsiphon*, *Daubenya*, *Polyxena* and *Whiteheadia*; descriptions of these will be found under the appropriate entry.

Melasphaerula (*Iridaceae*)

Cormous. There is only one species, *M. graminea*, which is from South Africa. It has erect, narrowly sword-shaped leaves and slender, tough, wiry stems which carry many small flowers in a loosely branched inflorescence; the flowers are slightly 2-lipped and creamy white to pale yellow. Although not showy, this is a delicate-looking plant and is extremely easy to cultivate so has its place as an interesting item for the winter/early spring months. It is a winter-grower so the corms should be planted out (in areas with mild winters) or potted (in cold-winter regions) in autumn in a sandy soil and placed in as much light as possible; it will grow and flower through the winter/spring and then die down for the summer months when the corms can be kept quite dry.

Merendera
(*Liliaceae/Colchicaceae*)

Cormous. A small genus from southern Europe and western to central Asia, sometimes merged with *Colchicum*, with erect, funnel-shaped white, pink or purple flowers in autumn or spring; they differ from colchicums in having no tube to the flower, the six segments all separate. Winter-growing, so plant or pot in autumn in well-drained, sandy soil in full sun; they are rather small so are better in a raised bed, rock garden or bulb frame, or in pots in an unheated glasshouse. The corms need to be warm and dry in summer; some species, especially *M. filifolia*, will sometimes stay dormant for several seasons without producing leaves or flowers – try giving a summer baking, remove or split the outer hard blackish corm tunics in late summer, then replant or repot and water profusely.

Milla (*Alliaceae*)

Cormous. A small genus of about 5–10 species from Central America, Guatemala and southern Arizona having long, narrow, basal leaves and a leafless stem bearing a few-flowered umbel of upright, long-tubed flowers; these have six segments spreading to form a flattish star shape; in the most frequently cultivated species, *M. biflora*, these are fragrant and white with a dark, usually green, stripe along the centre of each segment; the other, rarely cultivated, species have white, pink or blue flowers. Millas are summer-growers, so should be planted in spring for flowering in late summer. They are not frost-hardy and in cold areas the corms must be lifted for the winter and stored dry; in milder areas

78 *Dandya purpusii*

they can be planted out in a sunny position in well-drained soil and left undisturbed. Alternatively, they can be grown in deep pots of a sandy soil mix in the cool glasshouse or conservatory. The related Mexican genera *Bessera* (2–3 spp. with conical, pendent, red, pink or purplish flowers), *Dandya* (1 sp., similar to *Bessera*) and *Petronymphe* (1 sp. with pendent tubular yellow-green flowers) almost certainly require similar treatment in cultivation, as may *Behria* (1 sp. with tubular red flowers) from Baja California, but I have no firm details about the requirements of this; it might be a winter-grower, to be cultivated in the same way as *Brodiaea*.

Molineria (*Hypoxidaceae*)

Cormous/rhizomatous. These are similar in appearance to *Curculigo* (see page 82) and probably require much the same treatment in cultivation; they are mostly from the warmer parts of India and south-east Asia.

Moraea (*Iridaceae*)

Cormous. A large genus of well over a hundred species, all African, distributed widely from Ethiopia to South Africa but rather few (c. 15) in tropical Africa; most of them occur in the South West Cape winter rainfall region with also a considerable number (30 or more) in the summer rainfall, eastern part of southern Africa. They have flattened-rounded corms giving rise to very narrow to lance-shaped channelled, often rather tough, basal leaves and showy flowers in a wide range of colours; they have three large outer segments and three smaller inner ones, so they are somewhat iris-like to those who are more familiar with this northern hemisphere genus.

79 *Moraea fugax*

The method of cultivation of moraeas depends upon their origin: those from the East Cape are summer-growers and should be treated as such (and those from tropical Africa), planted or started into growth in spring after a winter rest period and given a well-drained position which is, however, well-supplied with moisture throughout the summer growing period. In very cold areas where the ground freezes to a considerable depth they will probably not survive, but they can be grown as container plants and taken under cover for the winter. Some of the species, for example the large, clump-forming *M. huttonii* and *M. spathulata,* are more or less evergreen in cultivation in mild-winter areas but the long leaves become rather unsightly by spring; it seems to do no harm to cut off the untidy tips, allowing the flower stems and new leaves to develop without the distraction of the old foliage. These summer-growers are, on the whole (obviously not the tropical species), much hardier than those from the South West Cape since they are at rest in winter,

and several inhabit cold-winter highland areas.

The moraeas from the winter rainfall areas of the South West Cape continue to be winter-growers when brought into cultivation, mostly flowering in winter and early spring, so should be planted or started into growth by watering in early autumn after a warm, dry, summer dormancy. They do well in pots in a just frost-free glasshouse or conservatory, planted in deep pots in a sandy potting mix; in frost-free climates they can be grown outside in well-drained, sunny positions but the flowers of many species are delicate and are better with at least some protection from rain. After flowering and seeding they can be dried off for the rest of the summer.

Muilla (Liliaceae/Alliaceae)

Cormous. About 3 species from the western USA, late spring-flowering with umbels of flattish white or greenish-white flowers, the tuft of the very narrow basal leaves dying off at flowering time. They are winter-growers, so plant in autumn and dry off in summer when dormant; grow in a well-drained soil in full sun; in damp-summer areas grow in raised beds, bulb frames or an alpine house.

Muscari (Liliaceae/Hyacinthaceae)

Bulbous. A familiar genus of spring-flowering species (one autumnal) from Europe and western Asia. The species fall into three main groups: the grape hyacinths have dense racemes of small, near-spherical or tubular blue (also white forms) flowers, mostly with constricted mouths, but *M. azureum*, *M. pseudomuscari* and their relatives are bell-shaped and not constricted (these are treated by some authors as genus *Pseudomuscari*). The tassel hyacinths, *M. comosum* and its relatives (separated by

80 *Muscari comosum* 'Album'

some authors as the genus *Leopoldia*) have generally looser racemes with dull brown, greenish or yellowish tubular flowers and a 'top-knot' of showy purple, blue or pink sterile flowers. The musk hyacinths, *M. muscarimi* (*moschatum*) and *M. macro-carpum* (these are sometimes separated as another genus, *Muscarimia*) have dense spikes of scented, tubular, whitish-brown, pale blue or yellow flowers which have angular projections around the mouth. They are all winter-growers so should be planted in autumn and allowed to grow through to the following summer when they die down for a rest period. Most of the grape hyacinths are very easily cultivated in sunny positions in reasonably well-drained soil; *M. neglectum* and *M. armeniacum* do well in partial shade. The tassel and musk hyacinths need a warm, sunny position which dries out in summer if they are to flower well; several of them have strong permanent roots (especially the latter) so take a while to settle in after planting and should not be disturbed too often; in areas with unreliably dry summers they make good subjects for a bulb frame, or for deep pots in an unheated glasshouse where they can be dried off in summer.

Narcissus (Amaryllidaceae)

Bulbous. A familiar genus, mainly from western Europe and North Africa,

extending into the eastern Mediterranean. There are, perhaps, about 50 species, but there is much variation within each 'species', with very different interpretations as to what it means, so the number of species varies widely depending upon which authority is followed. They have thread-like to strap-shaped, basal leaves and leafless flower stems bearing either solitary flowers or several in an umbel; the flowers consist of a central 'corona', which varies in size from a shallow cup to a long trumpet, surrounded by six perianth segments, the 'corolla'. All the wild species are white, cream or shades of yellow, or bicoloured (and one green-flowered), but the range in cultivation has been extended by breeding to include darker orange and apricot, and pink or reddish trumpets. All *Narcissus* grow in the predominantly winter rainfall region of the western Mediterranean so are essentially winter-growers for planting in autumn; after growing through winter and spring they die down for the summer and go into a period of rest, although quite a number of species do not fully lose their roots during this period unless disturbed.

Most of the trumpet daffodils, *N. pseudonarcissus* and its kin, and *N. cyclamineus*, need a lot of moisture in the growing season and these will mostly do well out in the open ground or in grass, the natural habitat of many of them; an open situation is best, although they will tolerate dappled shade. *N. triandrus* and *N. asturiensis* also need plenty of moisture, but combined with a well-drained, sandy/peaty soil which partly dries out in summer. The late-flowering *N. poeticus* is a plant of wet mountain meadows in the wild so it too requires moist conditions whilst in growth. The Jonquil, *N. jonquilla* and its relations, seem to like a deep, rich soil, reputedly preferring alkaline conditions but certainly thriving in our own garden which is acid enough for rhododendrons. Most of the

81 *Narcissus alpestris*

smaller species, for example *N. watieri*, *N. assoanus*, *N. rupicola*, *N. romieuxii* and *N. cantabricus* are really best grown in pots in an unheated glasshouse or bulb frame where their miniature beauty can be appreciated and there is more control of their growing conditions; some of them flower so early in the season that their delicate blooms would be damaged in the open ground; they need full length pots and a sandy/gritty potting medium which is kept well-watered during winter and spring, then allowed almost to dry out in summer. The autumn-flowering species such as *N. serotinus* need a real baking to induce them to flower. *N. bulbocodium* variants are also successful in pots but they can be tried in the open garden on a rock garden or in grass, providing it consists of fairly fine grasses, not broad-leaved, coarse or large, tuft-forming ones. The best colonies of *N. bulbocodium* are usually to be seen on sandy, acid soils, particularly on sloping ground where there is water seeping down the slope in the growing season. Some species are less frost-hardy and require a warm, dry summer period if they are to flower well; those with several flowers clustered in an umbel, *N. tazetta*, *N. papyraceus* and their relatives, fall into this category and in cold areas will need to be planted against a warm, sunny wall; these, and the selections and hybrids derived from them are good subjects for forcing indoors for an early display, and for this purpose it is necessary to buy good bulbs in early autumn which will have buds already formed inside; if bulbs from the garden are to be lifted for forcing it is best to dig up the clumps in early to mid-summer, sort out the largest bulbs and then store them in a warm, dry place until autumn; this will help to ensure that flower buds are formed.

Nectaroscordum (*Liliaceae/Alliaceae*)

Bulbous. A small genus of about 3 species from southern Europe and western Asia, related to *Allium* and having a strong onion/garlic type of smell when bruised; they have a rounded bulb producing long, narrow, channelled basal leaves and a tall stem bearing in summer an umbel of bell-shaped, green, purple or white flowers on long, arched pedicels so that they are pendent; in fruit, the pedicels become erect and make attractive dried decorations. The two seen most frequently in cultivation, *N. siculum* and its subspecies *bulgaricum* (*N. dioscoridis*) are very easily grown and will sometimes seed around far too prolifically. They can be grown in full sun or dappled shade among shrubs or other perennials, or in grass, and will tolerate quite damp heavy soils; they die down in summer but do not require a warm, dry rest period. However, *N. tripedale*, an attractive species from the Middle East, does seem to need drier conditions in its summer dormant period and is perhaps rather better suited to a bulb frame.

Nemastylis (probably = *Salpingostylis*) (*Iridaceae*)

Bulbous. A small genus of about five species from southern USA, Mexico and Guatemala. They are related to *Tigridia* and have similar erect, narrowly sword-like leaves which are pleated lengthways. The flowers are very short-lived, several produced in succession, and have either six equal segments or the outer three are larger than the inner three; they are flattish and starry in shape, in shades of blue, violet or yellow. These are summer-growers, suitable for growing outside in frost-free areas in a sunny, well-drained position which is, however, supplied with plenty of moisture in summer. In cold-winter areas they can be grown in pots in a slightly heated glasshouse or conservatory and partially dried in winter whilst dormant; a sandy, loam-based potting soil seems to give best results. The following related genera should probably be treated in the same way, but I have not tried them yet: *Cardiostigma* (c. 4 spp. from C. America, sometimes treated as species of *Sphenostigma*; flowers with 6 equal segments, blue or violet, dark-spotted in the centre), *Ainea* (2 spp. from Mexico; flowers white or violet with 6 subequal segments or the outer 3 larger).

Neobakeria
(*Liliaceae/Hyacinthaceae*)

Bulbous. The three species forming this small South African genus, *N. angustifolia*, *N. comata* and *N. heterandra*, are similar to, and now usually included in, *Massonia*. They are very rare in cultivation; if obtained, they should almost certainly be given similar treatment to species of *Massonia* (see page 118).

Nerine (*Amaryllidaceae*)

Bulbous. A well-known genus of 20 or more species from southern Africa, only a few of which are in general cultivation, but there are many colourful, large-flowered hybrids. They have thread-like to strap-shaped basal leaves, some evergreen, others dying away for the summer months. Nerines are mostly autumn-flowering with leafless stems bearing umbels of glistening pale to deep pink or red flowers (also white

82 *Nerine humilis*

forms) which have six narrow segments, often wavy or crisped at the margins and rolled backwards, leaving the stamens protruding conspicuously. Most nerines are winter-growers, flowering in autumn after a warm, dry summer dormancy and before the leaves emerge; the summer-deciduous species need to be dried out as soon as the leaves die off in spring/summer but the evergreen species should not be dried out completely for long periods, the watering just reduced in summer. In mild-winter areas nerines can be cultivated outside in warm, sunny positions where the soil dries out in summer, but in regions with slightly frosty winters only *N. bowdenii* and its selections and hybrids are at all hardy; even there, in cold winters when the ground freezes, the bulbs, and the leaves, are liable to be damaged. For this reason, the bulbs of this species are planted in beds at the foot of sunny walls where they get protection and a warm summer rest period. All others are best grown in a light, well-aired but frost-free glasshouse, either in pots or planted directly into beds; the smaller species such as *N. masonorum*, *N. filifolia*, *N. humilis* and *N. angustifolia* are excellent in pots. A gritty/sandy, loam-based soil mix is suitable, with liquid feeds of a potash-rich fertilizer at least once a month through the growing season. As long as they are doing well and flowering, it is best to leave them undisturbed, but when they become very crowded and stop flowering they should be split and repotted in early autumn before the first watering; plant with the tip of the bulb above soil level.

Nomocharis (*Liliaceae*)

Bulbous. Beautiful summer-flowering relatives of the lilies, comprising about eight species from China, Tibet and Burma; like lilies, they have scaly bulbs and leafy stems, the leaves scattered or whorled, and one to several large flowers in a raceme; these are flattish or saucer-shaped with the inner three segments broader than the outer three; the segments are often toothed or frilled at the margins. The colours range from pure white to pink and deeper red, often prominently spotted or blotched darker and with a dark eye in the centre. *Nomocharis* are plants from a cold dry winter, summer rainfall (monsoon) climate and, not surprisingly, are rather difficult to grow in regions with a relatively low rainfall and humidity. Here, in south-east England, for example, they do not thrive, whereas in the cooler and more humid conditions in parts of Scotland they often grow with great vigour. They do best when

83 *Nomocharis aperta* hybrid

given as cool a spot as possible in a deep, well-drained, humus-rich soil with the base of the plant shaded by dwarf shrubs – small rhododendrons are the obvious natural companions – and the top of the stem in the light; dappled shade is ideal in warm, sunny climates but they will take full sun in the cooler areas. They need plenty of moisture during the growing season, but not water-logged conditions, so this means good drainage with regular watering. As with lilies, pot cultivation can be a successful method of cultivation in places where they do not do well in the open ground, but, here again, a cool spot must be chosen.

Notholirion (*Liliaceae*)

Bulbous. A small genus of six species from Iran, Afghanistan, the Himalaya, Tibet and western China, related to *Lilium* and perhaps also to *Fritillaria* but quite different from both in having bulbs which are encased in brown papery tunics (they are loose-scaly and naked in the other two genera); the bulbs are also monocarpic, dying after flowering to be replaced by small offsets. Long, narrow, basal leaves are produced in autumn or winter, in some species these beginning to die back when the flower stem pushes up in late spring or summer; the flowers are pale lilac to pinkish-purple or a darker crimson and are pendent or horizontal, funnel-shaped with the six segments sometimes flared outwards at the tips. The main problem with the cultivation of *Notholirion* is the presence of leaves in the winter months. I find that, with those species I have tried, they are best grown in containers which can be placed in the frost-free glasshouse, otherwise their leaves can become severely damaged by only a few degrees of frost; on the other hand, they seem to need fairly cool-growing conditions in the spring and summer, so the pots are then placed outside in a semi-shaded position and kept watered and fed with a tomato fertilizer until they die down in mid- to late summer; after this they are dried out until mid-autumn, then repotted and started into growth again. I have to say, however, that they are not very free-flowering under these conditions, the bulbs tending to split into many small ones. The soil is a well-drained, gritty, loam-based mix with about one third well-rotted crumbly leafmould. In mild-winter areas they could be grown in the open ground and may be better for this.

Nothoscordum (*Alliaceae*)

Bulbous. A small genus from temperate South America, notorious because of the now world-wide, pestiferous *N. gracile* (*N. fragrans*, *N. inodorum*); there are, however, some very attractive species, well worthy of cultivation. They have very narrow basal leaves and slender stems bearing umbels (sometimes solitary) of starry, yellow or white flowers in spring or summer. The horticulturally interesting species such as *N. ostenii*, *N. sellowianum* (*Ipheion sellowianum*) and *N. dialystemon* (*I. dialystemon*) are winter-growers of untried hardiness at present. They can be grown in a bulb frame or in pots in an unheated glasshouse in a sandy soil mix;

84 *Nothoscordum dialystemon*

although they die down in summer and need to be warm, their bulbs should not be dried out excessively or they are liable to go into a prolonged period of dormancy which is difficult to break, and they may go for two or more years without leaves or flowers. *N. gracile* is very hardy and almost defies eradication; it is almost evergreen but behaves as a summer-grower in cold-winter areas, dying down for the winter.

Odontostomum (*Tecophilaeaceae*)

Cormous. A genus of one species from California, having long narrow leaves at the base of a much-branched stem which bears small, white flowers with reflexed perianth segments. It is a winter-grower, flowering in spring or early summer. Plant the corms in autumn in a bulb frame, or in deep pots in an unheated glasshouse, in a sandy soil mix; water until late spring then dry off for rest of summer; in mild areas with dry summers it could be tried outside.

Oenostachys (*Iridaceae*)

This African genus has now been merged with *Gladiolus* by Drs. Peter Goldblatt and Miriam de Vos.

Onixotis (*Liliaceae/Colchicaceae*)

Cormous. Previously known as *Dipidax* and may still be found under this name. A small genus of two species from the southern Cape region of South Africa, only one of which, *O. triquetra*, is cultivated to any extent and then mainly by specialists. The small corms produce erect stems with narrowly lance-shaped basal and stem leaves and spikes of starry, white or pink flowers which have a darker eye in the centre. They are winter-growers and are not hardy; in mild areas they may be grown outside but in cold-winter countries will need frost-free conditions under glass.

In the wild they grow in seasonally very wet places, so require plenty of water in the growing season, then less in summer whilst dormant; it has been suggested that they do well if grown in pots placed in a saucer of water in winter, then removed for the summer to dry out. A sandy/peaty soil mix seems to be suitable.

Orchids, terrestrial (*Orchidaceae*)

Tuberous. The orchids constitute such an enormous family (conservatively estimated at some 20,000 species) of monocotyledons that it is only right that they have societies and whole books devoted to them and their cultivation. A very large proportion of the orchids are tropical epiphytes, but there are a few hardy terrestrial species with tuberous roots that have perhaps entered more into the gardening realm of the bulb enthusiast than that of the orchid specialist. Several genera immediately spring to mind, those most frequently cultivated being *Dactylorhiza*, *Orchis*, *Ophrys* and *Serapias*; *Pleione* species and their hybrids, although they are perhaps more epiphytic in behaviour, are much-cultivated by alpine enthusiasts, usually under glass and kept just frost-free; some of the many fascinating *Pterostylis* species from Australia and New Zealand are similarly

85 *Dactylorhiza elata*

proving popular and are quite readily cultivated in pots in the alpine house. *Calanthe* and *Bletilla* are two further terrestrial genera which have become increasingly popular in recent years. In addition to these tuberous orchids, several genera of temperate, rhizomatous-rooted orchids are also very popular with hardy plant enthusiasts, notably the slipper orchids, *Cypripedium*, and a few species of *Epipactis*. I have cultivated a few species of each of all of the above genera over the years with mixed success, some very well, others less well and some total failures. I could make various general observations about each, but to try to deal with the cultivation of all tuberous and rhizomatous terrestrial orchids in a few pages would not make sense. I therefore have no hesitation in recommending the books of some friends and colleagues who know far more about the subject than I: *Hardy Orchids* by Phillip Cribb and Chris Bailes (Christopher Helm and Timber Press, 1989), and *Orchids at Kew* by Joyce Stewart (HMSO, 1992); the latter contains some useful cultural details, and a section on propagation from seed, weaning the seedlings, etc. *The Encyclopaedia of Alpines* (Alpine Garden Society, 1994) also has some very useful cultivation hints on the above genera.

Ornithogalum (*Liliaceae/Hyacinthaceae*)

Bulbous. A very large genus of over 100 species, widely distributed in Europe, especially the Mediterranean region, North Africa, western Asia and tropical Africa, south to South Africa where it occurs in both the eastern summer rainfall and south-western winter rainfall regions. They have basal leaves, varying from thread-like to strap-shaped or narrowly lance-shaped, and leafless stems carrying racemes of cup-shaped, saucer-shaped or flattish flowers; in many species the raceme has a flat-topped appearance caused by the stalks of the lower flowers being longer than the upper. The flower colour is predominantly white, often with a green stripe along the centre of each segment, but there are also species with green, yellow and orange flowers.

Cultivation depends upon the origin of a particular species. All of the Eurasian and North African species are winter-growers, fairly hardy and should be planted in autumn in an open, sunny position with reasonably well-drained soil; a few of the Mediterranean species are slightly tender, notably the large and impressive O. *arabicum*; this, I find, needs to be grown in a very sheltered, warm spot and is best in a bed in the unheated glasshouse.

Those from the eastern Cape are the reverse, needing to be planted in spring to grow and flower in the summer months; I have tried only O. *saundersiae* which is almost hardy here, surviving some winters, but to be on the safe side I lift the bulbs in autumn and store them frost-free for the winter, along with other marginally hardy summer bulbs such as *Tigridia*, *Galtonia* and some *Gladiolus*. In areas with milder winters these summer-flowering ornithogalums could certainly be left in the open ground permanently.

The South African winter-growers are not so hardy; these are grown in the just frost-free glasshouse, potted in autumn in a sandy, loam mix and watered through winter to late spring when they die down after flowering; a warm, dryish rest period follows, not too sunbaked though. I have not tried many, but they do seem to be relatively easy to grow and fairly trouble-free; some of the most attractive are in this group, such as O. *dubium* which has large, yellow or orange flowers and O. *thyrsoides*, the well-known chincherinchee which we see frequently as a cut-flower; this is usually a winter-grower but nurseries offer bulbs

86 *Ornithogalum nutans*

which have been dry stored over winter for a spring planting; these will flower later than normal, in summer.

The only other ones I have not commented upon are the tropical African species. Few are in cultivation and the only one likely to be met is O. *longibracteatum*, a widespread species (also in South Africa) which many people grow without knowing what it is! It is one of the bulbs most frequently sent to me (and to Kew) for identification, normally grown here as an indoor pot plant. The large, fleshy, green bulbs sit on the soil surface and have 'babies' appearing under the outer skins of the parent bulb, eventually bursting through; the leaves are long and strap-like, tapering gradually to the apex, and the greenish-white flowers are produced in a very long, slender raceme; it is very tender but in mild-winter areas it could be grown outside.

Oxalis (*Oxalidaceae*)

Tuberous/bulbous/rhizomatous. An enormous genus of over 800 species, very widespread but with concentrations in South Africa and Central and South America. They may be annual or perennial, some are shrubby and a few are aquatic; the rootstocks may be fibrous, tuberous, rhizomatous or bulb-like, producing lobed leaves (3 or more leaflets) in a basal tuft or scattered up the stems; the flowers are either solitary or several in loose to compact, sometimes umbel-like heads, and have five petals rolled like an umbrella in the bud stage, unfurling to a funnel shape, sometimes almost flat; the colours range from white to yellow, red, pink, purple and violet-blue. The tuberous species which concern us here are very varied in their cultivation requirements, some summer-dormant, some winter-dormant, some needing cool-growing conditions, others being tender and only suitable for frost-free climates or glasshouse cultivation. Some are extremely weedy, such as *O. latifolia* and *O. pescaprae*, and it is just as well to test all species in containers, especially in mild-winter areas, to see how invasive they appear to be before allowing them into the open garden; on the other hand, some species are very difficult to cultivate, notably some of the higher altitude South American species. As a general rule of thumb, the majority of 'bulbous' *Oxalis* can be split into three groups for cultivation purposes:

Those southern African species from the eastern (predominantly summer rainfall) region (e.g. *O. depressa* [=*O. inops*], *O. obliquifolia* and *O. smithiana*) and those from Central America, especially Mexico (e.g. *O. deppei* [probably = *O. tetraphylla*]) are summer-growers and need to be kept dryish and frost-free during their winter dormancy. These make good container plants and in cold areas need to be grown under frost-free glasshouse conditions, or they can be planted out in spring in a sunny, well-drained position.

Those South African species from the South West Cape (predominantly winter rainfall) region are winter-growers (e.g. *O. hirta*, *O. purpurea*, *O. versicolor*), starting into growth in autumn and flowering in autumn, winter or spring before becoming dormant for a dry, summer rest period. These grow well in a frost-free glasshouse with plenty of light and air through the winter months, and are excellent container plants in a sandy soil mix.

Those from the temperate and higher altitude regions of South America (e.g. *O. adenophylla*, *O. enneaphylla*, *O. laciniata*, *O. loricata* and *O. squamosoradicata*) are also treated as winter-growers, in that they should be planted in autumn to start root growth before winter. Mostly they do not make active growth above ground before the spring, flowering in spring and early summer. The lovely yellow *O. perdicaria* [*O. lobata*], however, produces flowers and leaves in autumn and rests in summer; these are on the whole much hardier than the South African species, some actually requiring cool-growing conditions in order to succeed. They are also good for the unheated glasshouse or frame, or they can be planted out on a raised bed or rock garden in a grit-humus soil mix which has plenty of moisture available in spring and summer; a position which becomes hot and dry should be avoided.

Pamianthe (*Amaryllidaceae*)

Bulbous. A small, tropical genus of only one or two species from moist forests in Ecuador, Bolivia and Peru; only *P. peruviana* is cultivated to any extent and even that is

87 *Oxalis* 'Ione Hecker'

rare. The bulbs have a long neck and strap-shaped, basal leaves; a few large, fragrant creamy-white flowers are produced in summer in an umbel; these are long-tubed with a central, funnel-shaped cup surrounded by six spreading segments; the cup has conspicuous teeth at its margin and prominent stamens. I have not had the opportunity in recent years of growing this lovely plant but my old notes say that *Pamianthe* is a tropical plant requiring warm conditions throughout the year (min. winter temperature 15 °C [59 °F]); during the summer it needs plenty of moisture, fairly humid conditions, and regular liquid feeds (potash-rich 'tomato type' fertilizer); in winter, slightly drier but never dried out completely; plant with the neck just reaching to soil level in a loose, 'open' mix.

Pancratium (*Amaryllidaceae*)

Bulbous. A genus of beautiful amaryllids comprising about 15 species from the Canary Islands, the Mediterranean region, tropical Africa and tropical Asia. They have strap-shaped basal leaves and leafless flower stems bearing umbels of large white, fragrant flowers; these each have six narrow segments surrounding a conspicuous funnel-shaped corona. Pancratiums are seldom cultivated, although the sea daffodil, *P. maritimum*, is familiar to many who visit the Mediterranean during the summer months, flowering in late summer sometimes in the sand just above water level; it is, however, not a good garden plant, not flowering very freely and having short-lived flowers; it is worth trying in a hot, sunny place where the dormant bulbs will get sun-baked in summer, either outdoors in mild-winter areas or in a frost-free glasshouse; try feeding with sulphate of potash in autumn and spring, and (suggested by Chris Lovell) perhaps a dash of sodium chloride! Much better and hardier is *P. illyricum* from Corsica and Sardinia;

this needs a similar position in the garden, but it flowers much more reliably and the flowers last longer; it is also good planted out into a bed in a frost-free glasshouse or conservatory, or in a deep pot; *P. canariense* also needs frost-free conditions. The tropical species are, of course, plants for a very warm climate and outside the subtropics need warm glasshouse treatment; I have only tried the African *P. tenuifolium* and this certainly needs to be kept warm and dry for the autumn, winter and spring (e.g. in the airing cupboard), then given a good watering to stimulate growth in early summer and kept at a minimum of about 18 °C (64 °F) whilst in growth; other tropical species probably need the same treatment.

Pardanthopsis (*Iridaceae*)

Rhizomatous. An eastern Asiatic genus of one (possibly two) species. The Chinese *P. dichotoma* is not uncommon in cultivation; it is allied to and similar in growth to the rhizomatous species of *Iris* (it has been called *Iris dichotoma*) in having flat fans of erect, sword-shaped leaves; the small, short-lived, iris-like flowers are carried on loosely branched stems and are white to purple, lined and spotted with dark brown-purple in the centre. It is a summer-grower, dying back in winter during its dormant period but not becoming completely

88 *Pancratium illyricum*

dormant. Although frost-hardy, this some-times succumbs to winter wet, so requires a well-drained, gritty soil in an open position, but during the summer growing and flow-ering season it does need plenty of moisture and will not succeed in warm, dry posi-tions. Young plants are best planted out in spring and then left undisturbed. This is also related to Belamcanda (see page 69) and will hybridize with it to produce a range of interesting intermediates which have been named x *Pardancanda norrisii*; cultivation is as for *Pardanthopsis*.

Paris, Kinugasa and *Daiswa* (*Liliaceae/Trilliaceae*)

Rhizomatous. These are usually grouped together under *Paris* and they are all rather similar in their characteristics. They are all Eurasian, *Paris* (about 4 species) wide-spread from Europe to eastern Asia, *Daiswa* (about 20) mostly from the Himalaya and China, and *Kinugasa* (one species, the white-flowered *K. japonica* from Japan). They have rhizomes, varying from short, thick ones like those of trilliums to far-creeping slender ones, which give rise to stems bearing a whorl of four or more leaves above which is held the solitary flower; this has conspicuous green, yellow or white sepals and narrow, often thread-like, petals which may be green, purple or yellow. These are all winter-dormant plants, growing and flowering in spring and summer; they are essentially woodlan-ders for a freely draining leafmould-rich soil in a cool position where they will get moisture throughout summer. The rhi-zomes should never be dried out, neither should they ever become waterlogged; if lifting them for propagation this is prob-ably best done in late summer or early spring, but on the whole they are best left undisturbed. Although also placed in the Trilliaceae, *Scoliopus* from California and Oregon is not all that similar in appearance;

there are two species, *S. bigelowii* and *S. hallii*; they have a pair of broad leaves on the ground and short, leafless flower stems bearing small upright unpleasantly scented flowers in spring; these have three broad, spreading sepals and three very slender erect petals; the colour is creamy or yel-lowish, heavily streaked with purple or brown. *Scoliopus* is easily cultivated in a cool, semi-shaded position in leafmould-rich soil, but will not tolerate severe frosts on its leaves in spring when in growth; it dies down for the summer.

89 *Paris quadrifolia*

Pauridia (*Hypoxidaceae*)

Cormous. A genus of one species, *P. minuta*, from South Africa; it has thread-like leaves and tiny white, starry flowers in autumn. I have not tried it but I would expect it to be a winter-grower, requiring similar condi-tions to the related *Spiloxene* (see page141).

Petamenes (*Iridaceae*)

Cormous. This African genus has now been merged with *Gladiolus* by Drs. P. Goldblatt and Miriam de Vos.

Phaedranassa (*Amaryllidaceae*)

Bulbous. A small genus of nine species mainly from Ecuador but also Colombia and Costa Rica. They are striking plants with broad, elliptic or lance-shaped basal leaves produced before the leaves in early spring; the leafless flower stems carry umbels of pendent, tubular flowers, mostly pink or red (rarely yellow) with green tips; they are similar in appearance to *Stenomesson* species, except for the leaves, and the stamens are not united into a cup at their bases. I have tried only *P. dubia* which was cultivated in the same way as the stenomessons (see page 142) but, since I have now lost it, this may not have been ideal! However, narcissus bulb flies attack most of these amaryllids and may have been the cause of its demise. Chris Lovell recommends frost-free, cool greenhouse or windowsill cultivation in pots, then stood outside for the British summer; in winter they are given a brief (up to 8 weeks) warm, dry, dormant period (in the airing cupboard!). Chris has used both peat-grit and cocofibre-grit potting soils with success and the pots are given a monthly 'Phostrogen' feed in summer. Paul Christian in Wales and Terry Hatch in New Zealand say that by giving alternate growing and dormant periods more than one crop of flowers can be produced each year (try 2 months dry, 4

months growing). Like the stenomessons, these could probably be grown outside in mild-winter areas.

Phycella (*Amaryllidaceae*)

Bulbous. A small genus from South America with about 5–7 species in the Andes; the size of the genus depends upon what is included, since some species are placed in *Hippeastrum* or *Rhodophiala* by some authorities. Phycellas have narrowly strap-shaped basal leaves appearing at or just after the flowers which are carried in an umbel and are tubular or funnel-shaped with six lobes flaring outwards at the tips; they are red, yellow or purplish, usually bicoloured, and appear in summer or autumn. Few of these are cultivated, in fact I have encountered only *P. bicolor*, and I have little experience with them; I suggest treating them as for *Rhodophiala* (see page 135). The same may be said of *Hieronymiella*, a genus of perhaps 4–6 species from Argentina; these have strap-shaped leaves and umbels of whitish, yellow, orange or red flowers with six segments surrounding a central cup; in very cold-winter areas, probably the best option is a frost-free glasshouse with the bulbs grown in long pots or planted directly into a bed, with a dry dormant period in autumn/winter.

Pinellia (*Araceae*)

Tuberous. A small genus from eastern Asia. They are summer-flowering, with entire or 3-lobed leaves and small, tubular, green or purplish-veined spathes, each with a protruding spadix. Plant in spring in partial shade in humus-rich soil which is well-supplied with moisture in summer; in areas where the ground freezes to a considerable depth it is safer to lift the tubers in

90 *Phaedranassa tunguraguae*

autumn and store them away from frost; alternatively, grow in pots in an unheated glasshouse or frame and place outside in summer whilst in growth.

Placea (*Amaryllidaceae*)

Bulbous. A fascinating genus of approximately five species from the Chilean Andes. They have very narrowly linear to strap-shaped basal leaves and, in spring, few-flowered umbels of funnel-shaped, white, cream, yellowish or pink flowers, usually striped or veined purple-red; they have a small cup in the centre. I have had only limited success with cultivating the genus, with *P. ornata*; they appear to behave as winter-growers, so should probably be started into growth in autumn after a dry, summer rest period, kept in growth with moderate watering through winter and spring and dried off in early to mid-summer; high potash liquid feeds are almost certainly a good idea. In mild-winter areas they could be grown outside but in places with frosty winters, frost-free glasshouse cultivation will be necessary; use long pots so that the bulbs can be planted fairly deeply; a well-drained gritty/sandy, loam-based mix should be suitable.

Polianthes (*Agavaceae*)

Tuberous. A fascinating genus from Mexico, only one species of which is cultivated to any extent, the tuberose, *P. tuberosa*. There are about 15 species, all with tufts of narrowly lance-shaped to strap-like leaves and wiry stems carrying loose racemes of white, pink or red, pendent to horizontal flowers which are curved-tubular with six, short, spreading lobes; the tuberose is noted for its delicious scent. These are summer-growers, dormant in winter and flowering in mid-summer; those which I have tried

91 *Polianthes geminiflora*

are not very hardy and gave the best results when planted directly into a frost-free glasshouse bed. However, the red-flowered *P. geminiflora* (*Bravoa geminiflora*) grew and flowered well for many years against a warm fence; it also performs well as a container plant. I find *P. tuberosa* very difficult to flower, the tubers splitting and forming clusters of small ones which are reluctant to grow on to flowering size. They appear to require a deep, rich soil with plenty of moisture and warmth available in summer; one of the old and very successful methods of cultivation involved making special 'hot beds' with manure but I have not yet tried this. *Prochnyanthes*, *Pseudobravoa* and *Hesperaloe* (evergreen) require much the same treatment.

Polyxena (*Liliaceae/Hyacinthaceae*)

Bulbous. There are reputedly only two species in this genus from the Cape winter rainfall region of South Africa, *P. corymbosa* and *P. ensifolia*, but the latter has many very different-looking variants. They are very low-growing plants, the former with very short, narrow, almost cylindrical leaves and short spikes of upward-facing pink or purplish flowers; the latter has narrow to broad, green to grey-green leaves and near-

stemless heads of upright, white to pinkish flowers. These are winter-growers, flowering soon after they are first watered in autumn and remaining in growth until late spring when they should be dried off for the summer. A well-drained, sandy mix is suitable; their size and lack of hardiness makes them best for pot cultivation in a just frost-free glasshouse, but in mild-winter areas there is no reason why they should not be grown outside.

Proiphys (Amaryllidaceae)

Bulbous. Formerly known as *Eurycles*, this is a small genus of only three species from south-east Asia and north-east Australia. They have broadly oval or oblong basal leaves developing before or with the flowers which are carried on leafless stems in umbels; they are white, long-tubed with a small, toothed cup in the centre and conspicuous stamens. *P. amboinensis* from south-east Asia and *P. cunninghamii*, the Queensland lily from Australia, are occasionally seen in cultivation but I have never encountered *P. alba*. They grow in and at the margins of forest and it is recommended that they are given a loose, open potting soil of loam, peat, leafmould and gritty sand with plenty of moisture available during the growing season, rather less during the dormant season, although never dried out completely. In temperate areas treat as summer-growers with a minimum temperature of 15 °C (59 °F) in winter; plant bulbs with their tips just below soil level.

Puschkinia (Liliaceae/Hyacinthaceae)

Bulbous. One or two species from western Asia, spring-flowering, with racemes of pale blue or white flowers with a darker stripe along the centre of each segment. These are winter-growers, so plant in autumn in well-drained soil in sun or partial shade, but in a position which does not become too hot and dry in summer or the bulbs may become desiccated.

Pyrolirion (Amaryllidaceae)

Bulbous. There are two or three species in South America, mainly from Bolivia and Peru, with large, yellow, orange or white, funnel-shaped flowers, the tips of the six segments curved outwards to slightly reflexed; these appear in spring and summer, followed by the narrowly strap-shaped leaves which last through summer and autumn before dying away for a winter dormancy. Only *P. tubiflorum* (*P. aureum*, *P. aurantiacum*, *P. flammeum*) is at all well-known in cultivation; this is a summer-grower, the dormant bulbs needing to be kept warm and dry (min. about 15 °C [59 °F]) in winter and then started into growth in spring. In Britain it is necessary to grow it in a deep pot (or planted into a bed) in a heated glasshouse; if in pots it could be placed outside once the warmer weather has arrived in summer. A well-drained, sandy, loam-based potting soil is recommended.

Ranunculus (Ranunculaceae)

Tuberous/swollen roots. A very large genus, worldwide, with perhaps as many as 2000 species, familiar for their cupped or saucer-shaped, yellow or white (rarely orange, pink or red) 'buttercup' flowers with a mass of stamens in the centre; the leaves are variably lobed or toothed. Only a small proportion of these are cultivated, and even fewer have swollen rootstocks capable of being dried out and treated as 'bulbs'; the notable exception is the eastern Mediterranean *R. asiaticus* which is widely grown, but mainly the large-flowered, double and semi-double cultivars; it has a swollen storage system in the form of a cluster of claw-like roots. This is naturally an autumn-winter-spring grower, flowering in mid- to late spring, then dying down for the summer. Bulb nurseries sometimes also offer dried roots in spring for summer flowering. *Ranunculus asiaticus* is not very hardy so in cold-winter areas where the ground freezes it will need a sheltered, sunny position such as a warm wall will provide, otherwise just an open, sunny spot will suffice, in a well-drained soil. After they have died down the roots can be lifted and dried, if dry soil conditions cannot be relied upon. The wild forms, with a single row of white, yellow, orange or red petals, are lovely plants for pot cultivation in the frost-free glasshouse or bulb frame. A few other Mediterranean ranunculus are treated in the same way.

The dwarf Eurasian *R. ficaria*, the lesser celandine, with its rounded or kidney-shaped leaves and yellow flowers in early spring also has a cluster of fleshy roots and this too dies down for the summer, although it is a plant of seasonally damp situations and a warm, dry period in summer is not essential; it is quite hardy and can be planted outside in any position in sun or partial shade where it will not become dust-dry in summer; in fact it is too successful in some places and can become quite a pest. There are various selections, with coppery or white flowers, single and double, and attractive, bronze-leaved forms, all worth growing; they make good container plants for an early spring display and this is a good way to keep them in check if they are mistrusted out in the garden. The related *R. kotschyi* from the Near and Middle East is a snow-melt plant in the wild, drying out in summer, and is much less invasive in cultivation; in fact, it is better in a bulb frame or pots, where it can be given a summer rest.

Rauhia (*Amaryllidaceae*)

Bulbous. There is just one species, *R. decora*, from Peru. It is evergreen with a pair of broad, elliptical, basal leaves and a leafless stem carrying a few-flowered umbel of narrowly funnel-shaped green flowers with protruding stamens. This is very rare in cultivation, in fact I have seen only one plant at Kew which flowered in mid-winter, followed by new leaf development. It appears to be similar in its cultural requirements to *Stenomesson* (see page 142), to which it is probably related; however, being evergreen, it would be best to just reduce the watering during autumn and winter rather than dry it out completely; then in late winter and spring give increased water and heat. The Peruvian *Pucara* (2 spp., also with tubular, green flowers), is probably not in cultivation; I would expect it to need similar treatment.

Rheome (*Iridaceae*)

Cormous. Three species are known from South Africa, in the South West Cape region and Namaqualand, related to *Moraea*; they have narrow, channelled leaves and short-lived, yellow or pinkish flowers in winter or spring; each flower has six free segments in a cupped arrangement. I have not tried to cultivate these but would expect them to require similar treatment to *Homeria* (see page 104).

Rhodohypoxis (*Hypoxidaceae*)

Cormous (?tuberous). A small genus of six species from the summer rainfall region of southern Africa, mainly the Drakensberg Mountains of Natal and Lesotho. They are dwarf plants with narrow leaves, producing a succession of pink, red or white flowers throughout summer; the flattish flowers have six segments, meeting in the centre, thus hiding the stamens. Most species are stoloniferous, producing rhizome-like outgrowths freely and quickly increasing into patches. The small corms should be planted or started into growth in spring after a dry, cool, winter rest period. Although fairly frost-hardy they may rot off in damp winters; thus, in wet-cold winter regions they are best grown in pots (pans are also suitable since they are shallow-rooting) so that they can be dried off in a shed or under the greenhouse bench in winter. The potting soil should be moisture retentive. In summer whilst in growth they need plenty of moisture to keep them flowering and some growers stand the pots in shallow dishes of water. *R. milloides*, in particular, needs lots of water and is a good plant for a 'peat garden' amid dwarf rhododendrons etc. If grown in the open ground, choose an open position in a gritty/peaty or sandy/peaty soil.

Rhodophiala, including *Rhodolirion* (*Amaryllidaceae*)

Bulbous. A horticulturally interesting South American genus of perhaps 30 or more species, closely related to *Hippeastrum* and sometimes included in that genus, although at present it is thought to be distinct; they occur mainly in the Chilean Andes and Argentina in winter rainfall (or snow at higher altitudes) regions. On the

92 *Rhodohypoxis*, a collection of species and cultivars

whole they have smaller bulbs than those of *Hippeastrum* and the leaves are much narrower; the flowers are funnel-shaped, carried in small umbels of 1-7 on leafless stems, mostly red, yellow or white, sometimes bicoloured. Since these are mostly from a 'mediterranean type' climate I have treated them (though I have tried only a few species) as winter-growers with a long summer dormancy; given this regime, they tend to flower in late summer/autumn before the leaves, so they are then kept watered through winter until the following spring/early summer. Although some should be frost-hardy, in cool-winter areas they do seem better in deep pots in an unheated glasshouse, although *R. bifida* has flourished at Kew, planted permanently outside in an open, sunny position and flowering freely in summer. Many of these are now coming into cultivation via the seed collections of John Watson and Anita Flores, and Jim and Jenny Archibald; they are lovely plants, more graceful than a lot of the *Hippeastrum* species and less subtropical in their requirements, so hopefully we will see a lot more of them in future.

Rigidella (*Iridaceae*)

Bulbous. A small genus of about four species from Central America, mainly Mexico, closely related to *Tigridia* and considered inseparable by some authorities; they are generally taller plants with red, pendent or erect flowers, having three large outer segments which are spreading or reflexed and three small inner erect ones; the leaves are erect and strongly pleated lengthways. These are summer-growers, flowering in mid- to late summer and then dying down in autumn for the winter months. They can be grown outside, planted in an open, sunny position which is well-supplied with moisture in summer, but in areas where the ground freezes the bulbs need to be lifted and stored for the winter in a frost-free shed or glasshouse in not-quite-dry peat. Like tigridias, it is best to pot the bulbs in early spring and start them into growth in a little heat before planting out; if planted directly into cold damp soil they sometimes rot off. If grown permanently under glass they are a little too vigorous to grow in pots and need to be planted directly into beds, but large containers would be suitable. The striking hybrid between *Tigridia pavonia* and *Rigidella orthantha* raised by Elwood Molseed may have been lost to cultivation but, if it is still around, should be given the same treatment as *Rigidella*.

Romulea (*Iridaceae*)

Cormous. A large genus of around 80 species with a wide distribution in the Mediterranean region of Europe, western Asia and North Africa, tropical Africa (on mountain tops) and South Africa, where there are many species in the winter rainfall area of the South West Cape and a few in the eastern summer rainfall area. They are small plants with one or two very slender, often wiry, leaves and one to several upright, funnel-shaped flowers like crocuses, in a wide range of colours from white to pink, blue, purple, red and yellow, often

93 *Romulea hirsuta*

with differently coloured zones in the centre. They are mostly winter-growers so the corms should be planted or potted in autumn and kept in growth through winter to late spring when they die down and need to be kept dry for the rest of the summer. Most of those from the Mediterranean region are frost-hardy, providing that the soil does not freeze solid for long periods, and do best in sunny situations in a sandy/gritty soil; they are also suitable for bulb frame or pot cultivation in an unheated glasshouse. It is important to grow them in as much light as possible in spring or the flowers will not open properly.

The tropical African species are not very striking and are seldom if at all cultivated. The South West Cape species are by far the most exciting with larger flowers in many striking colours. These are very successful in mild-winter areas and some of them can become almost invasive, but where there is the likelihood of sharp frosts they need the protection of a glasshouse with slight heat on cold nights; their size makes them ideal for pot cultivation, in a sandy soil mix. They need starting into growth in late summer/early autumn and will then flower in late winter/early spring. There are few from the eastern, summer rainfall part of southern Africa and only *R. macowanii* var. *alticola* (*Syringodea luteo-nigra*) is seen in cultivation to any extent; this is grown in Britain as an attractive yellow autumn-flowering alpine house plant.

Roscoea (*Zingiberaceae*)

Tuberous-rooted. Although not 'bulbous', even in the widest sense, these have thick, fleshy roots and go into a period of dormancy, and they are monocots, so are included here! There are about 20 species from the Himalaya and China, producing tufts of lance-shaped leaves and long-tubed flowers which have an upper, hooded 'petal' and a large lower lip; they range in

94 *Roscoea purpurea*

95 *Sandersonia aurantiaca*

colour from white to yellow, pink, purple and red. These are from summer rainfall (monsoon) regions with dry, cold winters, so they grow and flower in summer then die down for the winter. In gardens they need a cool position in sun or dappled shade in moisture retentive but well-drained soil; a mix which is humus-rich and gritty achieves this combination. In areas which have mild, very wet winters they may tend to rot off whilst at rest (the true *R. alpina* is very prone to this), so it may be necessary to provide some sort of cover (plastic/glass sheet) to keep off excess rain. Alternatively, they are good plants for deep pots or containers which can be moved into a shed or glasshouse for the winter. *Cautleya*, a small Himalayan genus with taller, leafy stems and terminal spikes of yellow flowers similar in shape to those of a *Roscoea*, is less frost-hardy and, in cold-winter areas, needs protection whilst dormant in winter; in mild areas it is easily cultivated outside in a semi-shaded bed which does not dry out in summer.

Sandersonia (*Liliaceae/Colchicaceae*)

Cormous. This is a genus of one species from South Africa, *S. aurantiaca*, not unlike

Gloriosa (see page 98) in its misshapen corms and growth habit but having smaller orange flowers which are pendent and urn-shaped. It is naturally a summer-grower and its cultivation needs are the same as those of *Gloriosa*.

Saniella (*Hypoxidaceae*)

Cormous. This has just one species, *S. verna*, from southern Africa in the mountains of Lesotho and the neighbouring Eastern Cape. It is related to *Rhodohypoxis* but its small, white, long-tubed, crocus-like flowers have visible yellow stamens protruding from the centre; the erect, deep green leaves are very narrow and channelled. Like *Rhodohypoxis*, this is a winter-dormant, spring/summer-grower and appears to grow best in a peaty-sandy soil mix, kept very wet during the growing season. As far as I know it has not been tested for hardiness out in the open garden but it is an interesting plant for pot or pan cultivation in an unheated glasshouse.

Sauromatum (*Araceae*)

Tuberous. Only two or three species, from tropical Africa, the Himalaya and India, well-known because of the 'voodoo lily', *S. venosum* (*S. guttatum*), which is sold as a curiosity for placing on the windowsill to flower without water. This has a twisted, lance-shaped yellowish or brownish spathe, spotted with deep red or purple internally, and a long-protruding, tapering, greenish or maroon spadix; a single large leaf with a blotched stalk is produced soon after and develops up to 15 lobes. This is a summer-grower, dormant in winter, flowering in early spring and then remaining in leaf until the following autumn. It is hardy in mild-winter areas and can be planted out permanently but where there are sharp ground frosts the tubers need to be lifted and stored dry and frost-free for the winter. When grown as a curiosity the tubers can be flowered indoors (if you can stand the smell!) whilst still dry, then, after the soil has warmed up in late spring, it can be planted out in the open garden for its not unattractive foliage. Alternatively it could be planted directly into a glasshouse bed or grown in a large container. I find that *S. brevipes* behaves in much the same way.

Scadoxus (*Amaryllidaceae*)

Bulbous. A small genus of about 10 species, formerly included in *Haemanthus*, occurring wild mainly in tropical Africa and eastern southern Africa but extending to the subtropical part of Arabia. They resemble *Haemanthus* in having showy umbels of many small flowers with narrow segments and very prominent stamens; the foliage, however, consists of an upright tuft of rather thin, green leaves, quite unlike the paired leathery leaves lying on the ground which are so characteristic of *Haemanthus*. Coming from more tropical areas, they are less hardy than *Haemanthus*. The only species likely to be encountered in cultivation are *S. puniceus* (*Haemanthus magnificus*), *S. pole-evansii*, *S. multiflorus* and its subspecies *katherinae*. They are summer-growers; the first has flowers in winter while still leafless, then produces leaves through spring and summer before dying down for a dry rest period in autumn; the others flower in summer with their leaves

and need plenty of moisture at this time. However, watering should be reduced during winter, although not stopped altogether since these are almost evergreen. In cold-winters areas, heated glasshouse conditions are necessary, using deep pots or containers and an open, well-drained gritty mix with leafmould; a minimum temperature of about 10 °C (50 °F) in winter is necessary, and much warmer in summer during the growing season. In mild climates they can be grown outside in partial shade.

96 *Scadoxus puniceus* (photo: J.S. Ingham)

Schickendantzia (*Alstroemeriaceae*)

The one species, *S. pygmaea* from the Andes, is usually included in the genus *Alstroemeria* (see page 60).

Schizostylis (*Iridaceae*)

Rhizomatous. There is only one species, *S. coccinea*, which inhabits the eastern, summer rainfall, area of Southern Africa. It has a cormous/rhizomatous habit and can form extensive patches of erect, narrowly sword-shaped leaves; in late summer or autumn it produces spikes of large, red, saucer-shaped to flattish, starry flowers, regular in shape with six segments joined at the base into a slender tube; in cultivation there are now several selections with flowers in varying shades of red and pink, and white; it is popular both as a garden plant and as a cut-flower. Although a plant of wet places in the wild it will thrive in cultivation in any reasonable soil which does not become too hot and dry in summer. It is tolerant of frost but the foliage becomes damaged during cold weather since the plant does not really die down completely in winter; however, even when damaged it usually recovers well through its extensive underground system of rhizomes. I have seen good patches on both alkaline and acid soils.

Scilla (*Liliaceae/Hyacinthaceae*)

Bulbous. A large, widespread genus, much-loved for the blue-flowered spring squills, *S. siberica*, *S. mischtschenkoana* (*tubergeniana*) and *S. bifolia*, although there many other species scarcely known in gardens. They have two or more basal leaves and racemes of starry to bell-shaped flowers, in various shades of blue or violet, rarely pink or white.

Most species occur in Europe, North Africa and western to central Asia; these are winter-growers, flowering in autumn or spring and dying down for the summer months. They should be planted in early autumn in well-drained soil. For cultivation purposes these fall roughly into two groups:

S. amoena, *S. bifolia* and its relatives, *S. bithynica*, *S. cilicica*, *S. greilhuberi*, *S. liliohyacinthus*, *S. messenaica*, *S. mischtschenkoana*, *S. persica*, *S. rosenii* and *S. siberica* and its relatives all prefer semi-shaded sites in humus-rich soil (preferably leafmould rather than peat); they will take full sun providing that the soil does not become dust dry in summer, or the bulbs will shrivel. *S. rosenii* is a high mountain plant and needs cold winters, followed by warm, spring sun to encourage rapid development; it is not very successful in mild-winter areas, as the stems do not develop quickly enough and the flowers try to open

97 *Scilla ramburei*

as they push through the ground. *S. persica* needs a damp position as it inhabits water meadows in the wild.

Species of the second group need sunnier positions, drying out in summer; they include *S. autumnalis*, *S. furseorum*, *S. hyacinthoides*, *S. litardierei* (*pratensis*), *S. lingulata*, *S. monophyllos*, *S. peruviana* and its relatives, *S. puschkiniodes*, *S. ramburei*, *S. scilloides* and *S. verna*. Some species in this group are rather more tender: *S. maderensis*, *S. latifolia* and probably also *S. haemorrhoidalis* from Madeira, the Canary Islands and North Africa, require frost-free conditions so in cold-winter areas must be grown in a slightly heated glasshouse; they are suitable for pot cultivation (large pots since they have large bulbs and vigorous roots), dried out somewhat whilst dormant in the summer months but never completely, for their roots are perennial.

The species from tropical Africa, the East Cape region of South Africa and India are summer-growers, dormant in winter. They are frost-tender and in cold-winter areas need to be stored in a frost-free place. *S. natalensis* is the most frequently cultivated; this is suitable for large containers, placed outside during the summer growing period and then removed to a shed or glasshouse when it dies down in autumn and kept relatively dry until spring. Many African species of *Scilla*, mostly those with striped or spotted leaves such as the frequently-cultivated *S. socialis* (*violacea*), have been transferred to the genus *Ledebouria* (see page 112).

Sessilistigma (*Iridaceae*)

Cormous. There is only one species, *S. radians*, from the South West Cape region of South Africa. It has a single basal, narrow, channelled leaf and a branched flowering stem carrying upright, flattish flowers, cream-coloured with a yellow centre, having six almost equal segments. I have not had the opportunity to try growing this but it is reasonable to assume that it is a winter-grower and will not be frost-hardy; if obtained, try growing it in a just frost-free glasshouse, potted in autumn into a well-drained, sandy medium and given plenty of light through the autumn-winter growing and flowering period, then dried off for the summer months.

Sinningia (*Gesneriaceae*)

Tuberous/rhizomatous. A large genus of more than 30 species from the warmer parts of Central and South America. They usually have tubers, producing soft, often hairy, leaves and tubular to funnel-shaped flowers in summer in a very wide range of bright colours; they are known mainly because of the cultivars and hybrids of *S. speciosa*, the familiar pot plant known as 'Gloxinia'. This, the florists' gloxinia, has large, rounded tubers and compact rosettes of broad, hairy leaves, producing several large, upright, funnel-shaped flowers which may be white, blue, pink or orange and red, often very conspicuously blotched or spotted inside, sometimes with frilled edges to the five petals. These are very tender plants, most frequently grown as indoor pot plants or in larger containers for the conservatory, although they could be grown outside in countries with very warm summers. Wherever they are grown, the tubers need to be dry and warm for the winter months; they are then started into growth in spring, either by potting them or encouraging them to break dormancy by placing them in trays of damp peat at a minimum temperature of 16 °C (60 °F); once they are showing signs of growth they are then potted or planted out into a light, open soil mix of loam, gritty sand and coarse leafmould or peat; the plant should not be grown in direct sunlight and it is best to water them carefully to avoid the hairy leaves; a liquid feed every other week of a balanced NPK fertilizer is helpful when grown in pots since they are quite strong growers. The rather more subtle and hardier *S. tubiflora* from Uruguay and Argentina is a lovely plant which I can recommend for the conservatory; it has fragrant, white, tubular flowers in summer. This grows vigorously in almost any sandy soil mix and when dried off for the winter can be kept anywhere as long as it is dry and frost-free; the tubers increase very rapidly in the course of one season.

Sparaxis (*Iridaceae*)

Cormous. A South African genus of about 12 species, endemic to the South West Cape winter rainfall region. They usually have narrowly sword-shaped leaves and unbranched or branched spikes of large, showy flowers, either regular in shape and flattish or irregular and appearing 2-lipped, with one larger, hooded upper segment (i.e. those which were in the genus *Synnotia*); they are often brightly coloured, in shades of red, pink, purple, orange or yellow or white and cream, often with contrasting zones or blotches. *Sparaxis* are all winter-growers so the corms should be started into growth by watering in early autumn; continue to water through to late spring/early summer when they die down, then dry off and keep warm for the rest of the summer. In mild-winter areas they can be planted outside in well-drained, sunny positions but they will not tolerate sharp frosts so in colder areas they will need glasshouse cultivation with slight heat on

98 Sparaxis tricolor

cold nights, either planted directly into beds or grown in pots. A soil mix which is rather sandy seems to suit those which I have tried. Give them plenty of light in winter as they can easily become etiolated. Some nurserymen offer corms of the colourful mixed hybrids for spring planting to flower in summer; these are not a special race bred for this purpose, they are corms which have been stored through winter to prevent them growing. For the first flowering season after planting they will grow in summer, but after that they will try to revert to their normal autumn/winter growing habit unless they are dug up at the end of that first season and dried off for the winter again. On the whole this does not work very well and, as they are fairly cheap, they are probably best regarded as summer bedding for one season only, then discarded.

Sphenostigma (*Iridaceae*)

Probably a synonym of *Gelasine* (see page 95)

Spiloxene (*Hypoxidaceae*)

Cormous. An attractive genus from South Africa, possibly as many as 25 species, but only a few are in cultivation. They have very narrow, often stiffly erect, basal leaves and flat, upward-facing starry flowers with six sharply pointed segments; they are mostly white, yellow or pinkish, often with contrasting zones of colour in the centre. I have successfully cultivated only *S. capensis*, which is a winter-grower, flowering at almost any time through winter and early spring; it is very showy, although needing good sunny days to encourage the flowers to open, not a feature of the average English winter! This does well in a sandy soil mix in a frost-free glasshouse, watered from autumn through to late spring, then dried out for the summer, although not baked and dust-dry, since spiloxenes are plants of moist areas in the wild; *S. aquatica* is an aquatic in the growing season and is best grown in a pot of sandy-peaty soil stood in a dish of water, then dried out in summer. In mild-winter areas they can be grown in the open garden.

Sprekelia (*Amaryllidaceae*)

Bulbous. The Jacobean lily belongs to a small genus – probably only one species – from Mexico. It has narrowly strap-shaped, basal leaves and solitary red, curiously-shaped flowers; the three upper narrow segments are spreading-recurved while the lower three are held closer together and downwards, forming a lip. The one species, *S. formosissima*, is a summer-grower, dormant in winter when the bulbs are best kept dry and frost-free, then started into growth in spring by watering and increasing warmth. It is often said that this is hardy in sheltered positions but it is certainly not here in south-east England. It is best grown as a pot plant in an open, well-drained soil, watered through summer when it can be placed outside once the warmer weather has arrived; it flowers in spring or early summer. In mild-winter areas it can be grown out in the open garden.

Stenomesson (*Amaryllidaceae*)

Bulbous. A large genus of up to 40 species from western South America, found mainly in the Peruvian Andes but also in Ecuador, Colombia and northern Chile. They produce narrow to broad, strap-shaped or narrowly elliptic basal leaves and leafless stems with few-flowered umbels of pendent, tubular or funnel-shaped flowers in yellow, green or shades of pink and red, often tipped green; the stamens are joined together at the base to form a cup. Since many of these are from equatorial regions they do not experience definite winters and summers so some of them flower at almost any time in the wild. In cultivation in mild areas they will carry on this behaviour but in cold winter regions it is best to encourage them to be summer-growers by giving them a dry, dormant period in autumn and winter, then start to water and provide warmer conditions in late winter or early spring through to autumn. Those which I have tried, *S. pearcei*, *S. aurantiacum* and *S. variegatum*, are grown in deep pots of an open, sandy, loam-based soil mix, kept in a slightly heated glasshouse (min. 8 °C [46 °F] in winter) and placed outside for the summer; they flower in spring or summer but are unpredictable in this. I have seen *S. variegatum* in flower in January in the mild climate of southern California.

Sternbergia (*Amaryllidaceae*)

Bulbous. A genus of about 8 species from the Mediterranean region and western Asia; they have upright, goblet-shaped yellow (white in *S. candida*) flowers in autumn (or spring in *S. candida* and *S. fischeriana*) and strap-shaped leaves, produced after, or at the same time as, the flowers. They are winter-growing, so plant the bulbs in early autumn and keep in growth until late spring when the leaves die down. They are best in warm, sunny positions in well-drained soil, left undisturbed to build up into clumps; alkaline soils seem to be particularly successful. If the bulbs are not warm and fairly dry during the dormant period in summer they will not form flower buds for the coming year. *S. colchiciflora* and *S. pulchella* are too small for the open garden and are best grown in a bulb frame or in pots under glass. The unique white-flowered *S. candida* has given variable results in cultivation; some people find it difficult to keep, or very shy-flowering, whilst with others it increases and flowers freely. Regretfully I have to admit that I belong to the former category! It appears to do best on deep, rich, alkaline soils.

99 *Stenomesson variegatum*

100 *Sternbergia clusiana*

Strangweia
(*Liliaceae/Hyacinthaceae*)

The one species, *S. spicata* from Greece, is now thought to belong to the genus *Bellevalia*. Cultivation is similar.

Streptanthera (*Iridaceae*)

Cormous. This genus is now included in *Sparaxis* (see page 140).

Strumaria (*Amaryllidaceae*)

Bulbous. This small genus from southern Africa is similar to and requires the same cultivation methods as *Hessea* (see page 103).

Synnotia (*Iridaceae*)

Cormous. Now included in *Sparaxis* (see page 140).

Syringodea (*Iridaceae*)

Cormous. A small genus of eight species of dwarf autumn/winter flowering *Romulea*-like plants from the South West Cape of South Africa with very narrow, basal leaves and upright, goblet-shaped, stemless (but long-tubed) flowers in shades of blue, lilac or violet, usually yellow or white in the throat. These are winter-growers so the small corms should be planted or potted and started into growth in late summer or early autumn in sandy, well-drained soil mix; they are not frost-hardy so in cold-winter areas they should be grown under glass with slight heat in winter to keep them just frost-free, but not too warm; when they die down in late spring water should be withheld for the rest of the summer.

Tapeinanthus (*Amaryllidaceae*)

Bulbous. The one species, *T. humilis*, is usually referred to the genus *Narcissus*. It is like a tiny, yellow, autumnal *Narcissus* but has no cup in the centre of the flower. It is winter-growing, so bulbs should be started into growth in autumn after a warm, dry, summer rest period. Best in a bulb frame or just frost-free glasshouse; feed bulbs with a potash-rich fertilizer if they will not flower.

Tecophilaea (*Tecophilaeaceae*)

Cormous. Two species from Chile. Flattish, white corms produce a short stem with few narrow leaves and funnel-shaped to flattish, brilliant deep blue, pale blue or violet flowers. They are winter-growers, so plant corms in autumn in sandy soil in full sun and dry off in summer. Not very frost-hardy (especially *T. violiflora*) so in cold-winter areas give slight protection of a bulb frame or just frost-free glasshouse; both species, *T. cyanocrocus* and *T. violiflora*, are good alpine house pot plants. Plenty of light is necessary to keep them as compact as possible.

Tenicroa
(*Liliaceae/Hyacinthaceae*)

Bulbous. A small South African genus, little known in cultivation, although probably worth trying. They have racemes of flattish, starry, white flowers with a pinkish line along the centre of each of the six segments; the leaves are very slender, almost thread-like, often many in a basal tuft. These are presumably related to *Drimia* (see page 86) or perhaps to *Ornithogalum*; I have not yet tried to grow them but, since they are from the south-western, predominantly winter-rainfall part of South Africa, they will, I imagine, be winter-growers; I would expect them to respond to being grown in a frost-free glasshouse (or outside in mild-winter areas), started into growth after a warm summer rest period and watered through winter until after flowering in late winter/early spring; a sandy, loam-based soil mix should suit them.

Tigridia (*Iridaceae*)

Bulbous. There are about 30 species from Central and South America, mainly Mexico and Guatemala; they have erect, narrowly sword-shaped, pleated leaves and very short-lived flowers with three large outer segments and three small inner ones; there is a succession of flowers which open only in the morning and they vary widely in colour from orange-red (only the largest species, *T. pavonia*, has such bright flowers) to white, yellow, brown and blue and purple, often conspicuously veined and spotted. The flowers are either pendent (e.g. *T. galanthoides* and *T. meleagris*) or erect (most others). These are summer-growers, some flowering early as soon as they come into growth (e.g. *T. dugesii*), but most are almost fully developed before they bloom. In mild-winter areas they can be planted outside permanently in sunny positions but where there is the likelihood of prolonged, even if slight, frosts, they need to lifted for the winter and stored in not-quite-dry peat in a frost-free place. I find it best to pot the bulbs in early spring and start them into growth in a little heat, then plant them out in a sunny, well-drained bed

when the soil has warmed. Otherwise they get off to a very slow start and sometimes rot off even before rooting if there is a cold, wet period in spring/early summer. They can also be planted directly into a bed in a cool glasshouse which is kept just frost-free in winter; the shorter species are also suitable for pot cultivation. The related Mexican *Fosteria* (1 sp., *F. oaxacana*, with small, yellow flowers spotted brown in the centre) and *Sessilanthera* (3 spp. with white or yellow flowers spotted yellow or purple in the centre) should be treated in much the same way, and probably also *Cobana*, which I have not tried, (1 sp., *C. guatemalensis*, with white flowers) from Guatemala.

Trifurcia (*Iridaceae*)

Now regarded as a synonym of *Herbertia* (see page 101).

Trillium (*Liliaceae/Trilliaceae*)

Rhizomatous. A large genus from North America, with a few species in the Himalaya and eastern Asia (sometimes regarded as a separate genus, *Trillidium*). They are very distinctive, producing stems with a whorl of three leaves and solitary flowers having three small outer, usually green, 'sepals' and three larger showy inner

101 *Tigridia seleriana*

102 *Trillium underwoodii*

'petals'; the flowers are either held above the whorl of leaves or on a stalk beneath them; some have beautifully mottled leaves. These are mostly woodland plants, flowering in spring. In cultivation the majority of them require dappled shade and humus-rich soil which has a plentiful supply of moisture in the spring/early summer growing period; they remain in leaf for most of the summer and should never be dried out altogether. Most do well in acid conditions but *T. nivale* needs a well-drained, alkaline soil and seems to thrive best in a pot in the unheated frame or glasshouse. The seeds take a long time to germinate, needing two cold periods, equivalent to two winters; however, the lovely dwarf *T. rivale* differs from the norm and needs only one cold period. One of the best times to move and divide trilliums seems to be in late summer, although it is also possible in early spring.

Trimezia (*Iridaceae*)

Bulbous/rhizomatous. A sizeable genus of perhaps 20 species from the warmer parts of Central and South America and the West Indies. They have iris-like fans of leaves (some species are evergreen) and tough stems bearing a succession of short-lived flowers not unlike those of *Cypella* (see page 83) with three large outer segments and three small inner ones; they are mostly yellow (sometimes purplish), spotted and banded with a brown or purple in the centre. They are very seldom cultivated but a few are grown, especially *T. martinicensis*; they are summer-growers, and not at all frost-hardy so require warm growing conditions (min. C. 12 °C [53 °F] in winter) in a well-drained, sandy-leafy soil mix and given a rest period in winter with slightly less water (but not dry). The related genus *Neomarica* (C. 12 species from Central and South America with similar shaped white, blue or yellow

103 *Trimezia martii*

flowers) is sometimes included in *Trimezia*; these are mostly large, evergreen plants and require plenty of moisture most of the year, and semi-shade. I have not tried *Pseudotrimezia* (C. 10 spp. from Brazil, like small versions of Trimezia, often with thread-like, wiry leaves) but I would expect them to be summer-growers requiring a sandy soil mix and a dryish period in winter.

Triteleia (*Liliaceae/Alliaceae*)

Cormous. About 16 species, from western USA, related to and sometimes merged with *Brodiaea*. They are late spring-flowering with umbels of funnel-shaped, blue, white or yellow flowers, with the leaves dying off by flowering time. Plant in autumn, dry off in summer when dormant. Well-drained soil in full sun. In damp-summer areas grow in a raised bed, bulb frame or alpine house.

104 *Triteleia* × *tubergenii*

Tritonia (*Iridaceae*)

Cormous. A primarily South African (extending to south tropical Africa) genus of nearly 30 species, few of which are in general cultivation. They have narrowly sword-shaped leaves, occasionally wavy at the margins, and spikes of flattish or saucer-shaped flowers, sometimes rather irregular in shape with a somewhat hooded upper segment and a prominent projection on each of the lower three segments; the colours range from yellow, orange to red, pinkish-purple and some-times white. These are predominantly winter-growers and are therefore planted or potted in autumn and started into growth and kept growing through winter and spring until they begin to die down in early summer, when the corms can be dried off and kept warm. They are not frost-hardy; in mild areas they can be planted outside in a sunny, well-drained position which dries out in summer; in areas which experience anything more than very light frosts of short duration they will need glasshouse or conservatory protection; several corms to a pot of species such as *T. crocata* make a good winter/spring display, planted in a sandy soil mix and given as much light as possible through the autumn/winter to prevent etiolation of the stems and leaves.

The tropical African species *T. laxiflora* behaves as a summer-grower with me, so its corms are dried out and kept frost-free in winter, then started into growth in spring; although very tender this could be planted out in the garden and lifted again for the winter. I grow *Radinosiphon* in the same way (4 spp. from south-east tropical and southern Africa with spikes of small, long-tubed, purple-blue or pinkish flowers like a tiny gladiolus); I would expect *Zygotritonia* to need similar treatment (c. 3 spp. from eastern tropical Africa with spikes of small orange or red hooded flowers).

Tritoniopsis (*Iridaceae*)

Cormous. Peter Goldblatt recommends that this should include *Anapalina* (see page 62). This is a horticulturally little-known genus of about 15 species from South Africa, from the South West Cape winter rainfall region. They have narrow, erect, sword-shaped leaves and spikes of pink, red, yellow or white flowers which are mostly irregular in shape with a hooded upper segment and the three lower ones forming a lip, not unlike some of the small *Gladiolus*. These are winter-growers; my limited experience with them suggests that they should be treated in the same way as other South West Cape bulbs such as *Sparaxis* (see page 140). They could prob-ably be grown outside in mild areas but in places with cold winters will require a frost-free glasshouse.

Tropaeolum (*Tropaeolaceae*)

Tuberous. A large genus of nearly 100 species from Central and South America, ranging from annuals to fleshy-rooted and tuberous-rooted perennials, very few of them in general cultivation. The tuberous species have become popular and sought-after in recent years. Most are climbers with rounded to variously lobed leaves and brightly coloured flowers produced in the leaf axils. These have five sepals, the upper of which is developed into a spur, and five petals which may be lobed or fringed; the colours range from creamy white and yellow to deep red, purple or blue.

The tuberous *T. tricolor* ('T. tricolorum') and *T. azureum* are both tender winter-growers, requiring frost-free conditions with as much light and air as possible to keep them compact; they make good winter- or spring-flowering container plants for a conservatory; a well-drained, sandy soil mix is suitable and they must be provided with bushy 'pea sticks' to climb

105 *Tropaeolum azureum*

on; in summer the tubers are dried off, then repotted early in autumn before the thread-like and easily damaged shoots start to appear. In the case of *T. tricolor* it seems that there is a spring/summer-growing form around since it is sometimes recommended for planting out in spring for summer flowering; the one which I grow cannot be treated like this, as it begins to grow spontaneously in autumn, even if the dry tubers are still in an envelope. In mild-winter areas, these could be planted out permanently.

The commonly cultivated vigorous climber *T. tuberosum* is a summer-grower, not hardy, but in cold-winter areas the tubers can be lifted in autumn and stored frost-free until replanting time the following spring; it is ideal for planting near a shrub, wall or fence to provide a splash of colour in late summer into autumn (the selection 'Ken Aslet' is slightly earlier, in mid-late summer).

The trailing *T. polyphyllum* and climbing *T. speciosum* are winter-dormant and much hardier, so can be grown in the open garden in quite cold areas; in fact the latter requires cool-growing conditions and does not grow here in south-east England with anything like the same vigour as it does in Scotland; it is said that it will not grow on alkaline soils, but whether this is caused by an intolerance of lime or because chalky/limestone soils tend to be hotter and drier in summer, I do not know. *T. polyphyllum*, on the other hand, seems to prefer a hot, sunny position in sharply drained soil.

Tulbaghia (*Liliaceae/Alliaceae*)

Bulbous/rhizomatous. There are over 20 species of these very allium-like plants from tropical and southern Africa; they are clump-forming with slender bulbs producing thread-like to narrowly linear, basal leaves and leafless stems carrying umbels of flowers, each with a short tube and six spreading segments with a small corona in the centre; they may be white, pink, purple and sometimes bicoloured with green or whitish segments and an orange or brown corona. Several species have become popular garden plants, although they are not reliably hardy; however, in areas which receive only light frosts they are suitable for sunny, sheltered positions, and in mild-winter areas they are very useful, easily cultivated perennials. Some of the smaller species, such as *T. cominsii* and *T. acutiloba*, make good pot-grown subjects for an unheated glasshouse, the former flowering for much of the year. Most of those in cultivation, for example, *T. fragrans*, *T. natalensis* and *T. violacea* (there are also variegated forms of this) are spring/summer-growers, dying down in winter; in borderline areas where frosty winters are sometimes experienced they should be covered with loose leaf litter, bracken, bark chips or something similar. The South West Cape species which are in leaf during winter are more susceptible to frosts and in cold areas are best treated as container plants for a frost-free glasshouse (e.g. *T. alliacea*). Tulbaghias do not seem to have any specific soil requirements, other than good drainage and a supply of moisture during the growing season; they will not thrive in hot, dry conditions.

Tulipa (*Liliaceae*)

Bulbous. A large familiar genus from (mainly southern) Europe, western Asia to Central Asia, and China and Japan if

106 *Tulipa ulophylla*

Amana (see page 61) is included. They are distinctive with upright, cup-shaped or funnel-shaped flowers, mostly red, yellow or white but a few are in shades of pink or purple. They are all winter-growers so should be planted in autumn and kept in growth by watering until the leaves begin to die back in late spring/early summer. Tulips need to be given warm, dry conditions during their dormant period if they are to thrive and flower well, so in damp-summer areas it may be necessary to lift the bulbs and store them, warm and dry, but not in direct sun. They need to be grown in full sun in well-drained soil and appear to be particularly successful on alkaline soils; the smaller species are very suitable for sunny positions on rock gardens or raised beds, or for pot cultivation in an unheated glasshouse.

Ungernia (*Amaryllidaceae*)

Bulbous. A small genus of eight species, mostly from the Middle East and Central Asia (one in Japan) having long-necked, blackish bulbs producing umbels of funnel-shaped, yellowish, brownish, pink or red flowers in late summer on bare stems before the foliage; the narrowly strap-shaped leaves emerge in spring in the wild, although in cultivation they often appear earlier in late autumn or winter. These are seldom cultivated and are, I find, not easy to please; those I have cultivated need a dormant period in summer during which they must be hot and dry; they tend to flower in late summer, even without the stimulus of water, and should then be watered sparingly through winter and spring until the leaves die back. Their long bulbs have thick perennial roots so they are not really well-suited to pot cultivation, unless in large containers; where dry summers cannot be relied upon (e.g. England), bulb frame cultivation is the best bet; in areas which have cold winters with snow cover and warm, dry summers they could probably be grown outside. A sandy/gritty loam-based soil seems to suit them.

Urceolina (*Amaryllidaceae*)

Bulbous. The two species of this genus from Peru and Bolivia, *U. peruviana* and *U. urceolata*, are placed by some authorities in the genus *Stenomesson*. They have broadly strap-shaped to elliptical, basal leaves appearing after the flowers which are carried in an umbel on a stout, leafless stem; they are urn-shaped, pendent and red or orange-red in the former, yellow in the latter. These behave as spring- and summer-growers, flowering in spring and early summer, producing leaves through summer and then dying down for the winter when the bulbs should be dried off and kept at a minimum temperature of about 8 °C (46 °F). In mild-winter areas they can be grown outside in sunny, well-drained beds but in cooler regions they are best treated as container plants, grown in a heated glass-house during the colder seasons and then placed outside for the summer. A well-drained, loam-based soil mix seems to suit them very well with an annual top dressing of new soil, leaving the bulbs undisturbed for as long as they are doing well.

Urginea (*Liliaceae/Hyacinthaceae*)

This genus has now been merged with Drimia (see page 86); however, the name *Urginea* for the Mediterranean species is still to be found in many books, particularly referring to the very common sea squill, *U. maritima*, the large bulbs of which many people see growing near the sea on their Mediterranean holidays. It makes clumps of large bulbs sitting on the surface, producing large, green to grey-green leaves, almost colchicum-like, in late autumn, winter and spring, following on from very long leafless racemes of many small, white, starry flowers in late summer/autumn. There are a few related species, mostly rather smaller, and some have attractively undulate-margined leaves; they are all winter-growers requiring a warm summer rest period, and are not very frost-hardy in my experience; a bulb frame or frost-free glasshouse provides suitable conditions in cold-winter areas, but *U. maritima* is a very leafy plant and does not really merit the space. In mild areas, in a warm, sunny position, a well-flowered clump would be an imposing sight for a short while in autumn; it would be worth trying in a heavy alkaline loam, sunbaked in summer to induce flower buds to form.

Vagaria (*Amaryllidaceae*)

Bulbous. A small genus of perhaps four species, mainly from North Africa but with one species, *V. parviflora*, from the Middle East; it is sometimes included in the genus *Pancratium* and does look rather like a small version; it has strap-like, basal leaves, dark green with a pale stripe along the centre, and an umbel of white flowers which have six narrow spreading segments; although there is no cup in the centre as in *Pancratium*, the stamens have their filaments widened and flattened in the lower part and have conspicuous teeth, giving the impression of a corona. I have cultivated only *V. parviflora* and this is not at all difficult. It starts to grow in autumn, flowering quite early, even in late summer, produces leaves in autumn which last through winter and spring, and then dies down for the summer; my plants have been grown in a just frost-free glasshouse, in deep pots of a sandy soil mix; they could be planted directly into a bed or in a bulb frame. In summer it requires a warm, dry rest period and will not flower if kept cool, so the pots should be placed under the glasshouse bench, out of direct sunlight, though in a quite hot position, for about 3 months. It appears to flower best if left undisturbed so that the bulbs increase (which they do quite rapidly) and fill the container; they are fed with a tomato fertilizer (potash-rich) in autumn and early spring.

Vallota (*Amaryllidaceae*)

Bulbous. The one species, *V. speciosa*, is now included in the genus *Cyrtanthus* as *C. elatus* (*C. purpureus*); cultivation notes will be found on page 84.

Veltheimia (*Liliaceae/Hyacinthaceae*)

Bulbous. There are only two species in this South African genus, both well worth cultivating for their tufts of bold green or greyish foliage and dense spikes of downward-curving, tubular, pink or red flowers, usually tipped with green or cream (a yellow form is also known). They are both autumn-winter-spring growers, flowering in winter; *V. capensis*, which has grey-green, very undulate-edged leaves, dies down for the summer months, whereas

V. bracteata, which has broader glossy green leaves only slightly or not at all wavy, is more or less evergreen. These make excellent pot plants for the window-sill or conservatory, or can be placed on a terrace in mild-winter areas, or even planted out in the garden in a sheltered position, but not in areas where there is even the slightest frost. The large bulbs need to be half-exposed from the soil and started into growth by watering in early autumn; during the autumn and winter, in areas where light intensity is naturally rather poor, they must be given as much light as is possible to keep them sturdy and compact, and this also has the benefit of encouraging stronger flower colours. They grow well in an open, freely draining, sandy potting soil. Even with the evergreen *V. bracteata* it is best to reduce watering in summer; plant with the bulbs half-exposed.

Wachendorfia (*Haemodoraceae*)

Rhizomatous. A small South African genus of c.3 species, seldom seen in European gardens but deserving of more attention, certainly in the milder climates; it is cultivated more frequently in Australia, New Zealand and milder parts of the USA where conditions are more suitable. The species most likely to be encountered is *W. thrysiflora* which has evergreen tufts of pleated, sword-shaped leaves and branched inflorescences in summer over 1 m (3 ft) in height with many sizeable yellow flowers marked with brown in the centre. In cold-winter areas this is not hardy enough to thrive outside, so really needs to be grown in a large container under glass, then placed outside for the summer; in mild areas it makes a good border plant if given plenty of moisture during its summer growing period. *W. paniculata* is said to be a winter-grower, dying down in summer after flowering, but I have not tried this one.

Walleria (*Tecophilaeaceae*)

Tuberous. A little-known genus in cultivation, comprising about three species from tropical and southern Africa. They have clustered tubers producing leafy stems, the leaves alternate and very narrowly linear to oval, the stem and underside of the leaves sometimes armed with prickles. The smallish pendent to almost erect flowers are produced in the upper leaf axils and have six spreading to reflexed, white to pale blue, deeper blue or mauve, perianth segments; six stamens protrude in a cone shape, bicoloured yellow and blue or violet. I have not tried to grow these but, given the chance, would try them as summer-growers, giving them a warm, dry rest period in winter and starting them into growth in spring in pots of a sandy soil mix; almost certainly they would need to be kept at a minimum of about 10 °C (50 °F) in winter, rising to 18 °C (64 °F) and above during the growing season.

Watsonia (*Iridaceae*)

Cormous. A southern African genus of over 50 species which are very striking, with erect fans of tough, sword-shaped leaves and showy flowers in very symmetrical spikes, sometimes branched; the flowers may be more or less tubular throughout or tubular in the lower part with the six lobes spreading out to form a funnel shape or a flatter saucer shape; the colour may be pink, purple, red, orange or rarely white, cream or yellow. Most of those in cultivation are from the predominantly winter rainfall region of South Africa so are winter-growers and should be planted in autumn; they flower in late spring or early summer and are then given a drier period in summer when they are growing less actively, although several are evergreen and should not be dried out altogether; winter-growers which are occasionally seen in cultivation include *W. aletroides*, *W. angusta*, *W. borbonica* (*W. pyramidata*, 'W. wordsworthiana* of hort') and its lovely white variant, *W. b.* subsp. *ardernei* 'Arderne's White', *W. fourcadei* (*W. stanfordiae*), *W. humilis*, *W. laccata* (*W. brevifolia*), *W. marginata*, *W. meriana* (*W. bulbillifera* is a form of this), *W. spectabilis*, *W. tabularis*, *W. vanderspuyiae* and *W. versfeldii*. In areas with cold, frosty winters these do not thrive, unless a very protected position can be found, such as a bed against a warm, sunny wall; I have grown several of them for years here in Surrey but, while they are not killed, they never build up enough strength to flower; if one is lucky enough to have a large frost-free glasshouse or conservatory with planting beds, this would be ideal, but they could be grown in large containers and moved out into the garden in spring. In milder areas they are excellent and stately garden plants for an open, sunny position in well-drained soil. The related evergreen *Pillansia* (1 sp., *P. templemannii*, from the South West Cape with branched spikes of orange-red, flattish flowers in spring) should, in theory, behave in the same way; I grew it for many years planted directly into a bed in a frost-free glasshouse but it never flowered; it is said to flower best after bush fires. I have never tried *Micranthus* (3 spp. from South and South West Cape with very dense spikes of small, blue, tubular flowers). These too should be interesting for a frost-free glasshouse or outdoors in mild-winter areas.

The *Watsonia* species from the predominantly summer rainfall regions of southern Africa make their main period of growth in spring and summer, flowering in mid- to late summer; these have not been tried out in cultivation to any great extent – unfortunately, since they may prove to be hardier than the 'winter-growers'; *W. densiflora*, *W. latifolia*, *W. lepida*, *W. pillansii* (*W. beatricis*) and *W. watsonioides* are all summer-growers.

107 *Watsonia coccinea*

Whiteheadia
(*Liliaceae/Hyacinthaceae*)

Bulbous. Only one species, *W. bifolia*, is known from the south-western winter rainfall part of southern Africa; this is rather like a *Massonia* (see page 118) in its growth habit, with two succulent green leaves, nearly flat on the ground, but instead of a stemless head of flowers it has a short, dense spike with many green, prominent, leaf-like bracts; the flowers are fleshy in texture and green or greenish-white with conspicuous stamens, appearing in winter. Cultivation is as described for *Massonia*.

Worsleya (*Amaryllidaceae*)

Bulbous. An amazing genus of one species from Brazil, *W. rayneri*, which is often included in *Hippeastrum*; it is very rarely seen in cultivation. It has large, long-necked bulbs producing fans of evergreen, grey-green, curved leaves and, in summer, umbels of large, widely funnel-shaped flowers in a lovely shade of lilac-blue, speckled darker inside. I am not the best person to recommend cultivation methods since I have always failed to grow it for more than a year or two from seed, but the following notes may help. It is a summer-grower, requiring a very open acid potting soil (bark chips, perlite, charcoal, rough peat and leafmould have all been recommended as a way of lightening the mix). In winter it is given less moisture, but never dried out, while in summer, plentiful watering and a humid atmosphere seem to be necessary. If container-grown, this must be large since it can have, when growing well, an extensive root system. The recommended minimum temperature is 15 °C (59 °F) in winter, rising in the growing season to 20–25°C (68–77 °F), with plenty of sunlight.

Wurmbea (Liliaceae/Colchicaceae)

Cormous. This seldom-cultivated genus has about 40 species, about half in tropical and South Africa and half in Australia. They have small corms, not unlike those of a Colchicum, slender, channelled leaves and loose to dense spikes of starry to funnel-shaped flowers, white, green, yellowish, pink, deep reddish-brown or blackish, sometimes with darker nectaries. Some species have fragrant flowers. I have not had much experience with these but they do sound interesting and worth a try; it is recommended that they (all species) are treated as winter-growers, starting the corms into growth after a warm summer dormancy for growing through the winter and spring months, during which time they will flower; a sandy soil mix would probably be best, but with plenty of moisture in the growing season since they inhabit seasonally damp places. Their small size means that they are best suited to pots, although in mild-winter regions they could be tried outside. The Australian Burchardia (5 spp. with umbels

of white or pink flowers) and South African Ornithoglossum (3 spp.) and Neodregea (1 sp.) should probably be treated in the same way.

Zantedeschia (Araceae)

Tuberous/rhizomatous. A small genus of about six species from southern Africa, from which many hybrid cultivars have been raised. They have bold leaves, often arrow-shaped and sometimes with conspicuous blotches, and leafless stems, each bearing a large, upright, funnel-shaped spathe surrounding a pencil-like spadix; this carries tiny flowers on its lower part, hidden by the tubular base of the spathe. The colour of the spathe may be white, pink or yellow, sometimes with a contrasting dark eye in the centre, but the hybrids are available in a much greater range of shades. In areas with cold, frosty winters, only the common Z. aethiopica is likely to be hardy, and even that gets frosted to the ground in, for example, southern Britain, although it survives and can be grown as a perennial for a moist, sunny position where it will flower in spring and summer; it can also be grown in water, up to 30 cm (12 in) deep. Grown frost-free, under glass or in mild-winter areas, it is evergreen and flowers at almost any time of year; in some parts of the world it has become naturalized and is a pest. It is always said that the cultivar 'Crowborough' is the hardiest but I have no personal evidence that this is any different from other clones in this respect. The other species and cultivars are less robust and are treated as tender plants for the heated glasshouse, or as summer-growers for planting out in spring for summer flowering; the tubers are then lifted and stored dry and frost-free for the winter. They can be also grown in large containers for standing out in summer. The soil or potting mix should be well-drained and rich; old rotted manure is a valuable additive, worked in thoroughly before planting, or, in the case of container cultivation, placed in the bottom of the container. It also pays to liquid feed (a balanced NPK) plants in containers during summer.

Zephyra (*Tecophilaeaceae*)

Cormous. One species (possibly two) from Chile. Flattish, white corms produce a sparsely leafy, aerial stem, loosely branched and carrying flattish flowers, clear blue outside and white within. Plant corms in autumn in sandy soil and dry off in summer. The corms sometimes stay dormant for several years; if this happens try a warm, dry period, followed by a drenching with water in late summer. They are not frost-hardy so in cold-winter areas require slight protection from a bulb frame or frost-free glasshouse.

Zephyranthes (*Amaryllidaceae*)

Bulbous. A genus of around 25–30 species from south-eastern USA, Central and South America. They have narrow, linear or strap-shaped leaves and solitary, funnel-shaped flowers, mostly white, pink or yellow. They are similar to *Habranthus* but in this genus the flowers are usually held at an angle, just above the horizontal, and have unequal stamens whereas in *Zephyranthes* the flowers are usually erect and have equal stamens. These are 'rain lilies', flowering in spring, summer or autumn after a period of dormancy as soon as it rains; some species are almost evergreen but in others the leaves appear soon after the flowers. The bulbs are best planted in a well-drained soil (a light, sandy soil is very successful) in spring, thus giving them time to settle in before the next winter; once established, they are best left undisturbed for as long as they are thriving. The most frequently cultivated is *Z. candida* which needs to be warm and dry through summer whilst it is dormant, otherwise it will not flower well; in cool-summer countries it is normally planted against a sunny wall where the soil temperature is likely to be higher. In mild-winter countries the pink *Z. grandiflora* sometimes becomes naturalized. *Z. flavissima* produces its small, yellow flowers over a long period and needs a lot of moisture in its summer-growing period.

Zigadenus (*Liliaceae/Melanthiaceae*)

Bulbous. A genus of about 15 species, mainly North American but with a few in Mexico, Guatemala and eastern Asia. They have a rather poorly developed bulbous base, giving rise to several narrow basal leaves and racemes or panicles of flattish white or green flowers which usually have conspicuous glistening darker green nectaries. These mostly occur in dampish places and flower in summer. They seem to do well in reasonably well-drained, sunny positions where they do not get too sun baked and dry in summer; I have also grown some of them with success on a peat garden. The Californian/Oregon *Z. fremontii* is one of the better species, horticulturally speaking, and this flowers rather earlier in the summer and then dies down, allowing it to tolerate drier conditions at this time; *Z. elegans* is large enough and vigorous enough to be planted with other perennials in a border, although not a showy plant. They are usually sold as growing plants in pots, so that they can be planted out at any time in autumn, spring or summer; the slender bulbs do not really contain enough reserves to allow them to be lifted and dried for marketing.

Index to genera

Plate numbers are given in **bold**